Charlie Kaufman

CHARLIE KAUFMAN
Confessions of an Original Mind

DOREEN ALEXANDER CHILD

Modern Filmmakers
Vincent LoBrutto, Series Editor

 PRAEGER

AN IMPRINT OF ABC-CLIO, LLC
Santa Barbara, California • Denver, Colorado • Oxford, England

Library of Congress Cataloging-in-Publication Data

Child, Doreen Alexander.
   Charlie Kaufman : confessions of an original mind / Doreen Alexander Child.
      p. cm. — (Modern filmmakers)
   Includes bibliographical references and index.
   ISBN 978-0-313-35860-9 (hard copy : alk. paper) —
   ISBN 978-0-313-35861-6 (ebook)
1. Kaufman, Charlie, 1958– 2. Screenwriters—United States—
Biography.   3. Television writers—United States—Biography.
4. Motion picture producers and directors—United States—
Biography.   I. Title.
   PS3561.A842Z75   2010
   808.2'3092—dc22   2010007209
   [B]

ISBN: 978-0-313-35860-9
EISBN: 978-0-313-35861-6

14 13 12 11 10   1 2 3 4 5

This book is also available on the World Wide Web as an eBook.
Visit www.abc-clio.com for details.

Praeger
An Imprint of ABC-CLIO, LLC

ABC-CLIO, LLC
130 Cremona Drive, P.O. Box 1911
Santa Barbara, California 93116-1911

This book is printed on acid-free paper ∞™

Manufactured in the United States of America

For Megan,
who always believed in Fatz and Billy

Contents

Series Foreword

The Modern Filmmakers series focuses on a diverse group of motion picture directors who collectively demonstrate how the filmmaking process has become *the* definitive art and craft of the twentieth century. As we advance into the twenty-first century we begin to examine the impact these artists have had on this influential medium.

What is a modern filmmaker? The phrase connotes a motion picture maker who is *au courant*—they make movies currently. The choices in this series are also varied to reflect the enormous potential of the cinema. Some of the directors make action movies, some entertain, some are on the cutting edge, others are political, some make us think, some are fantasists. The motion picture directors in this collection will range from highly commercial, mega-budget blockbuster directors, to those who toil in the independent low-budget field.

Gus Van Sant, Tim Burton, Charlie Kaufman, and Terry Gilliam are here, and so are Clint Eastwood and Steven Spielberg—all for many and for various reasons, but primarily because their directing skills have transitioned from the twentieth century to the first decade of the twenty-first century. Eastwood and Spielberg worked during the sixties and seventies and have grown and matured as the medium transitioned from mechanical to digital. The younger directors here may not have experienced all of those cinematic epochs themselves, but nonetheless they remained concerned with the limits of filmmaking: Charlie Kaufman disintegrates personal and narrative boundaries in the course of his scripts, for example, while Tim Burton probes the limits of technology to find the most successful way of bringing his intensely visual fantasies and nightmares to life.

The Modern Filmmakers series will celebrate modernity and postmodernism through each creator's vision, style of storytelling, and character presentation. The directors' personal beliefs and worldviews will be revealed through in-depth examinations of the art they have created, but brief biographies will also be provided where they appear especially relevant. These books are intended to open up new ways of thinking about some of our favorite and most important artists and entertainers.

Vincent LoBrutto
Series Editor
Modern Filmmakers

Growing Up Kaufman
and the TV Years

Riding his banana seat bike along the spring rain dusted sidewalk in the suburb of Massapequa, on the South Shore of Long Island, 10-year-old Charlie Kaufman was a lifetime away from the ostensibly glossier streets of Hollywood. At the time, he had no sense that one day in 2005 he would walk the red carpet leading up to the stage where he would receive an Academy Award for his original screenplay, and subsequently be expected to deliver a coherent acceptance speech. In fact, young Charlie's main concern in the thorny year of 1968, riding around his conservative, family neighborhood lined with newly planted trees, was why his older sister's bike had what was called a "sissy bar" on it. The baby trees, he thought, as he peddled past, merely looked like sticks shoved into the ground. In the years to come, summer after summer, they never seemed to grow.

Families shopped at Woolworth's and the A&P, and worshiped at Temple Judea. On special occasions, they stopped in for treats at Krisch's for homemade ice cream. However, behind the closed doors of the hardworking, puritan ethic that offered a car in every driveway and dinnertime as early as 5:30 P.M., when fathers emerged from commuter trains in white shirts and brown-striped ties, young Charlie suspected there was something more going on beneath the surface of this post–WWII, Levittownesque community. The hidden secrets were maybe not the kind of the darkly seductive, illicit "more" goings on that writer Grace Metalious suspected lurked beneath her own northeast small town (as detailed in her novel *Peyton Place*), but rather Charlie had an intuitive sense of the challenge of living a truthful life in the suburbs, despite the absurd expectation to fit in.

The concept of truth, in fact, would become Charlie Stuart Kaufman's calling. As evinced in grade school by his delight in the expansive world of science fiction and fantastical adventures, his interest in truth was not in the strict definition of truth as simple reality, but as a more essential authenticity. This true nature of honesty is more akin to Shirley Jackson's keen ability to scrape off a glossy veneer to unearth something dark and fantastic or Patricia Highsmith's powerful gaze into the very real mind of intense, psychological horror.

The other major influence on Kaufman's developing psyche was the particular zeitgeist in which he was raised. Born in November of 1958, the safety of newly minted suburbia would not shield him from the duality of the 1960s and 1970s, when he came of age. While war raged "over there" in Vietnam, the United States was adrift in the weed-soaked peace movement here (despite the culture of the nuclear family). What he was taught in school was incongruent with the underlying terror of those defining decades. His English teacher spoke about the romantic aspects of Jack Kerouac's America, illustrated in Kerouac's seductive treatise *On The Road*. When young Charlie's thoughts drifted from the classroom, he daydreamed that the writing life just might be for him. Kaufman would later attempt to reconcile that ethereal glimpse of a famous writer's life with the reality of Jack's personal demons, including the need for Dexedrine in order to produce the tangible manuscript, along with the lauded writer's drunken, surly appearances on the talk show circuit at the time. Kerouac was a staunch patriot and a former U.S. Merchant Marine, but the media often pinned him to the hippie culture. All of his fame never filled him up, and his slow suicide by way of the bottle, eventually released him from his tether to the earth. For the only time in his life, Charlie Kaufman would be too young to understand where Kerouac lived emotionally at the time of his fame. Kerouac's professional dilemma has parallels to Charlie Kaufman's experience in Hollywood. To the outside world, Kaufman has been nominated for two Academy Awards and eventually won the coveted Oscar, but he also spent years of his life lovingly dedicated to the dream assignment of adapting Philip K. Dick for the big screen, only to see his finished manuscript shelved for years by a studio, and eventually made without him, stripped of his name altogether. Kaufman did not yet understand what Kerouac meant when he said that fame is like a newspaper. Young Charlie was still safe in the suburbs of Long Island.

Kaufman was taught to read at a young age by his observant parents, who helped him cultivate what would eventually become clear insight into a person's true identity and hidden desires. Kaufman's father Drew, who worked as an engineer while he was growing up, certainly encouraged his children's intelligent curiosity and love of reading. Young Charlie's mother, who had studied social work and was working toward her master's degree, deferred school in order to raise her two children. Unbeknownst (or perhaps not) to his supportive, traditional Jewish parents, their youngest child had an early appetite for sophisticated themes, well beyond his years. Always precocious and eager for his parents to see him as an intellectual peer, he was soon digesting books from his mom and dad's private bookshelf. While some of the neighborhood children were throwing rocks at cats, Kaufman was reading Ray Bradbury's *Fahrenheit 451* and William Golding's *Lord of the Flies.*

As he entered the fourth grade, the future screenwriter began writing fiction. "We were binding our own books and we were supposed to pick an explorer. We were studying them and I decided I would write about my voyages with various explorers. Obviously, sort of a fictionalized idea of me. But I was traveling with these different real explorers and I illustrated it. I thought it was cool, when I was a little kid, that I was mixing this fiction [with fact]. I was very aware of the comedy of that. It was a joke, that all these explorers kept asking me to come with them on their trips, like I was a necessary partner to them. And there were lots of jokes about me getting sick and various mutinies."[1]

The budding student wrote the story for his beloved grammar school teacher, Sheila Goldberg, who encouraged his creativity, in particular, his interest in acting. As many a dedicated (and even the not-so-dedicated) student has experienced, a fond memory of grammar school includes wanting to marry a teacher. The experience of having a mentor who believes in you at such a young, hopeful age (other than good parents, bless them) can fill your life with love. And Miss Goldberg was to inhabit this role for young Charlie: she was the first woman he wanted to marry. "I thought she was beautiful, but it's because I felt like she loved me. I thought she wanted to marry me, too. I started out being interested in acting, and she's definitely the person who got me interested in that stuff and brought that whole thing into my life. She was just a really great teacher."[2] When Miss Goldberg suggested he play the role of a rooster in his school play, his whole life changed. As soon as he got laughs, he was hooked. That was the moment that defined his childhood. All he wanted to do after that was be in plays.

As he strutted across the stage embodying a cocky blustering rooster in a hen house, he suddenly had the newfound power to make his whole class laugh. This feeling opened him up to a whole new aspect of his developing personality. Heretofore he had been a shy, reserved child by nature. Playing a role that was the opposite of the introverted kid gave him a sense of freedom and joy. To this day, although the popular conception cultivated by the press has pinned Kaufman as a person suffering from crippling shyness, he relishes getting laughs on stage, such as during question and answer sessions to promote a film—especially if he can play off the host. Despite the endlessly cited recluse label (even after consenting to well over a thousand interviews with the press at this point), he enjoys competing for the most laughs amongst his colleagues and fellow filmmakers during seminars at screenings. He has always had fun in front of an audience.

Of his early school years and his innate talent for comedy, Kaufman has said, "I definitely loved, through that period, reading plays and either being in them or imagining myself playing these characters. There was something thrilling about that for me—somehow becoming somebody else in a convincing way. So at the same time I was writing dramatic and comedic stuff to perform, but I wrote prose, as well."[3]

At home, he and his older sister entertained his parents by staging plays for them in the living room and shooting short movies on a Super 8 camera. Kaufman loved to watch the Marx Brothers and Woody Allen. Growing up, he was attracted to "anything that took you out of what the convention is of being alive, of being a person, of the things that are just accepted. I think comedy, for me, when it's good, does that. It says, 'wait a minute, why are we doing this?' I think that's what I like about the absurdists, and it was just eye-opening to me, as a kid, to see that stuff."[4]

Later, he became interested in fellow Long Island native, Lenny Bruce. Controversial for his honest, obscenity-fueled rants, the progressive comedian appealed to Kaufman's need to uncover the truth of human nature, even if it wasn't pretty. Although much of the press, including *Variety,* condemned Bruce's work for its raw, undiluted view of the world, young Kaufman's taste found good company in the likes of the influential San Francisco columnist Herb Caen. In 1959 Caen wrote: "They call Lenny Bruce a sick comic, and sick he is. Sick of all the pretentious phoniness of a generation that makes his vicious humor meaningful. He is a rebel, but not without a cause, for there are shirts that need un-stuffing, egos that need deflating. Sometimes you feel guilty laughing at some of Lenny's mordant jabs, but that disappears a second later when your inner voice tells you with pleased surprise, 'but that's true.'"[5]

Although at the time Kaufman's hometown was indeed progressive, in the sense that it was one of the first templates for the new American suburbia, the plainness of the boxy uniformity left him with a yearning to be "from" a definitive, historically rich place. The homogeneous culture that the early suburbs aspired to made young Charlie envious of writers like Flannery O'Connor, who could specifically draw on her Southern Gothic roots for inspiration. Consequently, when asked about his childhood and how it has most informed his work, Kaufman has said that he is from the 1970s, rather than an actual place or Judaism.

In 1972, his family moved to Connecticut, where he continued to cultivate his passion for acting at the William H. Hall High School in West Hartford. He participated in several school plays. In November of his senior year, he played the role of Allan Felix, the genteel film critic who receives dating advice from the ghost of Humphrey Bogart, in Woody Allen's play *Play It Again Sam.* Kaufman's thoughts about his enjoyable experience were published in his yearbook:

> *Play It again Sam* was the most exciting and rewarding experience. You see, looking the way I do, I've always been cast in macho roles, for more than

obvious reasons. Directors constantly type-cast me in roles such as Stanley Kowalski, Othello, Bill Sykes, Emperor Jones, etc. It got so discouraging after awhile. "Why can't I play Elwood P. Dowd or the voice of Mr. Magoo?" "Sorry kid, you're too manly, too much gusto, but, I've got a great opening in a Tarzan movie." Then one day while I was crushing beer bottles—full ones—with my feet, one of my friends mentioned auditions for *Play It Again Sam.* "Any big brawny males in the cast?" I asked doubtfully. "No," my friend answered, "But try out, it's not going to kill you."

So I did. I don't know what Mike Jones saw in me, but he cast me as a divorced, frustrated, puny, oversexed twerp. I was ecstatic, but, there was no time for gaiety. Immediately I set to work destroying my body. Of course I couldn't shorten my hulking 6'5" frame, but a special trench was dug on stage that made me appear 5'4". Naturally I wore sunken cheek make-up and a fuzzy wig over my golden locks. My voice became a perfectly affected, effeminate, nasal twang and I WAS Allan Felix. At last my dream had come true; I wasn't a victim of my machismo physique. I was able to free myself, to be short ... to be somebody![6]

The teenaged Kaufman continued to foster his love of reading plays, acting, and writing. In high school, he read Luigi Pirandello's 1921 *Six Characters in Search of an Author* and was amazed that it had been written. The experimental play involves six characters interrupting a play rehearsal in progress. The characters are in search of an author to bring their stories and characters to fruition because they have been abandoned by their former writer and have been searching for closure or at least the chance to live out their fate. The manager of the play becomes increasingly frustrated by the blur between reality and fiction, as the hastily drawn "characters" have to deal with their own issues of loss, isolation, and bottomless questions about their existence. Much of Kaufman's work reflects these themes and yet even at a young age, he could recognize the twinkle of comedy in the Theatre of the Absurd he was studying. "At the same time there was stuff like Monty Python and *National Lampoon* in the 70s, Ionesco,—stuff that questioned what we accept as reality, sometimes in a very comic way. At the time I was thinking about comedic things."[7]

Another literary influence on the young Kaufman was William Golding's novel *Pincher Martin.* "When I first read it, it was like, Oh God, this is so cool. A guy is shipwrecked, his boat sinks and he is a sailor. He finds a little rock island and spends the entire book surviving on it, fishing and figuring out how to live, like Robinson Crusoe. In junior high school, when I read that, I thought it was the most amazing thing, the idea."[8]

Kaufman asserts that he was usually the go-to guy to beat up in school, although judging by the pictures of him in his high school plays, he seemed well liked. By acting in plays such as *Up the Down Staircase* and *Dr. Jekyll and Mr. Hyde,* and performing with an improve group called Upscene, he "could be somebody else, get laughs, and get attention without asking for it."[9] The sheer enjoyment of inhabiting someone else for a time, and his love of the tenuous and immediate nature of theater grew as he did. "I think the thing I like about theatre is the community of it, personally. I like audiences and I like rehearsals, just on a personal level that appeals to me. Theater is alive and exists in the present tense. Other performing arts do as well, but film doesn't and painting doesn't. But there is that thing where in order for [theater] to be good, you have to be cognizant of that and open to that."[10]

At Charlie Kaufman's high school graduation in 1976, he was one of the three students out of five hundred seniors in his class to be honored with the Diane T. Weldon Scholarship for Achievement Award, the school's drama award. In addition to acting in school, summer stock, and community and regional theatre, the precocious young Kaufman made several Super 8 home movies.

He still remembers the effect that seeing the film *Dog Day Afternoon* had on him as a teenager. Al Pacino and Dustin Hoffman inspired him. "Maybe part of the appeal was the feeling that they weren't conventional movie stars. I had a kind of attraction to the notion that they, like me, were little ethnic guys and yet they could star in movies."[11] Kaufman decided to pursue an acting career and enrolled in the acting program at Boston University; however, he soon became increasingly self conscious and eventually this thwarted his plans. Kaufman remembered a movement/dance class where he and his classmates wore the prerequisite tights. The only trouble was that he couldn't really dance around and exercise his "vehicle" freely when the giant, floor-to-ceiling windows of the classroom opened onto a busy construction site, with hardhats pointing and staring at him. He still loved acting, but as his classes progressed, he became more conflicted. "After a year, I somehow got really embarrassed by the notion of studying acting. Perhaps I secretly still wanted it, but decided to become a director and went to film school in New York instead."[12]

He found his film school experience to be "basically a giant workshop. I wrote this script which took place over one night about an insomniac trying to go to sleep. It's actually not that different from some of the things I would write now. It was fairly experimental in terms of structure, and the professor really loved it. I remember my classmate was Chris Columbus, and the professor held up our two scripts as shining examples of really great writing, but at the same time recognizing they were polar opposites. And of course Chris went off to become enormously successful immediately, and I couldn't get a job for eleven years after graduating."[13] But his change of heart from acting and subsequent transfer to NYU to study production would prove fortuitous both personally and professionally. It was at film school where he met his future writing partner, frequent collaborator, and the best man at his wedding, Paul Proch. Proch, the New York–based artist whose art appears in *Eternal Sunshine of the Spotless Mind,* shot his senior film at Kaufman's parents' home, as Kaufman served as Proch's director of photography. Kaufman divulged that when he was finishing his own senior project in 1980,

> School ended before the film was done, and I lost everybody and had to finish all myself. I rented space from young filmmakers on Rivington [Street]. It had twenty-five locations and thirty actors. In some ways, it was similar to *Eternal Sunshine* in that it's about an insomniac. It took place in his head as he was trying to fall asleep. At night he would have these fantasies—about women, different distractions. He also had this fantasy that he wanted to be a writer, and he had this fantasy of a book he was writing. Perhaps I am writing the same thing over and over, differently. [Laughs] I can tell you I tend to be an obsessive person and go over and over the same thing ... Different stories about the same thing, maybe, because I'm me ... and writing all these things that carry the same kind of consciousness.[14]

During his tenure as a film student, he also worked on several projects, such as a classic horror movie as well as a stop-motion animation that included boots walking. As a teenager, he had been heavily influenced by Woody Allen's penchant for chaotic storytelling and was eager to explore his interest in comedy. Kaufman and Proch went on to write articles for the groundbreaking, American humor magazine *National Lampoon.* "We started writing, submitting letters and wrote a bunch of articles, parodies, really weird stuff, very strange stories like 'White Pig, Black Pig,' about people migrating from body to body—and then moving into the body of Lou Costello, and when Costello died, it moved into Eddie Murphy. We also wrote 'Arsenic and Old Overalls,' which was about the death of [*Hee-Haw* star] Junior Samples, which led to a Bob Woodward investigation into his death."[15]

Payment for the articles amounted to approximately 25 cents a word then—a lot of money for young writers, and when Kaufman received his first big check from the *Lampoon,* he was so happy that he xeroxed it. Their names were in print! Encouraged by the validation, the writing partners also wrote a hysterical parody of a Stephen King–style horror story called "Eggboiler." The story is set in New England (naturally), and is about the plight of a psychic little girl and her father, who are on the run from government men in black. The child possesses the supernatural ability to boil eggs with her mind: her father plants said eggs inside the pants of the enemy. The yarn is replete with Stephen King doctrines such as a small town, a twin sister, astral projection, a blizzard, and New Englander character names the likes of Drs. Billy Jeff Scrimshaw and Barry Waldenpond.

> Pops saw all of Ebbets Field spread out below him like a living breathing Stratego board of humanity. The red and blue plastic pieces of the town jutting up all over, like so many spies and generals. The town square gazebo, where little Jimmy Macklin, Andy and Edna's youngest, had been brutally clubbed to death

in the fall of '63 by a man from Portland by the name of Ted Healy. No, he was not a vampire. He was not a ghoul, he was not an unnameable creature of the night. He was simply a man. A man with mental and sexual problems. And oh yes, he was a werewolf. But not on that particular night. On that night he was just a man with a club ... who had been bitten by an alien.[16]

Another Kaufman and Proch *National Lampoon* story, entitled "God Bless You, Mr. Vonnegut," was an ode to one of the 20th century's greatest American writers, Kurt Vonnegut, Jr., who is known for seminal works such as *Slaughterhouse Five, Breakfast of Champions,* and *Player Piano.* Kaufman especially identified with Vonnegut's themes of rootlessness and guilt. The son of a successful architect, young Vonnegut knew tragedy nonetheless, and lost his mother to suicide on Mother's Day. Just as Vonnegut had explored his sadness in his writing, Kaufman would go on to do the same. For example, Vonnegut's character Eliot Rosewater feels responsible for his mother's fatal accident. A postmodernist known for stories that included a vast array of topics such as the absurdities of life, politics, human nature, science, and technology, Vonnegut was however stigmatized by the label of science fiction writer.

In Kaufman and Proch's homage to Vonnegut, published in 1983, the title of the story itself is a nod to the novel *God Bless You, Mr. Rosewater* (also known as *Pearls Before Swine*). The writing partners play with Vonnegut's themes and cheekily emulate his style in order to create an affectionate parody. They begin one of their chapters with, "Wade Wetknees sat in the bar of the Holiday Inn in Boise, Idaho. It was a long commute from his job at the Illium Artificial Artery Factory in New Jersey, but he liked the player piano. He guzzled planter's punch and told his boyhood friend and manhood bartender, Ed Wyzyrbicki, about Saturn."[17] Kaufman and Proch made use of Vonnegut's metafiction style and even penned their own mantra, related to how their main character viewed the world: "And then some." This phrase is a reflection of how Billy Pilgrim, the main character of Vonnegut's *Slaughterhouse Five,* sums up his situation: "So it goes." Instead of the phrase Vonnegut's character Kilgore Trout shouts in the book *Breakfast of Champions* ("Make me young!"), Kaufman and Proch's line in *their* story is, "Make me a millionaire." To mirror Vonnegut's often pervasive theme of free will versus fate, Kaufman and Proch's narrator asserts several times, "He had no choice. Who does?" Throughout "God Bless You, Mr. Vonnegut," there are simple, felt-tip sketches, just as in Vonnegut's *Breakfast of Champions.* Another nod to Vonnegut's work appears in Kaufman's film *Eternal Sunshine of the Spotless Mind,* in which the main character Joel is "unstuck in time" and is able to view the past, present, and future, much like Vonnegut's Billy Pilgrim. Winston Rumford, Vonnegut's character from *The Sirens of Titan* was similarly preternaturally gifted (or cursed, as you see fit). At the end of their story "God Bless You, Mr. Vonnegut," Kaufman and Proch's sensibility and playfulness shines through with the lines: "Several months later, back in New Jersey once again, Wade woke from a deep sleep and found himself sitting on an insurance machine in the local airport. This was a common occurrence and as such did not alarm."[18] Kaufman explained,

> There was a certain type of comedy that I was drawn to at a young age. There might be a certain amount of messiness and absurdism to that comedy that has a much larger influence on my stuff than I'm even aware of. I'm really interested in chaos. You're often told by writing teachers that you should write from a distance. You're told that you should write about something that happened ten years ago because that's the only way that you can really understand it. But I think that perspective is storytelling. It's a lie! The reality, when you're in it, is a very interesting moment when I'm writing, rather than at a distance. I think that's the truth. It's life. It's always where we are. The other stuff is never where we are.[19]

Like Vonnegut, Kaufman showed a flair for writing about chaotic and absurd situations, though grounded in a familiar reality. Just as his literary influence had written himself into some of his surrealistic novels without the safety net of writing from an emotional distance, Kaufman would later take that same risk and insert himself into the screenplay *Adaptation*.

During the 1980s, while Kaufman worked at the Art Institute in Minneapolis (he was the voice on the public address system announcing that "the museum will be closing in 15 minutes"), he and Proch (who served as a guard there) wrote a play called *The Fat Zip*. The story involved "the most loved man in the world, who accidentally robs a bank and becomes the most hated man in the world," Kaufman noted. Their stage play was produced at the Broom Street Theater in Madison, Wisconsin, and was well received. Despite the show's popularity, Kaufman didn't think it was a good production. "We saw it the night the opening night audience saw it, and we were cringing. We couldn't believe how wrong it was in every way."[20]

The writing partners also penned a 204-page screenplay about film school, entitled *Purely Coincidental*. John Mitchell, the arts and entertainment editor of Massachusetts' *North Adams Transcript*, described it as "a brilliant attempt at building a story on coincidence and featuring lots of Don Knotts jokes."[21] The boys blindly sent it to the acclaimed actor Alan Arkin, and he "sent back a really nice letter telling them it wasn't a screenplay, but an 'insane tone poem,'" said Proch.[22]

Kaufman was thrilled and remembered, "Usually we got the stuff sent back to us, or we never saw it again. You know, the big thing was, you can't submit unsolicited manuscripts. We were always up against that. The only response we ever got was from Alan Arkin. He read it and wrote back this really lovely letter, which was so encouraging. He really liked it. And that somebody read it—that Alan Arkin read it!—was really an enormous deal for us."[23] The boys then sent the script to what they believed to be Steven Spielberg's house, but to no avail. Even if it had been the correct address, no one would read their unsolicited scripts without an agent.

They continued to collaborate on spec scripts for television shows such as *Married with Children* and *Newhart*. While Kaufman continued working odd jobs in Minneapolis, including a position as a clerk in the circulation department of the *Star Tribune* newspaper, answering phones for $6 dollars an hour, he continued to mail scripts to prospective agents. For four and a half years he woke up at four o'clock in the morning to catch the frigid pre-dawn bus downtown, where he sat in a basement office to field questions about missing or wet newspapers. Although the people he worked with were kind, the customers wanted to know why their paper was delivered dipped in ice water or missing entire sections. He recalled of those early days, "It was freezing and everybody looked really sad on the bus."[24] This brings to mind the opening scenes of the highly underrated film *Joe Versus the Volcano* (1990), in which the beleaguered employees trudge to work under gray skies, past a looming gray gate, to their gray basement offices. This was also the time in Kaufman's life when he started to find himself reading and rereading Franz Kafka's novel *The Trial*. The protagonist, Josef K., is arrested for a crime he is never informed of. He spends years protesting his innocence to a long line of misdirecting bureaucrats and a judge he never gets to meet. K.'s plight spoke to Kaufman's own frustration. He knew he was living life in a grinding loop in Minneapolis. Adding to his daily slog dealing with angry customers was the frustration of knowing he had the talent to change his lot.

Although Kaufman was disappointed with himself, he continued to write television spec scripts including one for *It's Garry Shandling's Show*, in which Garry's audience gets bored and leaves the show to go to a volleyball game at the beach. Since Garry can't do his show without an audience, he buys a laugh track and promptly becomes addicted to it. He loves the feeling so much that he begins to use it in all aspects of his life. Around the same time, Kaufman wrote a spec on *The Simpsons* called "Acrobart," wherein Bart runs away, becomes hypnotized by an evil ringleader, and joins a circus of hypnotized people to become a high wire act. Kaufman's second *Simpsons* script involved Homer going to Bart's school for career day to talk about his work. It doesn't go well, and Homer is so hurt from feeling like such a failure at career day that he wants to embark on something impressive, so he signs up for a secret agent school.

Kaufman disclosed:

When I turned 30, I was living in Minnesota and I realized this wasn't going anywhere and that I'd better figure out something or give it up. I didn't know how to get to be a screenwriter, which was what I was trying to do, but I saw that if you can write a spec TV show and get an agent interested, then you can get a job out of nowhere, especially at that time, because there were a lot of sitcoms. This was in 1990. So I thought, OK, I'm going to do this. I wrote a TV spec, and I had a friend who had an agent, who said that he was willing to read my script. I sent it to him, and he never read it. But he said he was willing to, so I called him every week for a year, which is also something that I never had the tenacity or the courage to do before—when people rejected me in the past, I just went away, because I was embarrassed and ashamed of myself. But I was at my wit's end, and eventually he read it about a year and a half later.[25]

It wasn't until Kaufman lost his patience from being ignored for so long and asked the literary agent's assistant if there was *another* agent he could speak to that he was finally taken seriously. In the end, it was one of his spec scripts on *The Simpsons* that eventually garnered him representation and the attention he deserved. When the agent suggested Kaufman come out to Los Angeles for meetings, the tenacious writer embraced the now-or-never attitude, borrowed $3,000 dollars from his father-in-law and drove his rusted-out 1980 Jetta (sans air conditioning) to Hollywood. For two months, his wife Denise waited for word back in Minnesota while Kaufman was in California unable to get so much as an interview. Just as he was ready to turn back and go home to Minneapolis for good, he received a call from the offices of the television show *Get a Life* (1991–1992), starring Chris Elliott. A meeting with executive producer David Mirkin sealed his fate. Kaufman remembered, "I'd gotten one other job offer, for a bloopers-type television show with Fred Willard as the host (*Access America*) that was [ironically] shooting in Minnesota. And Mirkin told me, 'Don't go back to Minneapolis.' Had I gone back, I don't think I'd be doing any of this—because I wouldn't have come out here again. I just wouldn't have. That was it."[26]

In an episode of *Get a Life* entitled "1977 2000," written by Kaufman and directed by David Mirkin, Chris Elliott's character invents a time travel drink in order to go back in time to prevent his friend Gus (played by Brian Doyle-Murray) from being fired from the police department. As in most time travel stories (with apologies to Michael J. Fox), things go awry. As the episode opens with Gus already having been fired, Chris Elliott delivers a speech suggestive of what Charlie Kaufman's character might say in the movie *Adaptation*. Chris says to his friend, "I mean, think about it, you're ugly and you're doughie and bursting with love like some kinda rancid wedding cake that was left out in a terrible rain storm by a drifter who's smelly, named Hank who lives in a storm drain and he wears five pairs of pants even though it's summertime and he'd be much more comfortable wearing five pairs of shorts." Classic Kaufman indeed. Later in the same episode, Gus exclaims, "Go back in time? No. Listen, I saw this *Twilight Zone* once. This guy goes back in time to keep his young son from getting killed in a car accident, but when he returns to the present, the kid had become the evil fascist ruler of the world, enslaving millions. The dad felt lousy. You get my point?"[27] This funny reference is similar to a scene in an early draft of the movie *Being John Malkovich,* when the character Lester (the leader of the Malkovichian cult) travels through the maligned portal/tunnel, and sees in a reflection that he is now Hitler. Then he quickly realizes that he is merely the *actor* in that *Twilight Zone* episode.

In the second *Get a Life* episode penned by Kaufman, entitled "Prisoner of Love," Chris Elliott's titular character meets his pen pal, Irma (played by Nora Dunn), who has been corresponding with him from jail. Chris asserts that he is merely going to casually and quickly meet this woman and not let her into his life, but of course as soon as he sees her, he falls madly in love. The script calls for "fall in love music" to play over the scene, as Chris dreamily views her as a beautiful vision in a white gown. His response calls to mind another of Kaufman's characters, Joel, in *Eternal Sunshine of the Spotless Mind,* who by his own admission, has a tendency to fall in love with any woman who shows him the slightest attention.

When Irma says to Chris that she just dropped by to say hi and "borrow like five-hundred bucks and get the hell outta here," Chris jumps in with, "No, no you can't, you have to stay here. You have to, I insist, in fact here, you can take the bed. I won't need it ... as long as I can just ... crouch in the corner and ... stare at you all night." Toward the end of the episode after Irma has taken Chris hostage, a jogger named Sharon comes to the rescue. As Sharon battles Irma in a *Mod Squad*–style fight, Irma shouts, "You're gonna kill me? Get real Heloise."[28] Irma may have used that name as a pejorative, to imply that Sharon was a meek 1950s housewife, but Kaufman has always had a penchant for the tragic love story of Heloise and Abelard, and he possibly chose the name as a nod to their story.

While *Get a Life* proved to be Kaufman's most exciting television work, his first few weeks on the job were nerve-wracking for him. In fact, during the initial six weeks of his first show business job, he did not say a word in the writers' room. Thrown into a room with very competitive comedy writers, he knew he must participate and every day he was convinced he was going to be fired. Every day. When he finally *did* speak, he was so shy that he was inaudible. However, when he was assigned an episode and it was well received within the writing staff, the feedback gave him the confidence to press on and bring more of himself to the table. Before *Get a Life,* he had trouble showing people his writing, but over time, the positive responses led him to reveal what else he had up his sleeve.

Soon Kaufman was writing for TV's *The Dana Carvey Show* but found that much of his work didn't make it to the sketch comedy stage. In October 2008, he told *Vanity Fair*'s Jim Windolf that,

> It was a very difficult show in that way for me. Not only for me, but for many of the writers. It was a hard show to get stuff on. Robert Smigel ran that show, and the stuff that got on was stuff Smigel had written or Louis C. K. had written or Dino Stamatopoulos had written. They all sort of knew each other going in, and occasionally the actors who were regular performers would

get things on, because they had come in with pre-made sketches, things they had done at Second City. [Stephen] Colbert and [Steve] Carell and those people had their stuff. I wrote a lot for that show, but I just couldn't get anything on and then we got canceled. I think a lot of us were brought on for a certain kind of conceptual thing that they thought we were good at ... I'm friends with Louis and I'm friends with Dino, but it was frustrating for me ... I wrote a sketch called "Fifty Years to Live," about a man who was injected with a very, very slow-acting poison—so slow that it wouldn't be detectable and it wouldn't look like a murder. He's a forty-year-old man and he spends the rest of his life trying to find the guy who injected him, so he can get the antidote.[29]

Although during the 1990s Kaufman wanted to write for such shows as *The Simpsons*, *Larry Sanders*, or *Seinfeld*, he toiled for many years in little-known vehicles such as *The Edge*, starring Jennifer Aniston and Wayne Knight; *Misery Loves Company* with Chris Meloni; and the dreary *Ned and Stacey*. Other conventional and unpopular fare followed, including *The Trouble with Larry*, starring Bronson Pinchot and Courtney Cox. Pinchot was just coming off his beloved hit television show *Perfect Strangers* at the time, and his former cast mate, Mark Linn-Baker, who had played his hapless American cousin, served as the new show's director. The network executives at CBS were perhaps not ready for the progressive content that now bankrolls cable television, for at the time, they found one of Kaufman's scripts for *The Trouble with Larry* so subversive, they preferred to forgo TV air time that week completely, instead of showing the episode. As relayed to *Wired* magazine, Kaufman disclosed, "The title character mistakes his archaeologist/roommate's rare child-king mummy for a pinata, and then has to replace it with an injured tightrope-walking monkey in a full body cast." A person on staff took Kaufman's joke quite literally, believing he wanted them to maim a real monkey, and the script was never produced. He continued, "I was like, 'Man this is the stupidest thing. It makes no sense any way you look at it. The monkey's in a human hospital. A mummy doesn't look like a pinata. Why can't we make a fake mummy instead of stealing the monkey?' That's what was funny to me about it. It was like saying, This form is such bullshit, let's play around with it."[30]

No matter. Not to be deterred, Kaufman, a prolific writer regardless of the medium, penned several pilots that never aired including *Depressed Roomies* for Disney and *Rambling Pants*. The former was "about two guys who live in a tenement apartment, and ... Well, it's kind of silly. [Laughs] They're absurdist, I guess. It got attention and people liked it, but it was weird, and it dealt with sexuality that was questionable for television at the time. And it didn't feel like a sitcom—it wasn't naturalistic. It was sort of theatrical."[31] The very funny pilot was about two 25-year-old men, Arthur and Alan, stuck in a postcollege rut, living in a low-rent apartment decorated with a sagging old couch draped in a patterned sheet. One could describe it as a male, surrealistic *Laverne & Shirley*, in which the two roommates pine over the same checkout girl and hit the floor wrestling to work out their problems until one of them grows bored. Perhaps the myopic TV network balked when one of the roommates (after much harassing by the other one) pretended to be gay to sweet talk a gay carpenter into carpeting the apartment upstairs to cut down on the noise. Who can say.

The television pilot *Rambling Pants*, on the other hand, was a story "about a traveling poet whose name is Pants. He was a very bad poet but he doesn't know that," related Kaufman. "He travels the country and gets into different kinds of adventures—again, pretty silly. And that one has a lot of singing in it. People break into song way too much in that one—like every fourth or fifth line. He has a sidekick who was actually a newspaper reporter, who kind of went astray, and looks to Pants as a hero—this very naïve, sort of dumb Jimmy Olsen kind of guy. And I wrote something for HBO which was about a relationship. I wanted to follow this relationship from its inception, but it's sort of anti-romantic—it's a couple in this sort of a gridlock situation, where people are together, but there's never really any clear reason why. And it was called *In Limbo*."[32]

Another pilot that never came to fruition was a show for Disney called *Astronuts* (not Charlie's title). Kaufman remembered that the executives were very excited about their *title*, but had no idea for a premise. None. The Disney deal came very early in his writing career, and he was thrilled to have such an opportunity. Without parameters for any kind of story premise, Kaufman penned "a throwback to the Monkees about a goofy rock band who were astronauts by day, and their biggest issue was getting back from space in time so they could make their gig."[33]

While on hiatus between television assignments, he continued to write pilots including *Animals Behind Bars*, a story about zoo animal characters that garnered the attention of HBO executives. HBO seemed a natural fit for Kaufman, as it was known for championing unique, idiosyncratic work. However, the project, which offered a more naturalistic view of a relationship, was never realized. Kaufman remarked, "I get really frustrated with sitcom romance and movie romance in general, because it doesn't seem to bear any relationship to my own experiences in that realm ... I think there's a lot of damage done to me personally by movies that don't reflect the real world—because I tended to feel 'less-than' watching movies, because my life is never like that. So I didn't ever want to be mocking of them—I have sympathy for it, so I thought it might be interesting to present that."[34] For example, once while picking up a girl-friend from the airport, a young Kaufman made a valiant attempt to convey a bit of classic silver screen romance by sweeping her off her feet, quite literally, and spinning her around. "It was so not our relationship. I don't even think that I had any feelings like that for her, but I wanted the experience of feeling that kind of magnetism and chemistry. Spinning someone around looks so cool in movies but it was horrible. I was hoping that maybe this would elevate the relationship to another place but she didn't know what the f**k I was doing. I was probably mad at her for not knowing what the f**k I was doing, for not knowing that I was doing a silly movie convention that you could still have fun with."[35]

Although the hyperrealized romance of television and cinema may have adversely affected Kaufman's early personal life, a lightning bolt of good fortune, plus years of perseverance, were about to combine to sideline his reality. In a page out of what could easily pass as fiction, the legendary Francis Ford Coppola read the fledgling screenwriter's first feature film effort and was so impressed, that he shared it with his then son-in-law.

Enter Spike Jonze.

2

Why *Malkovich?* Why Not

It was the first time I was in love. I learned a lot. Before
that I had never even *thought* about killing myself.

—Steven Wright

"Why does this guy hate me," the respected actor John Malkovich said upon
first reading Charlie Kaufman's screenplay for *Being John Malkovich*.[1] When
Kaufman was penning the script to use as a writing sample back in 1994, he
had never even met Malkovich. While the screenplay made the rounds to
studios and the powers that be in Hollywood, it was well liked and respected,
but deemed unfilmable; that is, up until Spike Jonze read it. Even as recently
as the 2008 Cannes Film Festival, while Kaufman was walking the Croisette,
he reiterated that no one could get *Being John Malkovich* made until Spike
came along. "It was unlike anything I had ever read," Jonze said. "Later,
Charlie told me that the script had gotten around, and everyone said it was
unmakeable. I guess I didn't know any better."[2]

Spike Jonze (aka Richard Koufay, nee Adam Spiegel, of The Spiegel Catalogue family fortune), the wonderboy visionary MTV video director and
a former Coppola by marriage, was the one to deliver the real live John
Malkovich for the job. Kaufman had sent the screenplay to legendary director
Francis Ford Coppola, who handed it to his son-in-law, Jonze. When Papa
Coppola put a call in to the real John Malkovich to ask him to discuss the
script, he said of Jonze, "In ten years we'll all be working for him."[3]

Long before Spike Jonze had even read the script, the real John Malkovich's
business partner perused Kaufman's screenplay and set up a meeting with the
writer. The meet and greet was more of a security check process rather than
a creative one, as the savvy executive wanted to rule out the possibility of
Kaufman being a stalker. Kaufman recalled,

I remember the conversation went, "And what's your relationship to John"
[laughs]. It was such a weirdly worded question, so I tried to dance around

it. I said, well, I've always been a big fan of his, and I think he's a great actor. And he goes, "Uh-huh. And why the 7½ floor?" Now, I had no idea what that meant, so I said, well, you know, I thought it was funny and interesting visually to picture this half-floor between two floors. And he said, "Did you know that John's apartment number in New York is 7½?" At that point, I felt a chill running up my spine, and I thought, there's no way they're ever gonna believe anything I say. It was just an enormous coincidence. I mean who has an apartment 7½? I thought about that for weeks, it's like, what does that even mean? I understand how people have half addresses, but why would you have a half apartment number, especially if you're John Malkovich?[4]

It's hard to say which ended up taking more of an emotional toll on the writer, the writing process or this selling process. Film school hadn't taught him to secure a literary agent, much less sell his own material. The movie that would go on to earn an Oscar nod for Best Original Screenplay, almost never happened at all. When Spike Jonze first contacted Kaufman, the writer was thrilled that someone wanted to make the film, but had no idea who the music video boy genius was, and he didn't really care. Someone wanted to make his movie! In fact, Kaufman initially believed that Spike Jonze was the son of the musician Spike Jones. No matter. Kaufman was excited when he boarded a plane in New York, where he was living at the time, to introduce himself to Jonze, whoever the young madman was, at a Los Angeles restaurant. Kaufman arrived a bit early, as is his wont, and ordered a glass of soymilk. He was presumably excited about the meeting, as well as exhausted from the filthy plane ride—why don't they ever clean them?—and calmed his nerves by discreetly taking slow, deep breaths. When his watch showed it was 12 minutes after their scheduled meeting time, Kaufman scratched at an itch on his arm and reasoned that this Spike person must just be running late. Jonze had a busy life. Kaufman sighed and looked at the newspaper he had brought with him. He hated not having anything to read while he was waiting for someone. It was now 30 minutes past their scheduled meeting time, and Kaufman found himself reading the same line over and over and still not registering it. He couldn't concentrate. And why should he? He had the right to bristle at the nerve of this person who couldn't even call the restaurant to let him know he was running late. Perhaps he did call and no one told him, Kaufman allowed, as he craned his neck to see if there was a house phone near the hostess area. Forty-five minutes had gone by, and now came the thought that he had been trying to occlude from his swimming mind the entire trip to Los Angeles: This probably won't even happen.

Kaufman had originally written the script only as a writing sample and had never even imagined that it would be made. It was a sample, for god's sake, an example of what he could conjure up. He was thrilled with the fact that Francis Ford Coppola (*Francis Ford Coppola!*) and the highly respected John Malkovich had even read it in the first place, and, said that *they liked it.* That was sort of enough. It had already served its purpose of getting him more writing jobs anyway—his agent had just told him about somebody wanting him to do an adaptation of the Chuck Barris book for something. So, it was fine. Right? Kaufman looked down at his half drunk soymilk, frowned at it, and wished he had ordered an iced tea.

Spike Jonze never did show. It was 1996, the time before cell phones, or at least, before Charlie Kaufman had a cell phone and apparently Jonze hadn't heard that restaurants had phones. Kaufman remembered, "I was like, fuuucckkk yooooh." He shook his head slowly, in mild disgust and added, "I hated him."[5] The writer thought it was horrible that he had flown all that way across the country only to be stood up. He went back to his charmless hotel, chastised himself for knowing better than to trust people by now, and packed to go home. Jonze eventually rung him and made apologies, saying he was stuck in an editing room, working on a commercial. The video prince asked if they could meet the following weekend, and Kaufman thought twice, or perhaps, eleven times about not going. It could have not happened at all. None of it. But thank God or Buddha or Lou Reed that Kaufman reluctantly swallowed his pride and, for the sake of the project, met with Jonze, and they began the fruitful collaboration we know today.

The video director savant made his mea culpas to Kaufman and subsequently invited him to his home (where Kaufman knew that Jonze would have to turn up at some point), and for four days they went through the script, line by line. Jonze suggested Kaufman revamp the third act, as the original screenplay called for the main character and the devil to have a puppet duel to the bitter death (involving building-sized puppets, like Godzilla vs. Mothra—the cerebral years). The devil's team would then invade John Malkovich's body and finally rule the earth. The End. Jonze encouraged Kaufman to write a less chaotic, more emotionally resonant ending, similar to the tone of longing and frustration found in the first two acts.

Kaufman spent months making revisions, and once he and Jonze began casting, the director had some reservations about the possible contenders. Kaufman noted, "He initially didn't want Cameron [Diaz] but she really wanted to do it and she was good friends with Catherine Keener who was cast in the film and she wanted Cameron to do it. Cameron offered to read, which someone in her position normally doesn't do. She was great and he loved her. I don't think she was cast because she was a movie star."[6]

John Cusack, who had recently worked with Mr. Malkovich in the movie *Con Air*, read Kaufman's script and was of course immediately grabbed by its originality. "The thing that I took away from the film was the culture of celebrity, and the difference between artistic integrity and fame. People who are artists want the wrong thing sometimes, and that was one of Craig's character flaws. He is a very good puppeteer, but he wanted more recognition than perhaps a puppeteer is worth. One of my favorite lines in the film is when Maxine calls up and asks Craig if Malkovich is appealing. Craig responds, 'Of course, he's a celebrity.' That's something to ruminate on."[7]

As for casting the main attraction (Malkovich himself), that took more convincing. After speaking with Francis Ford Coppola about the script, John Malkovich had offered to help produce the film, but he declined to star in it. He actually suggested William Hurt for the role. Due to this slight setback, the movie's producers asked that Kaufman change the name in the title to another celebrity. After being forced to draw up a list of possible actors to headline the movie, Kaufman and Jonze spent weeks trying to think of new names, but couldn't fathom anyone else for the job. They fleetingly volleyed the idea of customizing it for Willem Dafoe but believed that the name Malkovich was funnier to say repeatedly. They also talked about the idea of *Being Christopher Walken,* but Kaufman reasoned that the actor's name was so pervasive that audiences had a fixed idea of him, especially after his performance in *Annie Hall.* Subsequently, they made a pact to stand their ground with the original title. One of the reasons being, Kaufman liked the idea of naming it after John, because although he was a well-known actor, he made great pains to stay off the celebrity radar. Malkovich had shunned the Hollywood scene to live in Paris, where he would be granted privacy, and one would be hard pressed to dig up gossip about him. Kaufman also thought that there was always something unknowable about the actor, and that ultimately, that quality would best serve the story.

The initial tale of what would later become known as *Being John Malkovich* was essentially "a story about a man who falls in love with someone who is not his wife." One of his first ideas for the project was to explore the notion of a half a floor of a building: the 7½ floor. Kaufman explained, "At that point, Malkovich was nowhere to be seen. But you get these ideas that make it fun to write, and then you start to build a world, and justify a world and make it work; you put in odd stuff but you have to make it organic to this world."[8] Later, as he kept advancing the story, he eventually came up with the idea for a portal, and "as soon as there was a portal, it went into Malkovich."[9] Eventually, with Coppola's persuasion, the actor relented. "I didn't want to be the one that kept it from getting made. It was good. Really good. And they kept telling me they'd never get it made unless I agreed to be in it."[10]

Once the real John Malkovich was aboard, he encouraged Jonze and Kaufman to go even further with making fun of his celebrity status. Jonze related, "Not only did he liberate us to be mean, he said the meaner the better. On the shoot, he made everyone comfortable with playing with this character John Malkovich, not taking this character seriously, and it enabled all the other actors to feel very loose. There's this scene where Malkovich and Catherine Keener are having sex on the sofa, and she slaps him on top of the head, and it makes this really loud smacking sound, and I don't think she could've done that if John hadn't come into it with this attitude of having fun with it himself."[11] Malkovich explained, "I told them not to be shy of making fun of me. Because they must have been on a very precarious perch—writing this script which satirizes this person John Malkovich and then needing that same John Malkovich to be in the film to get it made."[12] Having said that, Malkovich later noted of making the movie and of working with Jonze specifically, "I found myself in the rather bizarre position of having him say to me: 'No. You wouldn't move like that. John Malkovich would do it this way.' But I never once said anything like, 'Look. I AM John Malkovich. I should know.' I played it the way he wanted. I see this as a character. Not me."[13]

The film opens on an exquisitely carved marionette whose features are so well defined that the wooden puppet looks as if deep in thought. After the marionette paces the stage, it looks up to realize it is being used and driven to act by a manipulative god named Craig (John Cusack). The puppet attempts to spring free of his strings by thrashing out in elaborate ballet maneuvers, but ultimately exhausts itself and falls down, resigned to its fate for now. The man in control, the string puller, allows his marionette to rest and the camera pulls back to reveal him taking a sip of beer, feeling strong and content; however, this happy moment is symbolic of only a small aspect of Craig's life. His crammed, run-down storage space, the backdrop for his alluring, highly contained fantasy world of wooden dolls is the only place he feels in control. In the next scene, this god-like confidence is juxtaposed with Craig's real life, in which he lives with his preoccupied, frazzled wife Lotte (Cameron Diaz) and a menagerie of sickly animals in a cramped, dingy, New York apartment. While the mangy animals are ostensibly Lotte's children, Craig doesn't even remember their names. When Lotte asks him to take a look at the ailing chimp named Elijah, Craig's response is, "Which one is Elijah again?"[14]

Kaufman's original screenplay begins in a similar fashion; however, the original screenplay had a more magical realism quality to the story, as the script opens with Craig sitting at a dusty, cheap, card table. He is looking at a book entitled *Sit,* and upon opening it, the audience sees that the word *sit* is repeated, filling the book's pages. Craig stands up, but then thinks better of it and merely sighs. He looks at the book again, but now it is now entitled *Die.* He opens it up and the word *die* runs through the book as the audience hears a rooster crow.[15]

In the filmed version, as in the original screenplay, Lotte encourages Craig to get a proper job, and she argues that by doing so he may feel more fulfilled or at least better about himself. Craig sullenly refuses, insisting he is only a puppeteer: he can't pretend to be something else. He points out that the famous puppeteer The Great Mantini (his perceived nemesis) doesn't need a day job. Amid the squawking, roaming house pets, the audience sees Craig watching The Great Mantini on the news on television. The TV announcer says: "The crowd is enthralled as Derek Mantini, arguably the greatest puppeteer in the history of the world, performs *The Belle of Amherst* with his sixty-foot Emily Dickinson puppet, directed by the inimitable Charles Nelson Reilly."[16] In this brief, blink-of-an-eye sequence, the audience is given entre into an elaborately crafted inside joke. Kaufman's subversive, clever allusion to the one-woman play *The Belle of Amherst,* written by William

Luce, evokes the themes of fantasy versus reality borne of a life of Emily Dickinson's isolation. The mention of The Great Mantini's director, Charles Nelson Reilly, is doubly funny as Nelson Reilly, perhaps best known for his over-the-top, comedy bits on *The Hollywood Squares,* also directed the Luce play on Broadway in 1976.

After the TV clip, Craig turns to Elijah, who has been clutching his stomach in pain, and tells him he is lucky he is a monkey, in that no one expects anything of him. "If I were a monkey, I'd be the happiest man alive. Nobody expecting anything of me. Just sit on a couch and moan all day. That's the life."[17] In a slight change of dialogue from script to screen, Craig adds, "Consciousness is a terrible curse: I think, I feel, I suffer."[18]

Craig assumes that the chimp has no consciousness, but Kaufman writes the pet, Elijah, as having a stomach ache because of unresolved issues with his family. The joke on Craig is that Elijah does suffer. The chimp's stomach ulcer is perhaps a manifestation of the trauma he experienced while in captivity. Elijah couldn't free his family from being enslaved, so he holds onto that guilt, which in turn gives him stomach pains. Lotte, big hearted that she is, anthropomorphizes her pets to the point where she takes Elijah to a psychotherapist to unlock the root of his pain. Like Craig, the chimp expresses human characteristics such as love, guilt, and the gnawing need to redeem himself. Even Kaufman's choice to give him the name Elijah implies that this is no ordinary monkey. Like John Malkovich, John Cusack has also eschewed the Hollywood tabloid press. He noted, "I remember thanking Charlie and Spike because I got to do a scene where I was sitting on a couch in a hovel with a monkey telling the monkey that I was an unappreciated artist. I did that looking straight into the monkey's eyes. All I could think was, 'My god—this is as good as it gets. There's nothing that can compare to this.'"[19]

Craig Schwartz goes to great lengths to prove that unlike the work of his bête noire, The Great Mantini, his own work is substantive, not just contrived to be popular. And as for Lotte's proposal that he get a "real job," well, he would rather suffer through a physical beating than put down his puppet strings. He is a real artist, not a commercially viable hack.

In the movie version, Craig performs a show on the streets of New York, and as people hurry by, his beautifully crafted puppets perform a piece from Alexander Pope's poem "Heloise and Abelard" (the work from which the movie *Eternal Sunshine of the Spotless Mind* is named). The man and woman puppets are separated by a wall, and Craig directs them to sexually undulate toward each other until a little girl's father abruptly ends the performance by punching Craig in the face and knocking him over.

In the screenplay version, absent from the film, Craig goes to even further extremes to prove he is a proper puppeteer, when he answers a classified advertisement for a female puppeteer to teach at a school for girls. He waxes his body, shaves, sews himself a dress, applies makeup, and does a good enough impression of a woman to charm the school's headmistress to secure the job. The story takes us through Craig becoming a well-liked and believable teacher, until a student notices he is riding a man's bike, in a bike race full of girls. The scene cuts to Craig, still in his dress, but now sitting in a jail cell while his wife, Lotte, bails him out. On the tension-filled ride home in the car, she asks him, "Why'd you do it Craig?" To which he replies, "I'm a puppeteer."[20] Despite the setback, he then applies for a job calling for WOMYN-TEERS, looking for an African American, lesbian, separatist puppeteer for community outreach. He again dresses up like a woman, but the scene cuts right to Lotte picking him up after he has been beaten to a pulp. Another job he applies for seeks a female puppeteer wanted for a nudist colony marionette staging of *Oh Calcutta!* This time when Lotte picks him up, in the car she says, "You know, maybe you should speak to someone about this."[21]

Kaufman related,

> I think you can be as outlandish as you want or as surreal as you want, as long as the characters are based in something real. You can put them in any situation or any reality as long as their reactions have something to do with human beings and you're focused on that element of it. I'm not interested in necessarily doing realistic things, obviously. I like fanciful stuff. But it can't be just fanciful without people in it. Then it's of no interest. If you decide that people are turning into carrots or something as your story idea, then I think that I would have to figure out why that's important to me as a person and why that story resonates in some way. Otherwise there's no story. It's just a gimmick.[22]

When Craig finally relents and answers an ad for what seems like a more appropriate job, or, at least, a less dangerous one, he interviews for a position at LesterCorp., located on floor 7½ of a corporate building.

Craig is the one who introduces the audience to this *Alice in Wonderland*–like half floor of an office where the furniture and vending machines are scaled to a smaller size, as if this is all perfectly normal. Not only did Craig need to mentally force himself to even apply for the job, but now the tall, hunched-over, depressed puppeteer is also physically uncomfortable in this new work environment as well. The audience is unsure if he will even get past the receptionist, Floris (Mary Kay Place), who is possibly hard of hearing or simply amusing herself by pretending to not be able to hear him. Despite the difficulties, Schwartz successfully impresses the randy, affable, centenarian boss, Dr. Lester (Orson Bean), and becomes gainfully employed. Dr. Lester apologizes for his alleged speech impediment, but Craig assures him that he understands every word he is saying. The elderly, though preternaturally robust businessman, is flattered by Craig's remarks but replies, "I'm afraid I have to trust Floris on this one...she has her doctorate in speech impedimentology from Case Western. Perhaps you've read her memoirs, *I Can't Understand a Word Any of You Are Saying.*" When Craig replies that he has not, Lester continues, "Pity. It tells it like it is. That's why the eastern, read Jewish, publishing establishment won't touch it. That's a quote from the book jacket. George Will, I think."[23] Although to the audience Dr. Lester seems quite capable of speech, he tells Craig that his disability has made him lonely all these years. Kaufman explores language and the nature of understanding in many of his films. In *Human Nature,* the project he worked on after *Being John Malkovich,* he continues to explore human communication and its inherent flaws; in fact, one of the characters gives up on speaking altogether. And in his directorial debut, *Synecdoche, New York,* communication meltdowns between characters cause a classical nervous breakdown.

Back in the employee training room at LesterCorp., Craig sits through the corporate video that explains that LesterCorp. is situated on a half of a floor because an Irish ship captain named James Mertin built the diminutive space for his tiny wife. A bored Craig looks around the room to see a beautiful, cold colleague, Maxine. When he tries to strike up a conversation with her about the absurdly amusing history of their building, she replies that it's bullshit. In a line that did not make it to the screen, Maxine adds, "The real story of 7½ is so evil that it could never be revealed to Americans raised on sitcoms and happy news anchors." When Craig asks if this statement is true, Maxine retorts, "Well, truth is for suckers, isn't it." This cryptic remark will be reiterated later by John Malkovich's close friend Charlie Sheen, when Malkovich questions his own sanity regarding his relationship with Maxine: "The truth is for suckers Johnny."[24]

Charlie Kaufman's own quest for truth runs deep and parallels the damage that pop culture can reek on real relationships and the chance for authentic connections. The writer has said of his process,

> When you're trying to conduct a scene between two people, it's very hard to sort of realize that what you're doing is a rehash of something you've only seen in a movie. I try to sort of remove those moments and focus on the ones that are true to me. My father said, my father Drew, when I was a kid, one of the things he taught me was that, if you can't be drawing from life, and you can't see it, don't draw it. There's a tendency, if you're going to draw this plant [Kaufman leans forward and touches the leaf of a plant], well you're going to draw this leaf and these leaves because you understand that they're there. But the fact is, you cannot see them. And you're starting to do symbols as opposed to an actual sort of representation of it. And so, to me that's the same thing as not having a moral or even an understanding of a larger picture when I'm drawing. I try to find that moment when I understand and capture it as cleanly as I can.[25]

Importantly, in the published script, though absent from the film, when Craig tries to properly introduce himself to Maxine, he tells her that he is just starting out at LesterCorp. To his delight, she quotes Emily Dickinson: "How dreary—to be—Somebody / How public—like a Frog—/ To tell one's name—the livelong June—/ To an admiring Bog!" But when Craig proudly knows her reference to Dickinson, she coldly remarks, "I wouldn't know," and walks away.[26] Instead of bonding around their mutual knowledge of the beloved poet, Maxine leaves him staring after her. Much like Lotte's parrot at home, Maxine is merely mimicking something she heard or read. In true Charlie Kaufman form, he chose an Emily Dickinson quote, as the poet exemplifies the notion of truth in art. She eschewed anything to do with public persona, or donning a mask to cover her true nature in order to better fit into the world. Unlike the character Craig, she never yearned for the label of celebrity and never even sought publication. While Maxine is a Lady Macbeth–type character who controls the strings, she also shares qualities with Emily Dickinson in the sense that she has no affectations and no interest in being anyone else or pretending to be something she's not. Neither woman has a need for external validation. The similarities end there, however, as Maxine is barely human.

In the film, when Craig returns home after his first day at work, Lotte's pet parrot yells, "Help! She's locking me in a cage." This statement reflects how Craig feels about his current situation in life in his cramped quarters and equally cramped mind. The bird's mimicking cry may be a foreshadowing of what will happen to Lotte, as well as Craig's fate if he continues to act as Maxine's smitten puppet. To continue with the themes of frustration and truth, LesterCorp's seemingly befuddled receptionist, Floris, has developed a crush on Craig. Her hearing problems only seem to dissipate when he rejects her. She hears him speak clearly when he gently tells her that he is only interested in friendship. His truthful words only serve to hurt her, and she may be the smartest character in the movie by only choosing to hear what she wants to hear. Like Dr. Lester's perceived speech impediment, this is an example of how Kaufman likes to play with communication and how its breakdown can fail some of his characters.

Maxine, like many of Kaufman's female characters, is a hurricane of a personality and far more worldly and clever than Craig. She is not shy about confronting him about his sexual attraction to her and even bullies him as he makes an attempt at polite conversation. When Craig confesses that he likes her but doesn't know why exactly, she retorts by deriding him, and he gets flustered by her aggressive honesty. She cruelly ridicules him by saying if he isn't attracted to her because of her breasts, then he is a homosexual and she will not waste her time. In the published script, but absent from the film, Craig replies, "I'm not a homosexual. I just like women for more than their bodies. Y'know, it's the eternal yin/yang. The male and female forces complement each other. One is never complete without the other. So I absolutely respect that which is feminine."[27] Craig may be attracted to Maxine, but it is not her femininity that drew him to her. Maxine exhibits very few traditional feminine qualities, especially in Craig's yin/yang definition. Rather, he is attracted to her extroverted personality, supreme confidence, and steely presence. She is a Barbara Stanwyck type, a femme fatale. She is everything he isn't, and to be like her would be the perfect escape from his own drowning nature. Though she is incredibly cruel to him, Craig is intoxicated with her. Unlike the classic leading ladies of noir film, Maxine seems to be charmless and is never coy. Craig is enamored of her strength and repeats her name over and over, as if it is a new mantra for his life, or a little prayer. Her name, as her strong identity, is fixed. Craig's name, on the other hand, is flimsy and maligned. When he first enters LesterCorp., Floris calls him Mr. Juarez, then Miss Warts. Maxine, whose name is even more masculine than Craig's, of course wants nothing to do with a man who plays with puppets.

While Craig's home life and relationship with his wife continues to fall apart, he plays with and directs a beautifully crafted puppet he has created in Maxine's image. This is the only time he has control over her (albeit merely a doll version of her) and speaks to the puppet as if it were truly her. He tries to convince the doll why puppeteering is a fascinating and valid skill. As he impersonates Maxine's voice while play acting, Craig explains, "Perhaps it's the idea of becoming someone else for a little while. Being inside another skin. Moving differently, feeling differently."[28]

This notion recalls the joy Kaufman experienced as a younger man when he performed in plays. While this idea of escapism is sensual and sexy to Craig, Maxine is already comfortable in her own skin and the way she chooses to navigates the world. She has no need for his fantasy role playing. Craig's explanation of puppeteering (and acting) directly parallels his experience in the portal, which allows him to be inside someone else's skin for a while. In an early draft, Craig tells his boss that he found the little door. It is a dark, membranous tunnel, symbolic of the birth canal. This discovery could be the re-birth Craig needs, or at least a new adventure. The unflappable Dr. Lester, however, doesn't show concern about Craig's discovery and merely tells him there is a short film on just that subject in the employee orientation room. This short film stars the previous actors also finding the little door at work. On the video, they've been told (and they accept) that this door simply leads to a small store room for merchandise. Craig's response to this explanation echoes what Maxine thought of the original orientation film: "Bullshit."

When Craig crawls into the wet, dripping tunnel, he finds himself being sucked through. Although he made the choice to enter, once he's inside, he has no control over where he is going. Kaufman's direction in the screenplay reads, "There is a flash of light." Then, the audience finds itself in a upscale dining room in morning light. "The point of view (POV) of someone reading a newspaper. The person lifts a cup of coffee to his mouth. There is a slurping sound. The person puts down the coffee cup and newspaper and stands up."[29] At this, Craig loses his balance and wonders where he is. Still holding the point of view from behind this stranger's eyes, the man goes to the mirror, and both the audience and Craig see that this is the actor, John Malkovich. The well-respected actor is now in a cab and is suffering the taxi driver questioning his identity. The driver recognizes that he is a celebrity and claims to enjoy his work, but can't quite pinpoint his name and certainly not his work. "Mapplethorpe?" the cab driver asks. While inside Malkovich's body, Craig screams in amazement at the absurd situation he finds himself in. The cab driver goes on to say that he loved Malkovich in the jewel thief movie. Malkovich had never played a jewel thief. In a scene redolent of what must have happened to the real John Malkovich and other famous faces over hundreds of times, Malkovich once told a journalist, "I was sitting in Piccadilly, y'know, when a guy came up and asked some directions. So I told him where to go and I went back to reading my book. But he kept saying, 'Don't I know your face? Aren't you an actor? What have you done?' And finally I said, 'Look, why don't you go wherever it is you're trying to find.' Which might kinda sound snotty. But, by the 60,000th time, it really starts to be a drag."[30]

In one of the great comic scenes of all time, the point of view from John Malkovich starts to fade, and Craig finds himself literally spit out, lying in a ditch on the New Jersey Turnpike. After making his way back to his office, he tries to tell Maxine how important his discovery is, saying, "Am I me? Is Malkovich Malkovich?" Craig's discovery could answer the metaphysical questions of René Descartes's theory of the mind–body split.

This first trip into the portal seems to prove that the mind and body are indeed separate. Craig tries to talk with Maxine about this, but Maxine is disinterested in such fundamental questions and on her way to a bar, yet Craig tries to impress upon her what this could all mean. "But Maxine!" he tries to explain. "Can of worms! End of the world! Illusory nature of existence!" In Kaufman's scripted lines in this scene that are absent from the film, Craig asks, "Was the Buddha right, is duality an illusion?"[31] Maxine remains unfazed by the news of Craig's newfound portal and what it may imply, until she realizes there is money to be made. Craig is against turning what could be the answers to the universe into a simple theme park, but once he realizes that his Machiavellian love interest is going to exploit his find with or without him, he relents. Kaufman makes a point of the commercial value of fame over metaphysical dilemmas, as it is decided that The Malkovich ride costs $200 a pop.

When Craig tells Lotte about his discovery, to his surprise, she immediately wants to take a ride in Malkovich. Kaufman draws the married couple as the most unhappy of the characters as they are dissatisfied with their current lives and choices in each other. Like embracing a new drug, Lotte is more than happy to abandon her identity for awhile, just for the sake of escapism. Once in the vehicle of John Malkovich, she is able to feel sensual and complete, maybe for the first time in her life. Although it is not *her* life, nor her body, she becomes addicted to this new feeling. While at dinner in Dr. Lester's mansion, instead of a bathroom, Lotte finds what looks like a shrine to the actor John Malkovich. The wall of the room is covered with memorabilia from Malkovich's real life, including high school football pictures and photos from his childhood that are obviously authentic. (The real John Malkovich told the film's producers to call his parents to get pictures from his childhood.) She drops to her knees as if in church, praying to a saint or before a god. Lotte doesn't tell Craig of her discovery in Lester's home, as she no longer trusts her husband and is growing confident in her newfound desire to become Malkovich. She also wants to keep this knowledge to herself as it provides her an intimate and private connection.

As Craig plays with his Maxine puppet at home, he removes the doll's head and replaces it with a puppet head made in his own likeness. He longs to be her, or own her, or both. When his wife unexpectedly visits him at LesterCorp., he is unnerved by having her in the same room as his new love, Maxine. When he asks Lotte why she isn't at the pet shop, where she would normally be at this time of day, in a few lines of dialogue from an earlier draft that were not filmed, she answers, "Fuck pets. Is this your partner?"[32] Everything that Lotte once lived for no longer matters. She used to be passionate about animals, but now her world has been irrevocably changed. The fact that she swears and shows such new resolve means she has already begun to metamorphose. The only thing important to her now is being someone other than her former self. Maxine is amused as Craig and Lotte's tension in the room is palpable. Lotte tells Craig that she has decided she is a transsexual and is going to Dr. Feldman about sexual reassignment. In an example of Charlie Kaufman's comic timing style, Craig blurts out, "This is absurd. Besides Feldman's an allergist. If you're going to do something, do it right."[33]

When Lotte meets Maxine, she is attracted to her for the same reasons her husband is. Maxine's sexy, bold, and extroverted nature is the polar opposite of Lotte, who is quiet, caring, and subservient. When Lotte is on the Malkovich ride, she crosses gender lines and relishes having a strong masculine exterior. Desperate to hold onto her newly discovered "self," she now wants a sex change because she believes that the feeling of being a man on the outside (what is presented to the world) reflects her inner feelings. The shell is what she is after: she never really becomes Malkovich on the rides because she always retains her own feelings as Lotte.

As a way to illustrate part of the actor John Malkovich's day-to-day life, Kaufman makes sure to include play rehearsals and the character's work preparations. In an early draft, when Lotte inhabits Malkovich, the actor is reading from Clifford Odets's play *Awake and Sing*, a story about a family in which the parents manipulate their children, while they seek their own dreams or identity. Malkovich practices his lines from the play, "So you believe in God ... you got something for it? You worked for all the capitalists. You harvested the fruit from your labor? You got God!"[34] The play underscores the dichotomy between idealism and literal materialism and enhances *Being John Malkovich*'s theme of the idea of celebrity.

In the final film version, the actor reads from Chekhov's play *The Cherry Orchard*, which is also about family machinations. In the scene, Malkovich reads about a character's disdain for materialism, while he comfortably sits in his well-appointed penthouse in New York. And just as the characters aren't really interested in John Malkovich (other than as an empty vessel to be used), Chekhov's characters don't really give a damn about the cherry orchard either. In reference to the choice of plays, Kaufman explained, "I knew I wanted Chekhov, and I went through a bunch of his plays to find lines that would be both overwrought and silly sounding. I also like that Lotte is learning the lines through Malkovich's eyes."[35] When Maxine calls the real John Malkovich on the phone for the first time, Lotte is residing in his body. The formerly subdued Lotte is enjoying the actor's confidence as he reads the play aloud before answering the phone. From inside Malkovich, she tries to convince him to indeed meet Maxine for a drink, although she is a complete stranger and this behavior is out of character for him.

The screenplay cuts to Craig and Maxine in the office, interviewing their first "real" client for the Malkovich ride. In dialogue from the published script, but missing from the movie, the potential candidate expresses a similar thought that Kaufman will further explore in the film *Eternal Sunshine of the Spotless Mind.* The client exclaims, "Oh this is just the medical breakthrough I've been waiting for. Are there any side effects? Please say no! Please say no! ... Long-term psychic or physiological repercussions?" All he wants to hear is that this unprecedented experience will be safe. Maxine supplies him with the answer, while applying her usual élan, "No. Don't be an ass."[36]

After a successful "trip," the client must have spread the word about the Malkovich ride to his friends, as the film cuts to a shot of a long line of heavy-set men outside Craig and Maxine's office. Although John Malkovich is everyone's "second choice" of portals, he is a big hit. At this point in an earlier draft, but not on the screen, Dr. Lester confronts Craig and tells him he is making a big mistake. Lester exclaims, "There are rules, boy, procedures, etiquette. This is not a toy. I've been waiting seventy years to utilize this room, grooming myself ... paying tribute, seeing all his motion pictures again and again ... and I am not alone. There are others. We are legion."[37] Just as Kaufman chose the biblical name Elijah for Lotte's pet monkey, he has Dr. Lester use the word *legion,* a biblical reference to the devil's followers. Back at Dr. Lester's mansion, the scene takes on a tone reminiscent of the film *Rosemary's Baby.* Lester addresses a room full of cloaked people, kneeling with candles as they all chant, "How much do we love you? We loved you in *Making Mr. Right.* That is how much we love you. We even own the director's cut on laser disk. Please accept us into your head as we have accepted you into our hearts ... Amen."[38]

Ironically, the people who choose to take the Malkovich ride don't mind that they experience the actor doing the same banal things of everyday existence as they do in their own lives. He orders bath towels and looks in his half-empty refrigerator like an average everyday citizen might, but his celebrity status hides the mundane or makes the blandness of life okay. He is a star, goddammit.

Although Maxine has no need for stardom, she is infatuated with Lotte and she uses Malkovich for her own reasons, other than using him as a business vehicle. Although John Malkovich thinks that Maxine is his lover, Maxine consistently waits for Lotte to enter the vehicle of Malkovich before she physically touches him. Maxine knows that Malkovich and Lotte are separate. Malkovich is flattered by the sexual attention and even goes along with Maxine's odd penchant for calling him by Lotte's name. After Lotte returns to their home after 4:00 A.M., Craig realizes she has been with Maxine, via John Malkovich. Lotte tells her husband that she values his friendship and wants to stay together platonically, if possible. In true classic Kaufman style, Craig answers, "I feel that somehow my parents never prepared me to make this particular decision. Not that I blame them. How could they know? Today's world is so complicated."[39] Ultimately, Craig realizes that he can only conquer Maxine through Lotte and takes his wife hostage. He binds her up in her pet monkey Elijah's cage and although she yells for help, the agitated neighbors, accustomed to the many animal noises and screams usually emanating from the Schwartz's apartment, merely yell back at them to shut up.

Meanwhile, John Malkovich is in full dress rehearsal on stage, playing the titular character in *Richard III*. He paces and ponders while he rants, "Was ever a woman in this humor wooed? Was ever a woman in this humor won?"[40] While Malkovich acts out these ironic lines, Maxine impatiently looks at her watch and signals him to stop the entire rehearsal because she is ready to be with him, or rather be with Lotte within the Malkovich vessel. Maxine wants to keep her scheduled time with Lotte. The nature of Richard III's frustration lends itself to the overall movie, and Kaufman chose that particular play because, "I liked the idea that Malkovich would have to rehearse in a hump."[41]

As the story unfolds, anyone may take a turn *using* Malkovich (for a small fee of course), but it is Craig who learns to actually control him as a puppet master would. With a little practice, Craig can now move Malkovich's limbs and even has sex with Maxine while she erroneously believes that Lotte is still inhabiting Malkovich. Once Craig is able to *speak* through the Malkovich vessel, the real John Malkovich finally realizes there may be supernatural powers at work here. When the distraught actor consults his close friend Charlie Sheen on the matter, Sheen chalks it up to John being stoned. As Charlie Kaufman himself might say, Malkovich yells, "I gotta know the truth Charlie," to which his friend replies, "The truth is for suckers Johnny boy."[42] The actor takes matters into his own hands and follows Maxine to the Mertin-Flemmer building. After he cuts to the front of the line that has formed outside an office, and confronts Craig, Craig tries to explain that their little business merely serves as a "simulation," but Malkovich insists that he experience this "ride." In a line of dialogue resonant of Philip K. Dick's short story, "We Can Remember It For You Wholesale," Craig answers, "You? Why I'm sure it would pale in comparison to the actual experience."[43] Charlie Kaufman has been an admirer of Philip K. Dick's writing since his friend from college Paul Proch turned him on to his work. In "We Can Remember It For You Wholesale," the main character's lifelong ambition is to visit Mars. Due to everyday work commitments and family responsibilities, he doesn't think he will ever fulfill his dream. Instead of the time and expense of traveling, modern technology in the time in which he lives offers the opportunity to have a "memory" of the experience implanted in his brain: it's a false memory, of course, and as Craig refers to the Malkovich ride, a simulacrum. When Dick's main character Quail asks if the memory will be convincing enough to satisfy his dream of traveling to a different planet, the technician tells him, "More than the real thing sir. Had you really gone to Mars you would have now forgotten a great deal; our analysis of true-mem systems— authentic recollections of major events in a person's life—shows that a variety of details are very quickly lost to the person. Forever." Quail reluctantly agrees to the procedure and relents that he'll have to settle for this operation instead of truly having the experience for himself. One of the salesmen at the false memory company quickly assures him, "Don't think of it that way. You're not accepting second best. The actual memory, with all its vagueness, omissions and ellipses, not to say distortions—that's second best."[44] The actor John Malkovich bravely insists on going into the portal, where he finds himself in a restaurant populated with incarnations of himself and only himself. He is horrified, and as if he is a fully conscious adult trapped in an infant's mind, he cannot communicate as all the other Malkoviches around him expect him to understand the only word they use to imply all meaning ... the word *Malkovich*. The Malkovich waiter asks him what he would like to order, while only repeating the word Malkovich. His date, a female Malkovich, smiles at him adoringly. The female lounge singer, also a Malkovich, warbles the lyrics, "Mahl ko vicchh." In an earlier draft, Kaufman included a psychedelic montage reminiscent of the tone of the classic horror film *Rosemary's Baby*. It calls for Malkovich to hurtle through swirling eddies of garish, colored lights, while naked elderly people point and laugh at him.

Back at the apartment, Lotte's monkey Elijah successfully unties her (and in doing so redeems himself from failing to save his family back in the jungle when he was younger). Kaufman writes Elijah as freeing his mind and himself from a caged existence in a way that Craig can never hope to. In an earlier draft, Kaufman went even further with Elijah's self-actualization and had him fight evil and preserve a part of paradise he finds with Lotte in the end. In the final script, when Lotte warns Maxine that Craig now has full control of Malkovich's body, instead of being moved to anger or hurt, Maxine is intrigued. She is no fool for love as her real interest is power. She is finally impressed with Craig's puppeteering skills, and since she herself can control Craig, in essence, she can also direct Malkovich's choices in life. The real John Malkovich tries to rebuff Maxine, but now that Craig has control, Malkovich is being consumed.

When the lost, wandering Lotte confides in Dr. Lester, he comforts her and explains that his real name is not Lester and that he is in fact the original Captain Mertin who found the magical portal. Charlie Kaufman may have named this character Mertin as a nod to the Trappist monk, Thomas Merton, who was known for his teachings on religious mysticism. Merton, who was an ordained priest but struggled against the vows of his vocation because he fell in love with a woman, is also symbolic of Craig's doomed love for Maxine, as well as the story of Heloise and Abelard that is so prominent in Kaufman's work. Moreover, Dr. Lester also often addresses Lotte as "my child" just as a priest would speak to one of his parishioners. Once Dr. Lester introduces Lotte to his "friends," a group of older worshipers also waiting to enter the Malkovich vessel, the film again takes on a *Rosemary's Baby*–like flavor, as the scene is filled with elderly people looking anxious but welcoming, as if they have something sinister to hide.

Although the real John Malkovich continues to attempt to throw off Craig's powerful, all-encompassing will within his body, Craig now has ultimate control of the previously imposed 15-minute limit to the vessel, proving that Andy Warhol can suck it. When Maxine provocatively tells Craig to do a puppet show in Malkovich, the slightly bulky actor performs a graceful and passionate dance, redolent of Craig's impossibly lithe puppets. He somersaults, pliés until exhausted, then folds into a heap on the floor. It is a magnificent feat for a man of any age. He proudly calls this piece, "Craig's Dance of Despair and Disillusionment."

In an early draft of Kaufman's script, in a departure from the final film, Craig excitedly tells Maxine that they should no longer hide the fact that he can control the famous actor. Instead, his idea is to make his talent known to the world and present John Malkovich as the world's most complicated puppet. Craig himself would be famous, as the only puppeteer man enough to work the strings. The Great Mantini would just faint. Following this storyline, Craig and Maxine furiously fill in the portal with cement. Dr. Lester and Lotte, followed by the Malkovichians, burst in on them but Lester wisely keeps Lotte from attacking Craig as he knows they must preserve "the vessel." Maxine and Craig leave the building unharmed as the elderly Malkovichians attempt to salvage the portal by clawing at the cement with their weak hands. Maxine and Craig (now permanently seen as Malkovich) visit Malkovich's agent. The actor informs him, "I'll get right to the point now Larry. I'm a puppet now—I'm being controlled by the world's greatest puppeteer, Craig Schwartz," to which the clueless agent replies and nods agreeably, "Oh yeah, he's good."[45] The newly packaged Puppeteer Malkovich's first show is in glittering Las Vegas as opposed to the filmed version, in which the audience sees him performing in a small-town, dusty supper club in the Catskill mountains of New York.

In a great comedic scene left out of the final film, Dr. Lester crawls through the portal again, but despite the Malkovichians attempts to salvage it, the portal is ragged and crumbling. Once he makes it through, Lester finds himself in a 1940s black-and-white scene with bombs dropping around him. He sees through someone else's point of view and is startled, but somehow this seems familiar to him. He walks past a mirror and exclaims, "My God, I'm Hitler in the bunker! Aaaahhh! Aaaah!" Just then, a director yells, "Cut!" and we see an entire camera crew around Dr. Lester. In voice over, Lester reveals, "Oh, I'm just that actor in that *Twilight Zone* episode."[46]

While Lester, Lotte, and the fellow Malkovichians think up a plan to rid themselves of Craig without hurting the real John Malkovich, Lester confesses that he is actually 205 years old. "Lots of carrot juice, little lady. That, and a deal with the Devil." In a 1999 interview with *The Boston Herald,* John Malkovich echoed Kaufman's scripted words when he explained one of his reasons he made the film. "What better person to know what's asinine about you than yourself?" Malkovich noted. "To me it was a pact with the devil, because in this case it's me, but it could have been William Hurt, Gary Oldman, whoever really. Sharon Stone." The actor continued, "You make a pact with the devil in that you subject yourself to a certain amount of ritual abuse and hazing so you can be part of making a point about the culture at large and the media and people's obsession with celebrity. To make these points, I'm the person whose life is laid open in a way. That concerned me—as so-called public people go, I'm a fairly private person—so that was a decision. I don't think this person Charlie Kaufman's intent was to flatter. But I loved the writing and my first response was to change it to Tom Cruise or you or anybody else."[47] In Kaufman's early draft, there is another really funny reference to the film *Rosemary's Baby.* Continuing with the theme that a celebrated actor sells his soul to the devil, Dr. Lester uses refrigerator magnets to explain to his followers that his name is an anagram—but it falls short of the correct spelling. Lester, now a little flustered, mutters, "It used to work, I'm sure of it."[48]

It is at this point in the story where Kaufman's original screenplay veers wildly from the screen version. The original third act was Spike Jonze's main concern, in that he felt it was too chaotic and set a different emotional tone from the first two-thirds of the story. In the final script, Maxine and Malkovich go on to enjoy his newfound fame as a puppeteer. In a television biopic covering Malkovich's transformation from respected, enigmatic theater and film actor to celebrated puppeteer extraordinaire, friends and celebrities such as Brad Pitt and Sean Penn make hilarious cameo appearances. Even director David Fincher, posing as Christopher Bing, the national arts critic for the *Los Angeles Times,* shows up in the documentary. A particularly funny scene that shows Kaufman's knack for writing comedy combined with pathos is evident in the clip from the TV biopic in which Malkovich teaches at Juilliard. Malkovich passionately instructs students on the art of puppe-teering. He quickly corrects one student by telling him that he must himself feel the pain, not simply force the puppet to move, but infuse it with sentient knowledge of emotion. Frustrated, he spouts to his students that unless they truly suffer, then their work is just a novelty act…"it's Topo Gigio. Nothing more."[49] This is a funny reference to the Italian children's hand puppet made famous on the *Merv Griffin Show.*

In Kaufman's previous version of the third act of the screenplay, Lotte decides she cannot join Dr. Lester and his followers as she now knows he is on the side of evil, and she returns to her beloved pet Elijah. On screen, Lotte chases Maxine through Malkovich's thoughts—through a series of childhood and teenage humiliations. The audience glimpses the young Malkovich being bullied after school, as well as an awkward moment with a girl during his young adulthood. Kaufman explained that although the characters are using John Malkovich, this is the closest they ever really get to him. "There's a moment when they go through his subconscious, but until that point, no one knows what he is feeling. They see through his eyes and they use his body, but he's still a mystery. I don't think anyone in the movie is particularly interested in Malkovich."[50]

Another added comic dimension that was cut out of the final film involves Dr. Lester and his business partner, Flemmer. Although in the film version, Flemmer is only mentioned as someone the company has lost track of over the years, in the script he is the real string puller behind the scenes, and Lester affectionately refers to him as "boss"—as in, "It's just me, boss, I brought croissants." Dr. Lester and his old friend Flemmer play out a funny exchange about the other characters: Lester tells Flemmer, "The kid's got talent. You've never seen Malkovich like this. Schwartz had him up there singing and dancing. Impressions." To which Flemmer replies, "Impressions? Those are hard." Lester adds, "Very talented son of a bitch. Too bad we can't kill him." Flemmer remarks, "I suppose I could come to him in a dream. I don't know. That's the best I can think of right now." Lester asks, "A scary dream?" Flemmer responds, "No, a sexy dream. Of course a scary dream."[51]

Kaufman's original third act called for Malkovich's new puppetering skills to become so renowned that Craig's nemesis, the great Derek Mantini, challenges him to a puppet duel. Mantini suggests they vie for the definitive title of World's Greatest Puppeteer, by pitting his building sized Harry S. Truman puppet against Craig's equally huge John Malkovich puppet. However, Mantini insists that they eschew Vegas-style special effects for a true performance: he suggests the puppets compete by performing the stage play, *Equus.* Although Craig (still in Malkovich's body) says he's never heard of it ("Sounds boring. Are there any songs?"), he accepts the challenge. "I'm not afraid. I toured for a year with the National Puppet Company's production of *Long Day's Journey Into Night.*"[52] Kaufman also makes a passing reference to this same Eugene O'Neill torture chamber of a play in the film *Eternal Sunshine of the Spotless Mind.*

While Kaufman's original script called for 60-foot dueling puppets to juggle chain saws and transform into literal swans in a packed auditorium, the filmed version shows Craig having to decide between leaving Malkovich's body to save the kidnapped Maxine from the Malkovichians or remaining in John Malkovich. He realizes that even controlling the world-famous John Malkovich has not merited true love. In addition, and perhaps more importantly, despite Craig's money and acclaim, he still isn't far removed from his state of mind at the beginning of the story. Regardless of his talent, he is just as anonymous as he was when he was a street performer. It is still John Malkovich who is famous, not Craig Schwartz.

Craig finally leaves Malkovich's body, and Dr. Lester and his flock are then able to enter the vessel. In Kaufman's early draft, Lotte and her noble monkey, Elijah (who speaks sign language) go on to create a paradise of their own, amidst the grey landscape and zombie-like city crowds yelling in the street, "Hail Malkovich, king of the damned."[53] Lotte knows that she alone must stop the cultists and returns to the Mertin-Flemmer building intending to bomb the portal. However, she finds a ragged-looking Craig, and they both realize it is too late to stop the Malkovichian rule. Lotte invites him to join her and Elijah in their little patch of paradise far from the dreary oppression of the city, just as Kaufman's script calls for the audience to pull back to see that the Great Derek Mantini is actually pulling the strings of the puppet posing as Craig. The script calls for the instructions: "Now we see filaments attached to Mantini's arms, and we follow them up to find that Flemmer is controlling Mantini. Flemmer throws his head back and laughs, 'One serpent, coming up.'"[54] Tellingly, the last page of the original draft includes a music cue for the song "Put Your Hand Inside the Puppet Head," by the band They Might Be Giants.

In the conclusion of the film version, Dr. Lester, his wife Floris, and his congregation all reside inside John Malkovich. It is implied that the real Malkovich has come to terms with this arrangement and even confides in his close friend Charlie Sheen as to how they can all go on living forever. "All of us. You, me, Floris, ... Gary Sinise maybe." Malkovich's manner, dress, and speech pattern now all match Dr. Lester's persona. While Lotte and Maxine are now a couple raising their young daughter Emily, the audience hears Craig's muffled voice and sees the two women from little Emily's point of view. The audience can infer that Craig tried to gain entrance to Malkovich once more, but did so only after the actor's 44th birthday (which is apparently the age limit for successful vessel jumping) and is now forever trapped behind the eyes and mind of this little girl. He is doomed to watch Maxine and his ex-wife lead their fulfilling lives as a family. Once a God-like master of an Oscar-nominated, celebrated icon, Craig is now condemned to helplessly watch Maxine and Lotte share a love that he was, and may forever be, denied.

Coming full circle back to the beginning of the story, Craig has returned to a cramped, claustrophobic cell of an environment in which he has no control. In the end, he is puppet.

When asked what the story means, Charlie Kaufman declines, because what is more important to him is that his audience have their own unique experience of his films without being colored by his own intentions. However, certain themes and ideas weave their way through much of his work. In *Being John Malkovich,* themes of mortality are explored through the story of Dr. Lester and his followers, as they bide their time on earth until they can reside in their god John Malkovich. Although Dr. Lester can only urinate sitting down and needs to relieve himself every 15 minutes, he tells Craig, "Nobody wants to die, Schwartz."

In Kaufman's film *Adaptation,* the accidental death of his character John Laroche's mother informs the rest of his life. In *Eternal Sunshine of the Spotless Mind,* Joel watches his memories blink out before him (his life flashing before his eyes as in the near death experience) as he desperately tries to snatch them back. And in Kaufman's magnum opus, *Synecdoche, New York,* Caden Cotard, obsessed with his own deterioration, examines his own mortality until his last breath.

The mind-body problem is also one of Kaufman's prevalent themes. The physical body is a hindrance, especially in the films *Being John Malkovich, Adaptation,* and *Eternal Sunshine of the Spotless Mind.* Many of the Malkovich-ride clients are physically heavy and see one of John Malkovich's good qualities as being "thin man extraordinaire!"[55] The character Charles Kaufman in *Adaptation* also berates himself for being overweight. In *Human Nature,* Lila can't live as a "normal" woman because her body is covered in hair due to hormones. Kaufman's characters believe it is their physicality, and not their neurosis about their physicality, that keeps them unhappy. *Eternal Sunshine of the Spotless Mind's* sad sack Joel lives in his mind and memory (or what's left of it) and doesn't seem to have any connection or use for his physical body either.

And to address the question that is still asked of Kaufman even to this day: *Why* name the movie after John Malkovich and build it around that specific person? It was simply the name that popped into Kaufman's head as he was writing, and he doesn't have an answer any more satisfactory than that. But the Oscar-nominated actor did of course wonder why him. "Spike didn't even know me. The writer, Charlie Kaufman, didn't know me. I just happened to be the one they chose. I kept thinking, if they made it about Bill Hurt or Bruce Willis, it would be hilarious. But that just isn't what he wrote, and they didn't want to settle for anything else."[56] When asked what themes reveal themselves and what the story means from his unique perspective, John Malkovich stated, "I think it's about acting—opening the door into the mind of someone else, and how escaping your own mind for fifteen minutes, you see the beauty and fascination and eroticism even in the most boring things, but what it really is about is something more sinister. It's the idea that we now lead virtual lives. We live our joys and sorrows through the lives of public people."[57]

Kaufman himself has said of the overall concepts of the film, "A lot of it comes from the idea of not wanting to be yourself and being envious of other people. There is for sure the idea of looking out in the world and feeling you don't deserve to be there. How do you come to feel you have as much right as anyone else to be on this planet, when you have a barrage of information telling you that you don't have a right to be here, or that you have to change yourself to be allowed to be here? I took each character and on an instinctive level explored how they would react to that anxiety."[58]

By the end of 1999, *Esquire* magazine called *Being John Malkovich* "The Last Great Movie of the Century." Their movie reviewer exclaimed, "Like Godard's *Breathless,* which copped to the truth that the movie-fed flimsiness of modern life was what made it exciting, *Being John Malkovich* is the kind of breakthrough that leaves every other movie around looking clueless; it's about all the things that they don't know they're saying."[59] In 2000, Charlie Kaufman was nominated for an Academy Award for Best Writing: Screenplay Written Directly for the Screen. Spike Jonze was nominated for Best Director as was Catherine Keener for Best Supporting Actress. Kaufman won the Writers Guild Award, and the film was honored with Best First Feature Film Award at the Independent Spirit Awards, as well as Best Screenplay from BAFTA (British Academy of Film and Television Arts) and the Los Angeles Film Critics Association. Although it was Alan Ball who would take home the Academy Award on Oscar night that year for *American Beauty,* Kaufman now found that he was on the world stage. Although he had worked for years writing for television, it was the success of *Being John Malkovich* that thrust him into the spotlight. Suddenly, the press was deeming him an overnight success; however for Kaufman, it had been a long night. That film alone had taken five years to make.

Beyond the Hollywood accolades, what surfaced to be most rewarding for the writer was his friendships with director Spike Jonze and Catherine Keener. More than just Kaufman's first film director, Jonze became a trusted confidant. Kaufman related, "I learned a lot from Spike. He does things without being afraid. He directed without having the experience and David O. Russell offered him an acting job and he did it. So it's a cool way to be in the world."[60] Catherine Keener, who was nominated for many acting awards for her role as Maxine in *Being John Malkovich,* would later prove just as important to Charlie Kaufman in his subsequent films *Adaptation* and, especially, *Synecdoche, New York.*

In the post-dawn of the Academy Awards ceremony, the pressure was now on to keep his momentum as a sought-after screenplay writer. Never again would he have to write for the sitcom world if he didn't choose to and soon he was taking on two to three feature film writing projects at a time. In his newfound autonomy as a writer, however, he missed his old friend Paul Proch. They were still friends of course, but their lives had changed. Kaufman revealed, "In the case of *Being John Malkovich,* which is the first screenplay I wrote by myself, I was trying to take two separate ideas and combine them. So I would see if I could surprise myself, if I could force myself into directions that were unanticipated. It was a conscious decision to try and duplicate that process of writing with someone else, but doing it by myself. But one of the reasons it's nice to have a collaborator is that when things get bad, you can have fun with it, you can make jokes about it."[61] In addition to missing the comfort of having a trusted friend to work with and bounce ideas off of, Kaufman also found himself butting up against both the moviegoers' and studios' expectations that his next movie would be something in the form of *Being John Malkovich 2.*

Human Nature Ain't All It's Cracked Up to Be

I awoke without having parted in my sleep with the
perception of my wretchedness.

—Pip from *Great Expectations*

The critical and box office success of *Being John Malkovich* swung Kaufman
into a new stratosphere in Hollywood. The writer was thrilled on behalf of
the hardworking and talented crew and cast of *Being John Malkovich* that
they were being appreciated for their many contributions to making that
project come to fruition. Their accolades were more than deserved. But personally, Kaufman was still the same person he had always been, and yet suddenly, industry executives who wouldn't have taken the time to sneeze in his
direction as little as a year earlier, were now inviting him to parties, to lunch,
to meetings in Paris. He found it hard to reconcile this new popularity with
the fact that he was still him.

When he was asked to write an introduction to the published script version of *Being John Malkovich*, he honestly told them he didn't know what to
say. The publishers told him to just write anything. They told him that some
of the people interested in studying the craft, also like to read about the
writer, and hope to glean advice. What he handed in was partly funny, partly
depressing, but completely honest: the nature of Charlie Kaufman. The introduction is written in three installments; the first one was written at three
o'clock in the morning: "The only thing I can talk about, the only thing
that's on my mind at the moment is that the human being can be a treacher-
ous creature. And that sometimes they can tell you they love you and they
care about you and maybe they don't. How terrible is that, to come to that
realization? Of course it makes sense. Nobody could really like me. I mean,
nobody ever has before. So I sell a screenplay and suddenly someone likes

me. Just a coincidence right? Yeah, right. If there's anything I can say about screenwriting, it's that you need to write what you know. And I don't know anything. I exist in a fog of confusion and anxiety and clutching jealousy and loneliness." In the second installment Kaufman apologizes: "Crap. That's my big finish? It's nothing. Almost like a joke. It's a punchline and not a very good one ... I'm sorry. I'm just an insignificant guy who wants to be significant. I want to be loved and admired ... I want everyone to think I'm brilliant. And I want them all to think I don't care about that stuff. There you go. Who I am. Now I'd better go down to the Kinko's in Glendale and email this to Faber and Faber before I change my chickenshit mind." In the last paragraph, he thanks all the people who "worked so hard to turn this screenplay into a movie. It was an arduous process and the creativity and tireless work of everyone involved was an absolute joy to witness."[1]

Since Spike Jonze had just been nominated for an Oscar for his directing work on Kaufman's first feature, suddenly everyone was interested in directing whatever else writer Charlie Kaufman had in his desk drawers. *Human Nature,* a spec script he had written early in his television career in order to garner more writing work (similarly to his original intent with the *Being John Malkovich* script), was to be his next screenplay to go into production. Like most of Kaufman's writing, the story is about characters isolated in their own existence without the ability to step out of themselves to view the world as a whole, beyond themselves. Because that is the nature of their existence, their myopic beliefs about themselves don't allow them to have meaningful connections with others. In *Human Nature,* Lila, a successful author who writes about nature, has a hormonal hair growth problem that prevents her from being traditionally feminine enough to find a male love. Dr. Nathan Bronfman is a gentle but severely repressed behavioral scientist attempting to teach mice table manners in order to help their evolution and validate his own absurdly regimented upbringing. Rounding out the trifecta of characters is Puff, a grown man who was raised as an animal in the woods by his mentally ill father who believed he and his son were apes. When Lila and Nathan find the ape man living in the woods, the story is set to explore disparate ideas about nature versus nurture, and cultural ideals versus mankind's predilection for our own innate, animalistic behavior.

"I think initially one of the things I was interested in was the idea of this pure being out of nature, who comes and teaches the civilized people the truth about what it means to be human," Kaufman related. "That stuff seems to crop up now and again in movies, and it's always seemed silly to me. But at the same time, there are human issues that I'm interested in—issues of isolation and feeling outside, and loneliness, and taking condemnation from a society and turning it on yourself; those are things I'm interested in on a smaller, more personal level."[2] The ideas for Kaufman's screenplay came from several places. He wanted to write about a feral man as well as an alienated woman. "I was thinking about those idolized portraits of pure people raised in nature that appear in movies a lot and I wanted to make fun of that. I also wanted to write about a woman who was on the outside and couldn't get in, so that was the hair thing, which seems to be a large issue in our country." Having a full head of hair has always been symbolic of beauty and good health. Conversely, an entire industry is based around depilating, waxing, threading, or lasering off unwanted body and facial hair. Kaufman noted, "You have to have it in certain places and you're not allowed to have it in other places. Especially with women, and it's happening with men now too; the idea that it's unattractive to have hair in places where you naturally have hair, just seems like such a culturally enforced notion."[3]

This approach to the story furthers one of the themes Kaufman began to illustrate in *Being John Malkovich:* the body gets in the way. In the case of his female character in *Human Nature,* society seems to have decided that women shouldn't have excess body hair. Only animals have body hair sprouting from everywhere. As Kaufman's work shows, a culture that is taught to hate its own nature is a sad, debilitated society. Self-hate becomes a form of hell. "I always write about people who are outsiders, people who feel unacceptable," relayed Kaufman. "The scientist character was inspired by reading about the behaviorist John Watson, who conducted the famous 'Baby Albert' experiments in which a baby was conditioned to fear white, fluffy objects. Kind of a Pavlovian kind of thing, but with a human being. It was sort of horrifying. (Watson) went on to become the father of psychology in advertising."[4]

While they were filming *Being John Malkovich,* Spike Jonze had introduced Kaufman to his friend and fellow video director visionary, Michel Gondry. Gondry, who was at the time perhaps best known to American audiences for his work with musical innovators such as Björk, Radiohead, and The White Stripes, had been in Los Angeles for over a year reading every screenplay he could get his hands on. The inventive Frenchman was looking to direct a feature film, but was bored out of his skull until he read Jonze's copy of *Being John Malkovich.* "It was the best script I had read," Gondry honestly effused. "Charlie Kaufman is a great writer, completely original. There is a very human dimension to the script, and I liked the characters immediately, even the ones doing terrible things."[5] When Kaufman watched Gondry's videos and award-winning commercials, he loved how beautiful they were. The two men felt an instant mutual admiration for their respective work. They also shared a similar sensibility. Gondry laughed, "I think we share a common negativity. Once I was talking to Björk, and she said to me, 'You're the most pessimistic person, but at least you're funny.' And I think that's something you could say about Charlie as well."[6]

Regarding the making of the feature-length film *Human Nature,* Kaufman explained, "I was interested in the idea of directing it myself, but what happened was, Michel Gondry really wanted to do something with me. So he came to me with this loose idea that a friend of his had: What if you get something in the mail that says you've been erased from somebody's memory? Michel started calling me about it, and my agent was going, 'This is an amazing idea. Oh, my God, this is so commercial, you have to do this. Do this!'"[7] Although Kaufman had never officially pitched a movie idea before, he and Michel Gondry drew up some material on the untitled "Memory Erasure Project," and made the rounds to meetings at the studios. Kaufman didn't think anything would come of the idea at the time, and was already in the midst of interviewing for work on an adaptation of Susan Orlean's book *The Orchid Thief*. Kaufman remembered, "I got the [*Orchid Thief*] job, probably a couple days before we sold the pitch for *Eternal Sunshine*. I was in postproduction on *Malkovich*, and I had to write *Adaptation* first."[8] To Kaufman's disbelief and perhaps dismay at the time, because he was already so busy, the boys sold their "Memory Erasure Movie" pitch to Focus Features and were given the green light to develop it. The only trouble now was that Charlie Kaufman had to write it. Kaufman remembered, "Michel was a little distraught that he would have to wait quite a while to direct *Eternal Sunshine*, so he said, 'While you are writing *Adaptation*, can I direct *Human Nature?*'"[9] Based on mutual appreciation for each other's work, and due to the fact that Kaufman was already up to his neck in writing projects and deadlines, he approved. However, since Spike Jonze was just coming off an Oscar nod for Kaufman's first film, the studio requested that Jonze helm *Human Nature* as well. Spike Jonze politely declined, but stayed on as an executive producer, and agreed with Kaufman that Michel Gondry be the one to take the reigns.

Human Nature's road to the big screen started back in 1996, before *Being John Malkovich* was even produced. Steven Soderbergh had optioned the script, and at one point was set to direct it. He was about to go into production with David Hyde Pierce to play Dr. Nathan Bronfman, Marisa Tomei to play Lila, and Chris Kattan to play Puff, when Soderbergh's schedule on the movie *Out of Sight* forced him to let go of the project. His contractual work kept him from committing to making anything new, and Charlie Kaufman bought back his option. Once Gondry and Kaufman went in to production on the project, the extensive audition process for *Human Nature* proved exhausting. Kaufman affirmed, "We went through a lot of people, because Puff has to be everything—he has to go from this very primitive person to this very sophisticated person. There were different actors who were really strong in different areas, but Rhys [Ifans] was strong and funny all the way across the spectrum." Kaufman added, "There are so many things that Puff had to deliver on that could have made for a disaster. Little things that you wouldn't even think about when you're writing a script—like the idea that this grown man has to appear in a diaper. How do you do that without it just being horrifying to look at? And you couldn't do that with a lot of actors, just because of their sense of self, you know. And because Rhys was so comfortable with it, it just became acceptable—and not even ridiculous."[10] Rhys Ifans, the complex and talented actor, understood the paradoxes he was asked to portray. He has said that "the movie is about the question of man being socialized. I think it's repulsive, but also necessary. We can't be animals. Animals kill. But then, if we have an army, if we condone death in the name of government, we are animals. [sighs] I have a punk-rock head and a hippie heart."[11]

The casting process for the key role of Lila Jute was just as thorough. When Kaufman wrote *Human Nature*, well before the movie was ever going to be made, he was told he would never find an actress who would agree to the part. However, he found his Lila in the intrepid Patricia Arquette. She jumped right in and her commitment helped in getting financing. Kaufman found her to be "courageous in a bunch of ways—because not only was she naked, she was also covered with hair in a way people might consider unflattering." Few actresses would be willing to dance around in a bodysuit made of fur, but Arquette managed to radiate quiet confidence and beauty. The body-fur suit was of great concern for the makeup and costume department, because although Kaufman and Gondry weren't concerned about the hair being beautiful, Kaufman explained, "We didn't want to be mocking of the character, because we don't feel that way about her, so we didn't want people to laugh at her. So it was kind of an issue, figuring out how best to portray this." [12] The film's budget was modest, and was not the type of project one might sign on to in order to pick up a paycheck. When asked whether it was more difficult to be completely naked on camera or to have certain parts of her body censored with fake hair, Patricia Arquette admitted, "it was hard on my ego to do it with hair, but then I thought, 'no one should apologize for (having) that hair.'"[13]

The Oscar-winning actor Tim Robbins, who has never shied away from a challenging or unlikeable role, was tapped to play the anal-retentive behaviorist Dr. Nathan Bronfman. Robbins's deep humanity is always evident in his work, and although the character Nathan is a strict disciplinarian and set in his belief that he can cure Puff of his ape-like qualities, he and Puff have parallel lives in that they are both victims of their extreme (though polar opposite) upbringings. Although Nathan's beliefs about what constitutes correct behavior are absolute, Lila's dogmas are just as militaristic. Extremes have nothing to do with Kaufman's way of writing and walking through the world. His work often explores the ways in which humans are more complicated than fixed labels, such as scientist or naturalist. Kaufman concentrates on the characters' struggles and how to make their plights sincere, whether he is writing comedy or drama within the script. Kaufman related, "Puff is a terribly manipulated human being from the beginning—his father is insane and raises him as an ape, you know? You can't get more manipulated than that. And then he's manipulated throughout the movie by everybody—including Patricia's character. So I have a lot of sympathy for Puff. He's tortured. And I think Nathan—Tim Robbins's character—is too. In a lot of people's eyes, Nathan is the least sympathetic character—but I never felt that way about him. He's also manipulated and tortured—by his family, and by his parents, and by his insecurities."[14]

Unlike many of Kaufman's other screenplays, the shooting script for *Human Nature* is only slightly different from his first drafts. In the draft dated May 20, 1995, the story begins with the direction of opening on a black screen to the sound of a gunshot. A crow screams, then the audience hears the flutter of wings. Just as our ears are waiting for another clue as to what is happening, the screen shows a bird's-eye view of a forest where we circle lazily above, until a break in the trees lets us glimpse a form lying dead on the ground. As the camera circles closer, we see that the form is a dead human body. In the beginning of the final version of the film that made it to the movie screen, the screen opens on two little white mice in the forest. We hear the sound of the gunshot and see the white mice scamper through grass as they are being chased by a black crow in hot pursuit. The audience is given the point of view of the mice, as they quickly decide not to cross water in their attempt to escape the crow, deftly run across a narrow branch as the crow nearly smashes into it, until they finally allude him by cleverly splitting up to run around a thick tree, causing the crow to smash into the center of it. The mice have escaped the predator, but they stop in their tracks (as does the hurt crow), as they suddenly come upon boots belonging to a prostrate human who seems to be dead.

Kaufman quickly sets up his themes of emotional isolation and the mind/ body problem as the audience is introduced to the character of Lila Jute being interrogated in a room by police. Although the audience does not yet know why Lila is in that situation, her dialogue and tone as crafted by Kaufman, informs the audience that she is a strong, beautiful woman who must have endured quite a dramatic story to land her in police custody with these fools. "So I spend the rest of my life in jail. So what? I've been in jail my whole life anyway. A jail of blood and tissue and coursing hormones ... a jail called the human body."[15] Kaufman combines comedy with pathos as one of the police men is so bored by Lila's monologue that he can barely stay awake, while the other smiles at her lasciviously when she mentions the words *human body*. The story then cuts to a dirty-faced, scraggly haired man, who is impeccably dressed in a crisp business suit. He holds a microphone and is addressing an audience. In opposition to Lila's fierce non confession, this man named Puff confidently asserts that he is sorry, and sorry for everyone involved. "Yours is a complicated, sad world," he tells the gathered crowd and press. Next the audience is introduced to Nathan, a man who sits alone at a table in a pristinely surreal white room. He confesses to the camera, "I don't even know what sorry means anymore."[16]

The story takes us through young Lila's preteen years in which her mother takes her to a doctor for her unnaturally hirsute body. The doctor tells her the condition is probably going to get worse and her mother tells her she better dedicate her life to the pursuit of knowledge or religion or something else, because no man is going to want her. In a scene absent from the final film, Lila's early adulthood is further illuminated when she is shown trying to fit in while in college. When her roommate rushes into their communal bathroom, excitedly trying to ready for a date, she is mortified to see Lila covered in shaving cream from head to toe. When the roommate claims to be hurt that Lila didn't confide in her that she had this problem and should appreciate the fact that she is even interested in her problems, Lila confronts her with knowledge of her faux concern. Now that Lila's secret is out, instead of freeing her, it only seems to compound her problem. Her roommate storms out the room, yelling to Lila that she is "fucked up," and "Why don't you fucking try electrolysis or something? Figure it out for chrissake."[17] The roommate articulates the disdain that Lila already feels about herself.

As Lila gets older, she spends time with lesbian separatists (a term Charlie Kaufman previously mentioned in an early draft of *Being John Malkovich*, when the character Craig answers a classified ad). She also joins a circus for a time, but still doesn't fit in. Just as she is about to kill herself in a bathtub, she spies a white mouse who seems to stop in its tracks to look at her with understanding in its beady red eyes. The animal saved her life, so she decides to go live among them in the woods. Ultimately, Lila becomes a successful nature writer, authoring a book called *Fuck Humanity*. The proceeds from her writing affords Lila the ability to live the way she wants to, and like the character Lotte in *Being John Malkovich*, Lila surrounds herself with animals who love her unconditionally. Kaufman often has fun with naming his characters and may have called the best-selling nature writer character Lila, because it resembles the name Lilith, who in certain mythologies predates Eve in the biblical story of the Garden of Eden. The character's last name, Jute, is a word defined as a strong fiber derived from a plant used to make burlap. The success of Lila Jute's book allows her to live in the woods permanently if she wishes and Charlie Kaufman underscores the character's happiness with the lyrics he wrote for his character. Lila emerges from her pup tent in the forest, looks around at all the furry, nonjudgmental creatures of the forest and feels accepted as one of them. The song is called "Hair Everywhere," and Kaufman was happy with the lines "I once thought god a creator diabolical. He have the nod to each one of my follicles. Now I'm free, no more cares. I've accepted my millions of hairs."[18] Patricia Arquette sings the lyrics softly and tenderly, and the lightness of the song shows the audience that she has finally found the freedom to be herself. She has found a home. The only thing that drives Lila out her happy paradise in the woods (by her own admission) is the need for sex with a man. In Lila's case, the forbidden apple she sold her soul for was sex.

The young Nathan's life is also traumatic and illustrated in a funny scene in which his parents take him to the zoo, and he is excited to see the monkeys, but his mother urges his father to tell him that we must never act like apes. Only a single chromosome separates us, but what makes us better than apes, Nathan's father explains, is, "Culture. Civilization. Refinement. If we do not have these as humans, then we might as well be living in pens and throwing feces about, masturbating in public." Nathan's mother quickly cuts off her husband with "Enough Harold." And then she adds, "Your adopted father and I whisked you away from a life that most certainly would have been one of degradation and alcoholism. Your part of the bargain is to never wallow in the filth of instinct. Any dumb animal can do that."[19] Nathan's parents ignore what is going on behind them in the scene—a man being dragged off by two uniformed attendants in the background, screaming that he is not a man, he is an animal! The screenplay notes that this man is Puff's father, who was finally committed to a mental institution after applying one too many times at the local zoo for the job of "apprentice ape." Another scene that further illustrates young Nathan's overly strict and traumatic upbringing is when as an eight year old he accidentally uses the wrong fork from a formal dinner table setting (always work from the outside in), and his punishment is to be banished from the table and go to bed without supper.

Lila tells her friend Louise (Rosie Perez), the woman who does her hair removal, that although she has achieved success and contentment on many levels, she desires to have a man in her life. When Louise tells her that her brother the therapist is treating the perfect candidate for her, Lila has doubts that the man can love her despite her excessive hormonal hair growth. Louise cheerfully assures her that the potential date has the smallest penis in the world, and therefore probably won't balk at her problems.

Although Nathan introduces his new protégé Puff to music, art, literature, and language, Puff learns to assimilate into his new world on a surface level, but cannot control his sexual urges. He knows when to applaud at the opera after Beethoven's *Fidelio,* he can sip wine properly, he trims his nose hairs, he reads Yeats, and he can perform the song "I Gotta Crow" from the play *Peter Pan,* but he can't prevent himself from humping a waitress like a dog. Nathan attempts to teach Puff to control his sexual urges and repeats something he learned from his father: when in doubt, don't ever do what you really want to do. Similarly, although Nathan is a well-bred, sophisticated scientist, he has no more willpower or moral center than the ape man, as he is easily seduced by his female assistant Gabriel (Miranda Otto). Gabriel pretends to be French and speaks with a French accent, a clichéd stereotype of femininity. Gabriel exists in the story as a device for Kaufman to show that the respected scientist Nathan is just as prone to his sexual desires as the ape man Puff.

Once the unlikely couple of Lila the naturalist and Nathan the behaviorist begin dating, they both try to be on their best behavior in trying to overlook each other idiosyncrasies. When Nathan brings Lila to his parents' home to introduce them, she tries to overlook the fact that his mother has differing beliefs about animals and nature than she does. In Kaufman's original draft, he adds the element of Nathan telling his parents they look terribly old and Lila admonishing him. His reserved, strict parents look at each other and laugh and explain to their son and his date that they have been performing a production of the play *The Gin Game* at the local community theater, and they have forgotten to wash off their makeup. It's funny to think of Nathan's parents acting in any play, but it is particularly funny to think of them acting in *The Gin Game,* written by D. L. Coburn in 1976, about two senior citizens in a nursing home who learn about each other and their respective families while playing a card game. Once the characters in *The Gin Game* become more familiar with each other, they use their intimate knowledge to belittle, embarrass, and humiliate each other. Kaufman refers to the play to underscore the emotional emptiness of Nathan's parents' relationship. Specific to *Human Nature,* the characters in *The Gin Game* also make choices in their lives that create a living hell of their own making. They are responsible for their own misery.

Once Lila's secret is exposed to Nathan, he can't get past the idea that her excess hair is not only unfeminine, but ape like. He hates apes. Lila is horrified that he now knows the truth about her, but she makes up her mind to do everything in her power to fight her own nature in order to save their relationship. She shaves all of her hair completely off, wears a wig, draws in high arched feminine eyebrows and starts donning frilly dresses. Her table manners are now impeccable, and emulating television housewives from decades past, she waits for Nathan to get home from work so she can be at his service to make him a drink. She makes all these changes because old-fashioned femininity is what he claims he wants, but her efforts are to no avail, as Nathan is still repulsed by her hair problem, which he equates with her inadequacies as a woman. However, instead of admitting he is unhappy, he tells her that she is exactly what he wants in a woman.

His assistant Gabrielle, on the other hand, is delicate looking, wears lingerie to work, and she's French! In a scene in which Nathan flees the home he shares with Lila to run to Gabrielle's apartment, the audience hears Gabrielle talking on the phone, sans her affected French accent she uses at work. Her apartment is a mess, she wears a stained pajama shirt, has pimple cream on her face, and ferociously picks her toenails while unconsciously watching TV. While Nathan knocks on her door, she jumps up to start straightening up the place and holds different lingerie up to herself to decide what will look better. In a funny reference to Meryl Streep, Gabrielle tells Nathan that he must chose between her and Lila, like in the movie *Sophie's Choice.* "It's like Sophie's choice. Only it is Nathan's choice. Did you ever see that movie? It is like that. Only it is this."[20] Ironically, despite the fact that Charlie Kaufman wrote the *Human Nature* script in 1996 during a hiatus from his television work, it would only be a few months after it was produced in 2001 until Meryl Streep herself would be cast in his next film.

Once Gabrielle quits her job with Nathan because he is afraid to tell Lila the truth about them, Lila volunteers to help him with his work. Although she was formerly against Nathan taking Puff out of his environment, caging him and attempting to socialize him, she has given up so much of her own ideals for Nathan that now helping him with his ape man experiment is feasible. She wants to be supportive of Nathan, which includes his work, however distasteful it may have been to her only a few months ago. In an excerpt absent from the film, but clearly important to Lila's transformation to please her man, she tells him that she has even decided to give up being a nature writer. Writing about nature was the one thing that validated her life and gave her the confidence and the means to live how she wished. The former best-selling author of the book entitled *Fuck Humanity* tells Nathan that her previous subject, nature, was silly, and that she is considering writing an article on quilting. In the next scene, Lila sits at the police station and says, "I had sold my fucking soul." The script then cuts to Nathan in a white space telling the camera that he indeed let her sell her soul. He confesses that he stood by as she did it and that it's inexcusable.

After a night when Nathan returns from having sex with Gabrielle, Lila asks him where he's been and he lies that he was having a philosophical conversation with Puff that went overlong. Charlie Kaufman's lightning wit shines through as Lila calmly replies, "That's funny. Because you know, I just went and picked him up at some flophouse on the lower eastside. He called me here when he ran out of his 'mad' money after spending an entire evening drinking, watching strippers, and fucking a whore." Then she adds casually, "Oh and what did you do tonight honey?"[21] When Nathan finally admits to Lila that he has been sleeping with Gabrielle and has fallen in love with her, Lila tells him that he has no idea what she gave up to be with him. Although absent from the film, in the ending to this scene from Kaufman's original draft, Nathan says that the human heart is a strange thing. Lila retorts, "How the hell would you know anything about the human heart," and then punches him in the jaw, sending him to land in a heap on the floor. Kaufman's original dialogue called for Lila to end the scene with, "How's that for ladylike, Nathan."[22] Lila holes up in a hotel room for awhile, and attempts to hide from the world until her friend Louise coaxes her to come to her home where she will help her recover her strength. In a sequence absent from the film, Kaufman's original script shows Lila bettering herself by eating a nutritious breakfast, struggling to do push-ups, getting electrolysis, reading Nietzsche, and jogging. The script calls for these scenes to be intercut with scenes of Nathan and Gabrielle on a lecture circuit with Puff on display making speeches to wowed audiences. Although the final film intercuts the lecture tour with Lila receiving painful hair removal treatments, the original draft continues to show Lila gaining strength for herself. While Nathan and Gabrielle retreat to their hotel room after Puff's lectures, Puff has to overhear the couple having sex. The original script calls for the movie to cut between shots of Puff sneaking out of the hotel at night to go to X-rated bookstores, watch pornography, and have sex with hookers with scenes of Lila in a Tai Chi class, now able to do one-handed push ups, in a boxing class, and on the ground rolling around with a rifle. Lila's training has paid off, and she and her friend Louise go to Nathan's lab to rescue Puff from the hypocrisy that has become his life. Louise's boyfriend Frank (Peter Dinklage) enters the premises with a gun and quotes André Malraux: "The attempt to force human beings to despise themselves is what I call hell."[23]

Lila takes Puff back to the woods to "retrain" him. When Puff says that he likes being human now, Lila uses the same technique Dr. Bronfman used and shocks Puff, sending him crashing to the ground. Once again, Puff will adapt in order to avoid being electrocuted. Lila's new rules in the forest include keeping talking to a minimum. Eventually, she wants to abolish it completely. In her frustration, Lila tells Puff, "Language was invented so that people could lie to each other and to themselves. There is no other reason." Puff is rightfully confused and adds, "I agree?" to which Lila answers, "Any answer is the wrong answer,"[24] and then gives him an electric shock.

Back in civilization, Nathan and Gabrielle's relationship has stalled. They attend dinner with Nathan's parents and Gabrielle tries to enlist them in asking their son what is bothering him. Absent from the final film, Nathan's parents are in clown makeup at the dinner table as their son asks them how their play *Godspell* is going. He is disinterested and simply trying to make polite conversation, but his parents giddily burst out into laughter and tell him the play is going great. They don't seem to mind that he is suffering in restrained silence. One can only imagine his repressed parents belting out the uplifting, life-affirming song "Day by Day" from the rock opera play, *Godspell*.

Although absent from the film, Nathan's reason to seek out Lila and Puff in the forest is motivated by the fact that he feels robbed of something that he worked so hard for, and that would have made him famous: making Puff into a gentleman. When he tracks down the couple, the behaviorist finds that Lila and Puff have abolished the English language from their world and communicate through primitive grunts and moans. It is their own form of communication, and they understand each other perfectly, without actual words. But when Nathan finds the couple living like this, he has a burst of jealousy, anger, and betrayal. He is hurt that although he tried to educate Puff as he would have his own son, this is how Puff repays him, by refusing language. Nathan shouts that he even taught Puff about Wittgenstein, but quickly adds the insult that it was obviously lost on Puff, and that the ape man never had any insight on their discussions anyway. Once Puff is confronted by Nathan, he feels he has to break his vow to avoid language, and delivers a monologue about how Nathan has done nothing but damage him with all his teachings. However, he then admits to his father figure that a certain word has been haunting him while he's been living in the jungle, and asks him what *simultagnosia* means. Nathan replies that it means the

inability to perceive things as elements of a whole. This failure of the characters to understand that they are each just part of what constitutes the *whole*
of human nature seals their miserable fate. Their lack of balance between
a civilized self and a naturalistic self keeps all of them in prison cells, both
literal and metaphysical, in life, and in Dr. Nathan Bronfman's case, in death
as well.

Kaufman, like many of the great thinkers of the world, believes there is
no joy in ignoring what is going on around you. Thinking there is only
one correct way in which to live creates isolation and extra barriers between
people. Embracing the whole of your truth, although parts of it are terrifying and sad, is more valuable than discounting the scary elements of human
existence. Even in sadness, a feeling of connectedness with that element can
be joyful.

With a nod to the irony of human nature, Charlie Kaufman creates an
homage to one of his literary influences, Franz Kafka, when Puff testifies at
a U.S. Senate hearing. Puff's funny scenes evoke Kafka's comical and ironic
short story "A Report to an Academy." Kafka's ape, who is never given a
name (as is the norm with many of the author's characters), presents a speech
before a group of powerful men in suits just as Puff does. Kafka's ape begins
his presentation:

> Esteemed gentlemen of the Academy! You show me the honor of calling upon
> me to submit a report to the Academy concerning my previous life as an ape. In
> this sense, unfortunately, I cannot comply with your request. Almost five years
> separate me from my existence as an ape, a short time perhaps when measured
> by the calendar, but endlessly long to gallop through, as I have done, at times
> accompanied by splendid people, advice, applause, and orchestral music, but
> basically alone, since all those accompanying me held themselves back a long
> way from the barrier, in order to preserve the image.[25]

The former ape tells the gathered audience how he first learned to shake
hands properly and drink liquor to show that he could fit in with humans.
He made the observation (that he kept to himself) that while on a cargo
ship, his captors drank the vile-tasting alcohol they offered him for amusement, in order to turn their minds off and revert back to a form of ape brain.
He hated the smell and taste of the humans' drink, but forced himself to
learn to accept it as a way to win them over. "It was so easy to imitate these
people. I could already spit on the first day."[26] When he learned the word,
"hello," he became part of the community of humans. Language was his
way out of captivity; however, at the end of the story, although the ape has
sufficiently proven that he is just as human as any other man, he is given a
choice to live out his days in another form of captivity. He can live at the
zoo, or at a music hall, where he will perform as "the smart" ape. During his
training to achieve his new goal, he went through many teachers and even
drove one mad. Much like Kaufman's Puff is trained by an electric shock to

his collared leash, one of Kafka's ape's teachers held a burning pipe against his fur. In trying to explain how he survived this trauma and prevailed, the ape man tells the committee, "Nowadays, of course, I can portray those ape-like feelings only with human words and, as a result, I misrepresent them."[27] Kaufman illustrates this same belief through his character Lila, who was once a celebrated author but then becomes so frustrated with words disguising real meaning that she refuses words to be allowed in her life with Puff. Before Puff murders Nathan, he painfully searches for the right words to convey all of his conflicted feelings for what he has experienced, but ends up with the frustrating conclusion that words are evil.

After the murder, it is Lila's wish for Puff to live freely in the woods, as she presumed he once did as a child, but first she wants him to testify before congress about the waywardness of man. As Lila watches Puff on a wall-mounted TV in the dayroom of a women's prison, Puff's speech resembles Kafka's ape, "And so, gentlemen, that is my story. I agreed to testify before this committee because I hoped to convey to the American public that there is indeed a paradise lost."[28] In addition to the Kafka reference, Charlie Kaufman may also be making a nod to Clifford Odets's play *Paradise Lost*. Kaufman mentioned Odets in *Being John Malkovich,* and in the case of *Human Nature,* Odets's premise of a false idealism is relevant. Although Odets's characters in *Paradise Lost* are well-meaning, educated people, they are never able to achieve their goals in life, because they are held back by the demands of basic survival.

The end of *Human Nature* circles back to the beginning of the story: Lila is in prison, and Nathan is in a hell or purgatory that looks like a bleached version of his parents dining room.

In an example of how the director of the movie, Michel Gondry, and Charlie Kaufman have a similar sensibility, Gondry's insightful reading of the screenplay helped shape the visual definition of Nathan Bronfman's life after death. It was Gondry's idea to have Nathan find himself in a white room and poke his head out the door on the right-hand side of it, so that the audience sees that this act immediately leads him through the door on the left-hand side of that exact, same room. He now exists in the same small, eternal space that looks eerily like a ghostly alternative to his childhood home. The dead Nathan delivers Kaufman's tragicomic treatise: "What is love, anyway? From my new vantage point, I realize that love is nothing more than a messy conglomeration of need, desperation, fear of death, and insecurity about penis size. But I'm not judging it. I know how miserable it is to be alive."[29] Puff, on the other hand, who has convinced congress and the press that he is through with man and will return to his true home in the forest, fools his enthusiastic fans of this plan, to jump into Gabrielle's waiting car to make his real escape. Although seemingly in charge of his fate, Puff, as played by the actor Rys Ifans, is a man who is ultimately trapped behind his own eyes. His accomplice, Gabrielle, is still pretending to be someone she's not as she coquettishly tells Puff in her fake French accent that he reminds her of Nathan. As they drive away from the woods, Puff takes a look back and seems slightly pained. Then he looks over at Gabrielle and evaluates her up and down with his eyes. Has he made the right decision? Will this new life of his be enough? Puff has managed to fool everyone, but like Kafka's ape, he may just be riding off into a higher form of captivity.

As Puff and Gabrielle drive off, the audience sees two little, white, trained lab mice by the side of the road attempting to hitchhike their way back to civilization. They hold up a tiny cardboard sign that reads "New York" as the second song Charlie Kaufman wrote for the film, "Here With You," plays over the scene. Like the first song in the movie, it is again performed by Patricia Arquette and starts out slowly and mournfully with the words, "As I lie here now, all alone, eyes, closed, gone now. We walk alone through fields of ruined heaven. We'll sing a song of love and eternity. I will not walk away." The camera stays on the little white mice and the melody and lyrics become comforting as Lila sings that she and her love are now unshackled, unchained, and understood. "I am you, I'm not blue. I'm back with you in the woods." Her love is free to stay or go, because wherever he may be, she sings, "I'll be with you forever, because you let me in to your heart."[30]

Throughout the film, Dr. Bronfman had Puff listen to audiotapes in his cage, narrated by a British woman on subjects such as culture, manners, and refinement. As the final credits roll, the female narrator from the tapes reads, "When some things are known, of which the one inheres in the other, or is locally distant from the other, or is related to the other in another way, by virtue of the incomplex cognition of, it is known immediately ... That we may not either stick fast in things already known, or loosely grasp at shadows and abstract forms, and not at things solid and realized in matter."[31]

This is part of a tape that Dr. Nathan Bronfman thought would help Puff develop mentally and socially. It features the teachings of the 14th-century philosopher William Ockham, who believed that our intuition is imperfect. He also wrote about abstract principles and parallels to our basic observations.

The quote playing over the ending scroll of credits is relevant, because before Puff shoots Dr. Nathan Bronfman, he says that he might kill him for revenge, which is an abstract thought he learned from Nathan. Ockham is perhaps most famous for his principle of simplicity known as Occam's Razor (a different spelling of his last name). This principle of simplicity is that the simplest explanations are usually best. The irony may be that Kaufman chose to include this passage in the screenplay, because as illustrated in his story, the reality of human nature is far more complex. Regardless, Kaufman has always been more interested in the questions, more so than the answers.

While *Human Nature* was being filmed, Charlie Kaufman made rare visits to the movie set and served as a producer, but felt it was important for Michel Gondry to have the freedom to work on his own. Kaufman believes it is unhealthy for the cast and crew to have two different voices informing their choices. However, in the way that Kaufman believed he found a colleague and friend with a similar view of the world, he may have also found a comrade in anxiety as well. Of the filming process in particular, Gondry remembered, "I thought I would die because I could never sleep, I had to take pills. I'm used to not sleeping until a job is finished, and with a commercial that's fine because a shoot lasts one week. With the film we had two months of it. Every stage of making a movie is difficult. You have all these rules to work around ... you go to bed later, wake up later. But the worst thing is the pre-production, you always believe it will never happen, so at least when you shoot, you know that the movie is happening."[32] To flesh out Kaufman's story, Gondry shot on a soundstage as well as on location. The combination helped shape the surreal and hyperreal quality of the characters' journeys. He affirmed, "Two thirds of it is shot on stage. The forest is shot in both ways, for romantic bin, on stage, and sometimes when it's more crude and realistic, outdoors. I wanted to recreate the 'feeling' of Hollywood movies from the 40s ... I remember this movie with a guy driving a car in front of a projection and then it cut to real shots, and that would give me a nice feeling."[33] Although the forest scenes are criticized for being too stylized and playful, the filmmakers were aiming for the magical quality they achieved. Kaufman came to Gondry's defense when he noted that if they (the filmmakers) had wanted the audience to think they were in an authentic forest, then they would have done just that.

Human Nature screened at the Cannes Film Festival in 2001 and some of the critiques were downright nasty. Mary Corliss of *Film Comment* wrote, "*Human Nature,* amateurishly directed by Michel Gondry, is a strained, manic parable of a wild child (Rhys Ifans) who is 'socialized' by a repressed scientist (Tim Robbing) [sic] and then liberated by the latter's erstwhile fiancée (Patricia Arquette). As in writer Charlie Kaufman's previous script, *Being John Malkovich,* the ripe imagination goes rotten long before the end; here, indeed, it never gets to bear fruit. And without getting clinical, let's just say that Ifans and Arquette are not the first two actors you might want to see au naturel."[34] Considering that the critic didn't even get Tim Robbins's name down properly, hopefully the filmmakers took the review with a touch of irony. However, similarly reductive reviews about Kaufman's personal script about isolation and alienation did tend to hurt his heart. Based on Kaufman's first outing, *Being John Malkovich,* some critics were expecting a stylistically similar movie with his sophomore effort, and could not get past the comparisons. A more reasonable prediction would have been to realize that directors Michel Gondry and Spike Jonze are very different people (both brilliant in their own way), and that Kaufman's second feature film, *Human Nature,* was never meant to be *Malkovich: The Return.*

Still, other critics saw beyond the film's literal story, to its universal themes. Rob Feld, who frequently writes for the magazine *Written By,* noted, "*Human Nature* continued Kaufman's funhouse-mirror reflection of society, sending up the notion that there's a utopian world someplace other than wherever one is. Utopia isn't in a state of nature, it isn't in society. The best that can be hoped for by Kaufman's fringe characters (which include a 30-something-year-old virgin with the smallest penis in the world, a man raised in the wilderness as an ape by a man who thinks he's an ape, and a woman suffering from a condition that covers her body in hair) is contentment with where and who they are."[35]

Kaufman responded to the harsher evaluations by saying, "When people criticize *Human Nature,* it's usually over what they see as this simplistic idea that nature is better than civilization. In actuality, that has nothing to do with what the movie's about. In fact, the movie was mocking that simplistic idea. The movie is a parody of that stupid notion."[36] When an interviewer mentioned that *Human Nature* is reminiscent of François Truffaut's *The Wild Child,* the passionate Michel Gondry replied, "*The Wild Child* is a lie. I saw the commentary on the case, which we examined when we worked on *Human Nature,* and Truffaut is a liar. Because the real wild child never learned to talk, and as soon as people who were funding the research on him discovered that he would not go further, he was sent back to his family and he had a miserable life. The movie should have talked about that in a more interesting way."[37] Kaufman added that he was inspired by movies that suggest there's a 'pure' state for humanity that we need to try to achieve. He has also always wanted to write about a feral man. There's a mock seriousness about it, although he wanted the characters to be real for people to have real feelings for them. As he did earlier in *Malkovich,* he was playing with philosophical notions just for fun. On collaborating with Kaufman, Michel Gondry has said, "It's very challenging because Charlie always wants to have an explanation when you're working with him. Sometimes I just have a feeling that an idea is going to work, but Charlie wants to know why. If there's something that Charlie doesn't like, he can get extremely particular about why it's not working. I like having someone around who can articulate precisely what's wrong, because through this process, you can find the best solution."[38] Although Kaufman never had any doubts about Gondry's capability as a feature film director and was happy with the end result, the fact that the movie only made approximately $600,000 dollars at the box office put the fear of God in the writer. He was confused about the reception of the film and wondered if he would work again. To his mind, *Human Nature* should have made the actor Rhys Ifans a star.

To make matters worse, the filmmakers felt betrayed by the distribution of their project. Michel Gondry especially wanted to participate in the way the film was marketed, yet his ideas were pushed aside. He passionately explained, "To me, the poster for *Human Nature* is hideous. The guy who decided to do this image, especially for the DVD, I made him promise to apologize to me after the video came out and didn't rent well. Because he promised me it would be a success ... We had worked on this film for four years. I wanted to go paint his house." To which Kaufman jerked his head a bit and volleyed, "You wanted to paint his house?" "Yeah," Gondry continued to roll, "Like paint big X's on his house. He put a fake naked Patricia Arquette on the cover to attract guys who probably wouldn't like the film, because he thought it would rent more ... Talking to him on the phone was so hard because he'd give you a little hope that you had some kind of control over how it turned out. Then as soon as it turned out that you're not in agreement, it was like, 'It was nice talking to you but I'm going to do it my way anyway.'"[39]

Despite the filmmakers being ousted from control over the movie's distribution, Kaufman's writing merited him the Best Screenplay Award from the National Board of Review. Both he and Gondry would soon move beyond the underrated film and box office failure of their first joint effort. Ultimately, they succeeded in making a film about the struggle to make a real connection with others and trying to make a place for yourself in the world. This theme is also central to another project Charlie Kaufman was struggling to write while *Human Nature* was in production. It was proving to be a difficult few years for Kaufman, and he worried that the financial failure of *Human Nature*, plus the solipsistic road he was going down with his next movie, *Adaptation*, might spell out the end of his career.

A Worthy *Adaptation*

Orchids are not built, they are a product of a long
complicated organic evolution—nations are the same way.

—George Will on *The Charlie Rose Show*

"You are what you love, not what loves you. That's what I decided a long
time ago." These are the words of Donald Kaufman, the cowriter of the
2003 Oscar-nominated screenplay *Adaptation*. A tall, enthusiastic, warm,
and welcoming person who has a talent for knowing what a modern movie
audience wants, D. K. (as he is affectionately known) embodies the type of
man who would have a promising career in Hollywood. His twin brother
and colleague Charles, on the other hand, is admittedly more of an intro-
vert. In subsequent interviews with journalists who only wanted to help
promote the brothers' award-worthy work and share in the excitement,
Charles was somewhat remote and inhospitable, but in his brother's eyes,
he was more like a man who had simply lost patience with being misun-
derstood. Donald is the more approachable, available of the two, but admires his brother's earnest writing and intensity. When, in an earlier draft
of the screenplay (before Donald came on board the project), his brother's
characterization of him was less than positive, Donald's generous nature
was evident when he explained that his twin, Charles, must have had his
reasons: he's an artist.

Though Donald may have an easier going personality, the gift of gab,
and an innocent way of putting others at ease, he supports the fact that his
brother's generosity is clearly in his writing. By offering his true life's experiences, such as having a hard time in first trying to adapt the screenplay
in question, Charlie is giving all that a writer has to offer the world. The
openness with which he shares his weaknesses and flaws is to be appreciated.
One twin is no better than the other. They are symbiotic, and together they
balance each others' light and dark.

When Charles Stuart Kaufman was first interviewing for the job of adapting Susan Orlean's *The Orchid Thief*, he was still in postproduction on his first feature, *Being John Malkovich*. Once *Being John Malkovich* looked to be a strong horse to bet on, Kaufman's literary agent was inundated with every project that seemed kooky or called "Kaufmanesque." *Being John Malkovich*'s influence was palpable, and Kaufman was deemed the go-to oddball screenwriter at the time. A possible project that stood out for him among the novelty acts, however, was the chance to adapt journalist Susan Orlean's book *The Orchid Thief: A True Story of Beauty and Obsession* into a feature film. It wasn't like the reams of "quirky" material he was being sent in the mail: it was well-written and straightforward, and he was learning things about a subject he never would have studied on his own.

Already a published author at the time, Susan Orlean was also a staff writer for the *New Yorker*. *The Orchid Thief: A True Story of Beauty and Obsession* was based on a series of articles she had written about the highly competitive, tightly nit, incestuous world of orchid growers in Florida. Before the book was even written, while still in its magazine stage, filmmakers Jonathan Demme and Ed Saxon bought the rights to her story, seeing through the surface value of flowers to the unbeknownst and provocative notion that the orchid business was no average day in a garden. With the working movie title "Passion," the filmmakers wanted to flesh out Orlean's story of her own quest for what drives passion in the context of the real-life, unique characters and environment she encountered while covering one of Florida's closely held secrets.

In a similar way that Charlie Kaufman had never heard of Spike Jonze, Orlean had never heard of Kaufman when she first heard that Hollywood producers wanted to make a movie out of her book. When her own literary agent broached the idea of a screenwriter adapting her novel, Kaufman's name was so thoroughly anonymous to her that she thought his credits included a movie called *Killing John Malkovich*. However, once she focused on this new idea that her personal story might be made into a movie, she began to fantasize about who would play her—people like Julia Roberts, Nicole Kidman, Holly Hunter, Jodie Foster, or Cate Blanchett. Ironically, neither she nor anyone she knew ever mentioned Meryl Streep, probably because she seemed larger than life, Orlean noted. And yet, in a bit of irony or in evidence of support for Charlie Kaufman's belief that we are all on a continuum, Susan Orlean once played an extra in the film *The Deer Hunter* (1978), starring Meryl Streep.

Once Kaufman got the job of adapting Orlean's lyrical, free-flowing tale, he vowed to stay true to the writer's original tone and vision. Who better to respect the quality of her intimate writing? He immediately understood and sympathized with her lovely, searching *tone* . . . But what was the right vision for his version?

He instinctively returned to his source material, Orlean's book, which contained essays from her attending flower shows, the history of orchid evolution, catalogue entries of the names of flowers, a list of plant crime clippings from *The Miami Herald* newspaper, and subsequent poaching diary entries:

January 10, 1991—Tree Missing.
February 12, 1995—A $250 palm tree was stolen from a yard. Someone dug up the tree, filled the hole and left with the fifteen-foot palm.
July 27, 1991—Orchids Stolen.
May 16, 1991—Orchids Stolen.
March 10, 1991—Orchids Stolen.

Kaufman looked at the ceiling, then turned the book over and looked at the author's photo as if to ask her, "How do you write a screenplay, based on a novel, based on a series of magazine articles about flowers?"

You don't.

He went back to his agent's office and had a meeting much like he described in his screenplay entitled *Adaptation*. Had the producer's check already cleared? He had accepted their money, and now needed to show something for it. He tried to explain to his agent, that in addition to his structural problems in attacking the project properly, he didn't know how to reconcile the fact that he needed to give the real people in Orlean's book a made-up, cinematic twist. Susan herself and one of her many subjects, the colorful orchid specialist John Laroche, were not fictitious and how could he speak for them and then be able to sleep at night. Kaufman clarified, "One of the main reasons I got stuck, and one of the main reasons I included myself in it, was because I was in a position that felt enormously unethical to me. Because I was putting words into real people's mouths and I didn't know how to do that. I'm not going to say, 'Susan Orlean said this,' and I'm not going to say that she had this happen to her when she didn't. So I came up with the idea that the only way that I can frame this, is to say that *I'm* saying that she said this. This is clearly a fiction. And then I felt comfortable saying whatever I wanted—like that she was a murderer."[1]

Once he put *himself* into that specific world, along with the other people in question, his mind was freed up to make things up and create. Plus, Kaufman readily admitted, the book was great, sprawling *New Yorker* stuff, but there was no plot.

By writing himself into a working story, like the writer Kurt Vonnegut, Jr., before him, Kaufman was asking the audience to participate in his own surreal self-analysis. What surfaced was the unveiling of any pretense surrounding his first failed attempts. He wrote honestly about his doubts that he could supply what he presented himself as being capable of, and included every little flaw, down to his cringe-worthy and brutally honest sexual fantasies about Susan Orlean and the other women in the story. Hollywood was never so honest, and he undertook this path of adapting the novel with the full knowledge that he would probably fail. Putting his true fears out there for his agent, a studio, and perhaps all the world to see was not something he embarked on lightly. Hadn't he already ripped open a vein for audiences in revealing that he always wanted to be someone else in offering the story *Being John Malkovich*? Hadn't he already asked his wife to wait out the period in which he was trying to first get work in Los Angeles early in their marriage, while she stayed back at their home in Minnesota, waiting for word from him? Why couldn't he just write the damned book adaptation, turn it in, and move on?

Though he berated himself over and over for not having the stomach to cash Jonathan Demme's check with a light and worthy heart, once he made the decision to write himself into the screenplay, his writing started to flow. He was honest with himself in that he still of course had doubts, but he was no longer stymied. "Who am I?" he asked himself. "No one knows who I am. I'm going to put myself in a script and they're going to make a movie of that? I thought it was completely self indulgent or at least would be perceived that way. Then I was being very brutal on myself, which is also a little scary but at the same time exciting, because I felt like I'm honest and that's a good thing to be, I think."[2]

Prior to this creative breakthrough, Kaufman admitted,

> I was getting nothing done. I was going out of my mind. And then I came up with this idea to include myself in the story, because it seemed that my energy was in the paralysis of not being able to write. But I didn't want to tell anybody my idea because I thought they would say no. And I didn't have any other ideas. None. Zip. So I went with it and I started to see connections. The book is about natural selection and adaptation with orchids, and here I was. I was adapting my ideas, and I was adapting this other person's work, and I was changing. I liked the way it all seemed very risky. I like to kind of explode the structure and put something in that people will feel like, What? Wait a minute! What is this guy doing in the movie that he's supposed to be adapting? It seemed like the ultimate risk, to put myself out there. I really needed to do it this way. I mean, I was waking up every morning freaking out. I thought my career was over.[3]

Not only did Charlie Kaufman take the risk of putting himself into Susan Orlean's story, but he wrote in a twin brother as well. Initially, Kaufman wrote a brother in to the story so that his main character would simply have a friend to talk to. The character named Charlie was a writer who lived alone, worked alone in his house, and didn't seem to have any friends come calling. Adding a twin with a polar opposite personality would better serve the themes of duality, dichotomy in nature, and differing passionate interests. Once the real Charlie Kaufman included Donald, he found the device that would help him crack the adaptation. What if this diametrically opposed twin brother, now living with the already struggling Charlie, said that he also wanted to be a writer?

Writing about Donald was fun for Kaufman and opened up further avenues and possibilities in the story. Unlike the intense Charles, his twin Donald did not seem to be bogged down with the weight of the world. Even on Charlie's own film set, when he tells Donald not to embarrass him in front of the cast and crew, his twin is more at ease with the dynamics than Charlie seems to be. Donald pleasantly and nonchalantly flirts with the makeup woman working on the set, as Charlie watches him nervously. Donald's view of the world and easier going personality attracts others and makes people comfortable, while Charlie's pain creates a barrier and evokes apathy. Donald is also the slightly thinner one.

During the screenwriting process, Donald proves to be a thoughtful sounding board, whether his brother likes it or not. And when he announces that he's going to be a writer too, he adds to Charles's sense of dread, but also instills a fire in him. He gets angry that Donald is using industry terms ("Don't say pitch," he admonishes), and that Donald blathers on about structure. Living together, Donald has personal access to his brother, and can ask the already established writer in the house for constant advice. Though Donald is goofy and moves through the world like a big puppy (when his back isn't bothering him), he has no trouble when he sits down at his computer to work on a story. Charles, in turn, resents that his brother and now apparently neophyte writer twin can bring his idea for a screenplay so quickly to fruition. Unlike Charles's writing process, Donald seemed to be able to conjure a cohesive script at will.

While Orlean's book began with a description of one of her most colorful subjects John Laroche: "a tall guy, skinny as a stick, pale-eyed, slouch shouldered, and sharply handsome, in spite of the fact that he is missing all his front teeth,"[4] Kaufman chose to open his adaptation with a male voice playing over the opening credits at the bottom of a black screen. The disembodied voice begins, "Do I have an original thought in my head? My bald head? Maybe if I were happier my hair wouldn't be falling out. Life is short. I need to make the most of it. Today is the first day of the rest of my life ... I'm a walking cliché."[5] The rant continues for the length of a page, then the scene quickly lights upon the busy, working movie set of *Being John Malkovich*. The actors, cinematographer Lance Acord, and his entire crew are shooting the film. The writer, Charlie Kaufman (played by Nicolas Cage) is on set as well, but looks uncomfortable and feels he is in the way. He *is* in the way. In a scene drawn from Kaufman's real-life experience, the 1st assistant director on the set tells him he's in the eyeline and asks if he can please get off the stage. Dejected, he leaves to stand outside the production area. Instead of this visit bolstering his confidence, as the creator and writer of the damn movie, being on his own film set only underscores his feeling of alienation and disenchantment. He is the reason that anyone on that movie set even has their current job, and yet in voice-over, the Charlie character mutters, "What am I even doing here? Why did I bother to come here today? Nobody even seems to know my name. I've been on the planet for forty years, and am no closer to understanding a single thing."[6]

Back at his desk in his home office, he slumps at the computer screen. He knows better than to wait for the gods of inspiration to arrive to help him, so he dives in to his screenplay, starting with the beginning of the world, or at least our world, imagining the previously barren earth, then a lightning strike, which brings murky pools of water. A single cell organism pulses in the water then rapidly multiplies. Suddenly there is the ocean and gelatinous sea creatures. Soon ancient mammals crawl around on land, ice ages push time forward, prehistoric man arrives through to a modern city being built, culminating in a close-up of a crying, newborn baby, Charlie K. Creation. Evolution. It is Darwinian evolution set to time-lapse photography, and the world is created in a few blinks. Compared to that feat, an individual's problems, especially a screenwriter's, are rendered petty. The next scene introduces us to the other kind of adaptation explored in the movie, as Charlie is shown at a lunch meeting with a film executive, who is in charge of helping a book transmute from page to screen. This screenwriter, however, known for standing up for personal truth, is averse to the successful policies of his chosen field. The executive suggests that a translation of the book in question, *The Orchid Thief,* could benefit from the main characters falling in love. It is a conventional note, yes, and lazy writing, sure, but it takes money to make movies, or to make anything for that matter, and incidentally, it is called show business, not show art. Cage's Kaufman sweats, and sums up his feelings for this Hollywood custom with a politely controlled, authentic passion that he can't hold back, because it is not in his nature: "Okay, but I'm saying that I don't want to cram in sex, or guns or car chases, or characters learning profound life lessons, or growing, or coming to like each other, or overcoming obstacles to succeed in the end. The book isn't like that and life isn't like that. It just isn't."[7] What about fidelity? he asserts. But Hollywood is no place for a writer, unless he can find something to fortify him, like strong drink. But Charlie Kaufman knows all this, as this is part of what haunts his work and life.

In an early draft of the screenplay dated November 21, 2000, Kaufman begins the story with a slightly different structure than the big-screen version. He starts with a subtitle: "The Earth," and shows us how the planet looks from space. It is brown and meteor scarred. Then the camera moves in to show an endlessly barren, lifeless surface until volcanoes erupt, lightning strikes, and bubbling water forms. This is shown in silence. In this early script, we see that Charles has birthday cards on his mantel that read "To Our Dear Son on His Fortieth Birthday." As in the final film version, the main character still employs the voice-over, and berates himself using the words old, fat, and bald. Then, rather than taking the audience straight to the *Being John Malkovich* set, the earlier draft quickly changes from Charlie's self-abusive voice-over to scenes that include our first introduction to John Laroche, careening purposely in a beat-up white van down the Florida highway, cutting through swampland. Kaufman shows Laroche like Orlean presented him, and surrounds him with books and objects that will inform the reader and moviegoer as to his character traits. Before Kaufman shows us the man's face, we follow his van around at great speeds, while gardening soil, trowels, an audio cassette of the *Writings of Charles Darwin,* computer parts, and various digging tools strewn around his car jostle and crowd around him. He doesn't seem to mind the clutter; it is more like a part of him and he looks to be a man on a mission. While his van screams around the curves of the road, the driver intently listens to a British narrator on audio cassette explain: "As natural selection works solely by and for the good of each being, all corporeal and mental endowments will tend to progress toward perfection."[8] Humming along in his van, John Laroche is closely followed by a green Ford carrying three young Indian men, passing a joint between them and blasting a Nirvana song. They can barely keep up with Laroche's erratic van ahead. Kaufman's next scene shows us that we are now in a New York skyscraper, which houses the *New Yorker* magazine. It is late at night and most of the employees have gone home hours ago, yet we hear a light but steady *click click click* coming from a typewriter.

Other than a writing assignment on the world of Florida orchid breeders, the real-life Susan Orlean's book became a meditation on the nature of passion and what drives it. She turned her search for the answers to passion in art, orchids, and writing, into a metaphor for life. In addition to Orlean's original posits on passion, Kaufman's script also explores the literal process of adapting Orlean's book as well as the whole definition of adaptation on a large scale. Both writers asked themselves if John Laroche's quick ability to transmute a crushing experience, such as being responsible for his mother's fatal car accident or losing his life's work to a hurricane, was an example of adaptation or passion. His way of mending himself was admirable, but was it true emotional recovery or just a ferocious need to block out pain in order to move on and adapt, or was recovery and forgetting the same thing? Orlean and Kaufman both wondered how someone so devoted, obsessed, and passionate about a subject or person could so completely renounce it. Is it personal evolution or a way of refusing to acknowledge the pain of loss and the life experience as a whole? Kaufman was supposed to write a movie about flowers, but his source material included many questions of philosophical constructs.

As in many of Kaufman's original scripts and the final cut versions of his films, references to literature and philosophy abound. In an early draft of *Adaptation,* Charlie's friend Margaret makes a reference to William Blake when she asks him if he knows Blake's line about seeing heaven in a wildflower.

Margaret also mentions Hegel and his *The Philosophy of History*, and his argument that history is a human construct. The dialogue between Margaret and Charlie, however, does not make it to the final film. Neither does an early scripted scene that would have provided the audience with a richer history of what Laroche's mother meant to him and how much she influenced his career and life decisions. The dropped scene shows a 10-year-old boy at a pet store in North Miami. Young Laroche's mother, a sweet, frumpy, learned woman, tells the boy he can choose any animal he likes, while she gently strokes the hair of his frail, glassy-eyed little sister nearby. When he chooses a turtle, his mother informs him he has made a wonderful choice and that his decision is even spiritually meaningful, in that the Native Americans believe the whole world rests on the back of a turtle. This lost scene goes a long way to flesh out the mother-son dynamic, and the pain of John Laroche's eventual loss and guilt becomes even more profound. In yet another dropped childhood scene, we see Laroche's father in a back brace watching TV while his mother cares for the ailing sister. His mother gently prays for the child as we see a little Hindu alter in the room. When the young John enters the scene, he passionately tells his mother that he feels he must collect every kind of turtle in the world (he knows the Latin name of each) and that his life isn't worth living if he can't. Instead of telling her little son to calm down, and redirecting his interest to something more practical or shooshing him away, she replies, "Well we'd better get started, huh, baby." Her encouragement knew no bounds of frustration. The adult Laroche the audience knows from the film shows Susan Orlean his abiding love for his mother when he proudly tells Orlean that he and his mom had the largest collection of 19th-century Dutch mirrors on the planet. His palpable pride for their work and partnership shines through as he prompts Orlean with the line, "Perhaps you read about us. *Mirror World* October '88? I have a copy somewhere…"[9] His early childhood focus on personal goals eventually leads him to plod earnestly through a swamp until he finds his current obsession: a rare, uniquely sought-after symbol of singular beauty, that is, the ghost orchid. Among the mosquitoes and the looming threat of an alligator in the background, it is clear that this man will not stray from his mission. Although "the ghost" is the name of the elusive orchid Laroche seeks, it is also perhaps a veiled reference to an impossible quest and the ghost of his mother.

Just as John Laroche's childhood scenes are left out of the final product, so too are scenes of Charlie Kaufman's imagined version of Susan Orlean's lonely upbringing. Kaufman shows us how as a little girl growing up in Canton, Ohio, Susan would write in her diary while holding a flashlight in bed at night. She would pretend to be asleep when her tipsy mother visited her girlhood room and sat on the edge of her bed, crying quietly. Although the real writer Susan Orlean is certainly not a murderous drug user, Kaufman's version of Susan does have a longing and sadness about her that is informed by his created childhood for the character. While Kaufman also designed

scenes in which Orlean's marriage was under strain, these too were fictitious, but also prescient. The real Susan Orlean admitted that at the time of
Kaufman's writing, her marriage was indeed coming apart. This couldn't have
been something the writer Charlie Kaufman would have known about, or so
she thought. When she read about her relationship waning in the screenplay,
she said, "I almost passed out."[10] Perhaps Kaufman's close reading of her
book gave him true insight, or his crafted marriage scenes just illustrate his
precognition.

Another added dimension in the draft from 2000 is Kaufman's inclusion
of his therapy sessions with a female counselor. He tells his therapist that he
could tell women he is a screenwriter and probably win their affections that
way; however, he wants people to like him simply for being him, not because
he is in show business. About women specifically he opines, "I want them to
like me. The way I like them. The way I'd do anything for some woman walking down the street. I don't need to know what their job is. I don't need to
know them at all." A terrible sadness comes over him as he tells his therapist,
"No one will ever love me like that." The therapist scenes deftly switch from
drama to comedy, as it becomes clear that some of the character Charlie's
inadequacies stem from his inability to connect with the women in his life. It
therefore becomes comical that he feels free to open up and relate his most
intimate details to a woman in an authority position. When he mentions
in a counseling session that he is concerned that he has been masturbating
"a lot ... not a lot a lot," while fantasizing about a new woman he is fixated
on, the therapist asks him, "So do you think you'll talk to this one?"[11]

Quite the opposite of Laroche's passionate expressions for his beloved
collections, the character Charlie adores women but only fantasizes about relationships with them. Similarly to the way Laroche has catalogued the original names of the many different classifications of orchids, so too has Charlie
compartmentalized the beauty of women. Just as all orchids are different and
take on a human equivalent, Charlie lists in his mind some of the women he
sees. One looks "like a school teacher, one looks like a gymnast, one looks
like a Midwestern beauty queen, one looks like a New York intellectual with
whom you'd do the *Sunday Times* crossword puzzle. One looks like that
girl in high school with creamy skin. One has eyes that dance. One has eyes
that contain the sadness of the world."[12] However, as Laroche's passion adds
purpose and zeal to his life and knowledge, Charlie's remote adoration only
leads to more alienation for him.

When the Charlie character can not shake his writer's block and sees that
his brother is making progress with his own writing, he reluctantly decides to
enroll in Robert McKee's legendary script writing class. His brother was able
to dash off a screenplay about a serial killer with multiple personalities, called
The 3, and sold it for six figures. The real Charlie Kaufman who has been
an admirer of the author Philip K. Dick's work since college, may be referring to Dick's 1965 novel *The 3 Stigmata of Palmer Eldritch,* which includes

"evolution therapy" and a fictitious hallucinogen. In *Adaptation*, Kaufman's characters undergo their own personal evolution, and he adds the cinematic, fictitious twist that Laroche harvests ghost orchids for a drug they produce. The name of Donald's screenplay could also be a reference to Kaufman's own unproduced adaptation of Dick's novel *A Scanner Darkly*. The nod to Dick is relevant as both writers include the themes of personal identity and the social construction of reality throughout their work. In another self-referential moment with his brother, the character Charlie tries to explain to his twin that his premise, especially if going to be shot for the screen, is ludicrous. It seems "unfilmmable," which is a word that the real Charlie Kaufman heard time and again when film executives and development people were reading his screenplay for *Being John Malkovich*.

While in Robert McKee's seminar, Charlie can't shake his thoughts that by even being there he is selling out. Hadn't he passionately told Donald that a writer's job is to discover something new and not simply input data into a formula? And serial killers! (heavy sigh), hadn't that been done to death? Will Jack the Ripper never get old? Part of him wants to flee McKee's audience while part of him has to acknowledge that Donald might be on to something. Whether Charlie agrees with it or not, he also can't deny that McKee himself is full of passion for his work. In opposition to his original mantra of avoiding Hollywood cliché, Charlie ends up *learning* something from McKee about writing drama, and perhaps about life itself. In stark comparison to Charlie's life, McKee's staunch supporter Donald is the one who is able to come to town, make friends, find a girlfriend, and quickly sell a lucrative screenplay.

Although the Charlie character is at odds with McKee's workshops as a way to embrace writing, the real Charlie Kaufman has obvious respect for McKee as a person. In no way was it his intention to belittle the teacher or his students on screen. In fact, the real McKee seemed flattered to be characterized in Charlie Kaufman's screenplay and understood his process from the onset. "When they came to me with this draft, I realized of course what Charlie was doing," McKee acknowledged. "The story needed an antagonist. And I said, 'I'm happy to play your antagonist.'"[13] Indeed, when the filmmakers needed to ask McKee's permission to use his name as a character in the film, his only request was not about himself, but that he didn't want his students made fun of. Regarding Kaufman's written interpretations of the real people for the movie (including himself), and blurring the line between reality and fiction, McKee noted that "truth is not what is, but what we think about what is. We who were portrayed realized from scratch that none of us were, in any real sense, actually in the film. Kaufman was after something else, not fact, not us." He added, "The guiding impulse in Kaufman values freedom over restraint, the unusual over the usual. He wants to push the cinema against the grain into hidden humanity, to take it through the frayed synapses of the mind, complete with spiraling free associations and compulsive, self-critical repetitions." Though the popular writing teacher warns against the possibility of making a story too personal in that it runs the risk of alienating the audience, he believes Kaufman already knows about that danger and that he needed to take that risk. "For at the heart of Kaufman is that dreaded voice of authority, his artist's conscience telling him that like it or not, one way or another, he has to tell the story."[14]

And in telling the story, he also has to tell the truth. Not the exfoliated, smoothed, and then polished truth, but the raw, bumpy authenticity of an honest life. For example, Kaufman doesn't include masturbation scenes in the *Adaptation* screenplay because he wants to embarrass himself or a reader or moviegoer, but rather because masturbation is part of the truth of the frustrations he was living at the time. Conversely, it is also symbolic of Darwin's point that self-pollinated things die, while its cross-pollinating brothers will thrive. Learning to understand Darwin's theory is the only way the Charlie character will develop as a writer and person. John Laroche (the real one and the fictional version) instinctively understands what the character Charlie lacks. During a day at an orchid show, Laroche stops to appreciate the flowers and impart his wisdom to Susan Orlean who is following him around scribbling his words on a notepad,

> There's a certain orchid that looks like a certain insect. So the insect is drawn to this flower, its double, its soul mate, and wants nothing more than to make love to it. After the insect flies off, it spots another soul mate flower and makes love to it, thus pollinating it. And neither the flower nor the insect will ever understand the significance of their lovemaking. How could they know because of their little dance, the world lives. But it does. By simply doing what they're designed to do, something large and magnificent happens. In this sense they show us how to live. How the only barometer you have is your heart. How, when you spot your flower, you can't let anything get in your way.[15]

The camera captures Orlean's facial expression as she takes these words in. Maybe she can learn something from this oddball, know-it-all flower stealer, the way Charlie can learn from his twin brother. Orlean's character, like Charlie's, is slow to grasp the bravery of emotional growth, and they both seem caught in their stubborn brains. When Laroche grows inpatient with Orlean's expectations and needs, he yells at her to find her own interests, stop leaching off him, and find her own way home. The grizzled, rangy Southerner with no teeth is telling the sophisticated New Yorker exactly what the great thinker Voltaire said in *Candide*: cultivate your own garden.

Just as Kaufman built a parallel emotional arc for his characters Charlie and Orlean, so too did he unify his antagonist and anti-hero, Laroche and Donald. The orchid thief himself and the twin brother have much in common as they are the characters who can readily adapt as the world demands. They are of like minds as they both choose to create their own experiences in the world. Both of them even create new names for the other characters. In the screenplay, when Donald is in scenes with his brother, he calls him

Charles, although everywhere else, that character is referred to with the more commonly used name Charlie. Common is not a word Donald would use to describe his twin brother, and calling him Charles implies the respect that the more formal moniker carries. Laroche also gives the learned, urbane Susan Orlean the affectionate nickname of Susie. He gives her a new name of his own choosing that is specific to their relationship. One can only imagine that there aren't that many people in the best-selling author's and *New Yorker* staffer's life with the balls to call her "Susie Q." In Laroche's eyes and when she is around him, Susan Orlean can become something different and have a whole new identity. Both Laroche and Donald have a unique relationship with their significants and identify them with personal, intimate names.

In the real Susan Orlean's book, a story element that Kaufman circles as something interesting he might be able to use in his adaptation was a mention of a "Swamp Ape." Orlean wrote: "There are certainly ghosts in the Fakahatchee—ghosts of rangers who were murdered years ago by illegal plume hunters, and of loggers who were cut to pieces in fights and then left to cool and crumble into dirt, and for years there has been an apparition wandering the swamp, the Swamp Ape, which is said to be seven feet tall and weigh seven hundred pounds and have the physique of a human, the posture of an ape, the body odor of a skunk, and an appetite for lima beans."[16] Kaufman made use of Orlean's allusion to this swamp ape in the Florida Everglades in the second draft of his script dated September 24, 1999. In the third act of this version, it is John Laroche instead of Susan Orlean who wants the character Charlie dead. When the brothers Kaufman intrude upon Laroche and Orlean at their love-nest drug shack, the couple confronts them but the boys jump into an airboat to attempt escape, before being chased by wild pigs. One of the wild hogs manages to jump aboard the boat but Charlie kicks it into the water as Donald steers. Laroche and Orlean give chase in their van while shooting at the brothers and a stray bullet hits the boat's tank, sending the boys flying into the air in a firey explosion. Underwater, Charles is attacked by an alligator but his brother Donald manages to decapitate the gator with a boat propeller blade. Donald helps his brother to shore, while Laroche and Orlean continue to pummel them with gunfire.

One of Laroche's neighbors, Mike Owen, sees the fire and hears the commotion, and jumps in his truck, headed toward the mayhem. Donald and Charlie have trudged to the shore, but Donald is hit by a bullet. In a touching and funny moment, as Donald lays dying in his brother's arms, he tells his twin to save himself and escape, because he's got an awesome third act. Charlie breaks down to his dying brother and says that he wishes he got to know him better: "See it's just I thought I knew you already. I thought you were me. And I hated me."[17] Donald succumbs to death and his distraught brother "screams heavenward." Just then Laroche's van swerves out of the bushy swampland, aiming right for them. Charlie rolls his brother's body out of the way and limps off as the van smashes into a tree. Laroche and Orlean, still toting guns, rush after Charlie into the swamp.

Mike, the good neighbor, finds Donald's broken body and lifts him into his truck. Charlie limps out of the swamp just as Mike sees him in the truck's headlights and is confused by seeing a double of the broken man he was just carrying. The breathless Charlie tells him that people are shooting at him and he needs help! Before Mike can make sense of the situation, his truck is flipped over and Donald's body flies into the water. Suddenly Mike and Charlie are staring up at a giant man-like beast. Kaufman's draft describes it as repulsive, covered in algae-matted fur. Mike and Charlie run, but the creature grabs Mike and breaks his neck. Now turned around in the chaos, Charlie runs smack into Orlean who is still high on ghost orchid dust and exclaims, "Hey, it's the screenwriter!" As he tries to warn her that a beast is in the swamp, Laroche puts his gun to Charlie's head. Suddenly the beast resurfaces, grabs Laroche, and pulls him into the swamp. Laroche calls out to Orlean, "Susie! Susie!" but she didn't see what happened and fires blindly into the marshland.

A lumpy mass of man and beast slumps toward Orlean and she and Charlie realize both the swamp creature and Laroche are dead. Orlean cries softly and pets Laroche's head. Kaufman feels her pain and gently tells her he used to look at her book jacket picture and know that she was sweet and smart, and that he imagined she was a little lost and lonely like himself. He gingerly takes her chin in his hand and redirects her thoughts onto him. Orlean looks at him deeply and tells him he is really wonderful and that she can see inside his lonely soul. Orlean coos, "It's raining inside you. I want to run through your dripply dripples. It's so beautiful. I love you. I do."[18] Charlie sits down on a rock, and in a Charlie Brown–defeated tone utters, "It's the drugs." Once her high fades and Charlie tries to walk away from her, she yells at him and says she can't let him go: she can't make this public. As just a few minutes ago she was loving and lovely, she now calls him all the miserable names he called himself at the beginning of the story: pathetic, fat, and bald. She also adds that he doesn't even know how to write. She begins firing bullets again and Charlie falls to the ground, but Clint Eastwood like, gets up and keeps walking. She takes aim again but is suddenly thrown to the ground by a bloody heaving creature. Charlie screams out, "Donald!" and limps backward as Donald and Orlean grapple on the ground. Donald passionately yells at her, "My brother is not fat. He's not bald. My brother is a great writer! He was trying to do something important!"[19] Suddenly the gun goes off and when Charles reaches them, they are both dead. The scene ends with him falling to his knees.

As morning breaks over the swamp, the scene is now filled with police cars and an active tow-truck. Charlie is wrapped in a blanket near an ambulance. He explains to a cop who the bodies are: Mike Owen, John Laroche, Susan Orlean, and that he doesn't exactly know what the swamp ape thing is. About his brother, he explains that they are twins and that Donald saved his life. When the sympathetic police man says that they really look alike, for the first time in his existence, he proudly answers that, yes, they do. In the beginning of the story, Charlie was embarrassed to look like his brother, mostly because he served as a direct reflection of how he felt about himself.

The last scene of the draft ends with Charlie back in a casual restaurant working on his writing with Robert McKee's book, *Story*, by his side. Alice, the waitress he fantasized about before, notices the book and volunteers that she loves McKee. She then recognizes Charlie from the last time he was there and quickly becomes reserved, but this time, Charlie is relaxed and comfortable with himself and doesn't drive her off. By comparison to their first encounters, now Charlie's character is calmer and seems to have found some peace with himself. He has evolved, or mutated, but his mind has been made unstuck, regardless. Alice asks if he has been studying, and he amiably replies that he has been working on a screenplay for Sony Pictures: "About being yourself and that all life from the flower to the human being is a miracle."[20] He relates that his brother was murdered and now it's essential for him to show people that life is important. Alice is so in awe of this newfound wisdom and the evolved Charlie that despite her being on the clock at her waitressing job, she asks if she can sit down with him and talk for awhile. This version ends on a hopeful note in that once Charlie became comfortable with his own truth, his changed energy attracts like-minded people like a magnetic force. The draft ends with the direction to show a quote from Shakespeare's *Julius Caesar* in white text on the black screen: "Let me have men about me that are fat; / Sleek-headed men and such that sleep o' nights."[21] The quote is followed by: *In Loving Memory of Donald Kaufman.*

When director and friend Spike Jonze read this early draft, similarly to the way he suggested that the original third act of the *Being John Malkovich* script be changed, he wasn't thrilled about the swamp ape in the ending, coming in as a deus ex machina. Funnily enough, as Donald Kaufman would know, Robert McKee's very first commandment is: Thou shalt not take the crisis/climax out of the protagonist's hands. More importantly, because Kaufman doesn't view his drafts as sacred and therefore fixed, he wasn't married to the idea of the swamp ape and went into rewrites. Consequently, the final film's ending is still dramatic, but even more poignant. Donald needed to die so that the Charlie Kaufman character could learn to accept himself, incorporate parts of Donald into his life, put his self inflicted fear aside, and embrace the world fully, regardless of rejection, pain, and loss. His fallen twin had taught him that you are what you love, not what loves you, and no one can take that away from you in the end. Just as Darwin's cross-pollination made it possible for the world to evolve, Charles and Donald needed each other to create their *Adaptation.*

In Kaufman's world, the John Laroche character could feasibly die in the story as well, because the Susan Orlean character had finally learned about passion. Her wish as she describes it in *The Orchid Thief* was to want to be as passionate about something or someone as Laroche was. He was the answer to her quest and his death enabled her to feel the full range of passion, including grief. She is forever changed because of her time with Laroche and knowing him pushed her past her numbing, remote filter from which she safely observed and reported on her surroundings. She and the Charlie Kaufman character had both processed through the painful road-going of personal adaptation. Susan Orlean's book ends with a badly planned day in the swamp with John Laroche giving up on the search for the ghost orchid and leading her back to her car; Kaufman's final version of his screenplay veers into a designed culmination of all he loathed in a commercial Hollywood blockbuster: a car crash, hostage situation, dramatic death scene, and redemption.

Kaufman turned in his screenplay (months past his deadline) and didn't hear back from the producers immediately. In the back of his mind, he didn't think this script would ever see the light of day. He had spoken to his friend Jonze about his problem doing the assignment when he was already five months in and had only managed false starts and dead ends. Jonze was immediately intrigued and supportive of the new imaginative tact Kaufman had on his mind. In fact, they were on the 7 and ½ floor set of the *Being John Malkovich* movie when Kaufman broached the subject. The conversation was rife with anxiety, but Jonze's enthusiasm for the new idea helped give Kaufman the strength to see the project through. However, Kaufman never told the other producers and certainly not the studio that he was taking their assignment in a new direction. He kept that to himself at the time, as he rightly assumed they would have balked: Mr. Saxon had hired him to write a faithful adaptation of *The Orchid Thief*. What he handed in was not the assignment he was given. As the days went on and the phone didn't ring, his nerves grew frazzled. Could he explain that he wanted to stay true to Susan Orlean's vision and that he believed he wrote best when he connected with what he was thinking about at the time? The only problem is that what he was thinking about at the time was that he didn't know how to write a movie about flowers. As the waiting continued, he was certain his choice would prove to be the end of his career. He freely admitted that he was terrified.

Film producer Ed Saxon, who had optioned Orlean's series of magazine articles years ago, then waited more years for her to write the book, then searched for a screenplay writer who he could trust to make the damn flowers interesting (because the book ended up reading like a seemingly unadaptable dear diary essay), was not amused. Kaufman winced as he remembered, "He was angry and confused and wanted to know who Donald was, and why I had farmed out part of my script."[22] And no wonder. He hadn't waited all this time to let the ball stop with him. Not on his watch. Saxon threw out his chest and brought the script to his lunch meeting with Susan Orlean. She remembered the meal taking an inordinately long time, especially for showbiz. When was he going to hand it over? He explained to her that it wasn't exactly like her book and that some of the characters in it were not in the book. After a lengthy, drawn-out dessert, he asked her to just read it and to call him immediately. When she went in to her office and opened it up to the first page she saw that a character named Charlie Kaufman had the first line of dialogue. She confessed that her first thought was, wait, "Isn't that the name of the screenwriter?"[23] She told the *New York Times* that initially she was astonished and that it "seemed completely nuts."[24] She was now a *character in the movie?* As she flipped through it she kept seeing the name Orlean Orlean Orlean on top of dialogue. They had her having sex with one of the subjects of her book, John Laroche, snorting drugs, lamenting the breakdown of her marriage, and wielding a gun. She was a writer for the *New Yorker* for god's sake. Now she was Patty Hearst? She didn't really understand what was going on. When she eventually returned Saxon's call after a few days, she agreed that the *story* was interesting, but didn't want her name in it: she didn't want to be a character. They could of course leave the character in it, just use a different name. Saxon had anticipated this, but wasn't going to accept this answer. He was part of the original producing team that had optioned Orlean's magazine articles in the first place. He had waited while she wrote the book to flesh out the story and found that it was not easily translatable to the screen. The project needed an imagination like Charlie Kaufman's. While Saxon understood Orlean's position, he tried to explain that every one else in the movie was going to use *their* name, for example, Robert McKee and John Laroche. Orlean explained, "But I feel funny. Here I am using drugs and having sex with my subjects." Saxon replied, "Susan, look at Charlie. Charlie is masturbating through the whole movie using his name." And she thought, "You know, he's got a point there. What am I complaining about?"[25] The other reason she relented was because she realized that if the filmmakers did change the character's name, then people might think *The Orchid Thief* book was written by someone else.

While Charlie Kaufman and director Spike Jonze were relieved that Susan Orlean had consented, they then faced the issue of casting. Jonze remembered, "We talked about a lot of people and read with people. It took a while to let go of the idea that I was casting somebody to play Charlie and get in my mind that we were casting someone to play his part in the script. Also to find somebody who could play both of those characters, who are subtlety different. Nicolas [Cage] has the qualities of being very self-loathing and getting worked up and anxious. He also has the qualities of being able to put those aside and be a goofball and loose. Those qualities, besides loving him in other movies, made us realize [he was the one]."[26] When Cage asked to meet the real Kaufman and spend some time with him, he also asked if he could sleep over at his house for a few days to learn what made him tick. "I was gonna bring my sleeping bag," the actor laughed. "But that wasn't something Charlie was going to do. So I invited him to go with me on a fishing trip to Mexico. And that also wasn't something he was going to do."[27]

What Kaufman did agree to was an exhausting round of many tape-recorded interviews, which he was hoping Cage would burn in the end.

In casting Meryl Streep, neither Kaufman, Jonze, nor Susan Orlean could believe their good fortune. Streep noted of Kaufman's screenplay, "He really writes out of pain and he is willing to express that, but I was very impressed with him. I think his work was in the script and it's gorgeous. It's very ambitious and very brave." Upon first meeting Charlie Kaufman, she remembered, "I found him to be very guarded as only somebody who's laid his entire interior self out in a movie can be. I'm shocked that he's done that, put his anxieties out for everyone to see. I was struck by how thoughtful he was and willing to discuss it and clear. I met him with Spike and they were clear about the tone of the piece and how they really did want it. They didn't want some smart aleck sort of cool look to this."[28] In later years, Streep would go on to work with Kaufman in his sound plays written for the stage.

For the casting of the eminent McKee, several giants of the screen were considered including Albert Finney, Christopher Plummer, Terence Stamp, and Michael Caine; however, because McKee had given the filmmakers permission to use his copyrighted material on screen and because he was so easy and great to work with, the producers asked him who he would cast to play himself if he could. His answer was the sublime Brian Cox, "because unlike the others under consideration, Cox never has a 'love me' subtext to his work."[29]

John Turturro was approached for the role of the dynamic, charismatic ball of perseverance that is John Laroche. Ultimately, it was Chris Cooper who would step into the orchid thief's squishy boots, but the decision did not come easily to the highly respected actor. Initially, he confessed, "I didn't think that I was capable of fulfilling the role." He admitted his wife pushed him to do it, telling him, "Often the roles that you shy away from are the ones that you'd better pursue."[30] The Coopers' sentiments mirrored the spirit of Kaufman's screenplay, and with that, the casting of the film was complete.

The film was shot in under 60 days but Jonze and his editor Eric Zumbrunnen, A.C.E., took 10 months to edit it. Every time the filmmakers fashioned a new version, Nicolas Cage needed to loop a whole new narration. Just as the beginning of this project had its failed starts, so too did the end. Jonze revealed, "I definitely knew that this was going to be a complicated editorial, because we were trying to make so many disparate ideas, characters, and moments come together. But I don't think we thought it was going to be as hard as it was. The intention of the script never changed, but how it's come together and how the sequences and scenes fit together—how much you intercut, or when you intercut between the multiple characters, where things happen in the story—there was a lot of flexibility."[31] Once they were relatively happy with the final cut of the film, they wrapped postproduction and sent the movie out into the world. Susan Orlean's bestselling nonfiction book had been transmuted for the big screen. It was now a combination of both fiction and non-fiction—a hybrid, much like the orchids. How it would be received was now out of Kaufman's hands. The sealed film canisters were shipped, the audience cued up for movie tickets, and as promised, Nicolas Cage burned the interview tapes.

When the film opened in 2002, it seemed to be the year of Charlie Kaufman as that same year saw the release of three films based on his screenplays: *Adaptation, Human Nature,* and *Confessions of A Dangerous Mind. Adaptation* met with mostly stellar reviews. *Rolling Stone* summed it up thusly: "Smart, inventive, passionate and rip-roaringly funny is a rare species. So all praise to Charlie Kaufman, working with director Spike Jonze to create the most original and outrageous film comedy since the two first teamed on *Being John Malkovich.* Cage is a double-barreled marvel, nailing every laugh as well as the emotions that run deep in the twins. It's a kick to see Streep let go with rich comic material," and "expect Oscar to chase Cooper. Best known for character roles (*American Beauty*), he gives a bust-out star performance that brims with magnetism (not easy if you're acting with no front teeth)."[32] The *New York Times* professed it was "gleefully self-referential an exercise in auto-deconstruction as you could wish. But it is also, more deeply, a movie about its own nonexistence—a narrative that confronts both the impossibility and the desperate necessity of storytelling, and that short-circuits our expectations of coherence, plausibility and fidelity to lived reality even as it satisfies them. Common sense suggests that there could never be such a movie, but if there could, it would have to be one of the slipperiest, most fascinating and, by any sane reckoning, best movies of the year."[33]

But as with all of Kaufman's deeply personal and therefore open-veined work efforts, *Adaptation* did have some opponents. Stephanie Zacharek of *salon.com* noted,

> *Adaptation* doesn't offer us a real story, just a bloated thesis. The movie doesn't reach out to anything or anyone; it's most interested in its own pinched vision. The movie's Band-Aid subtheme—the thing that gives its title a double meaning—is that human beings must adapt in order to grow. Life changes us a bit day by day, and we need to recognize those changes and act accordingly. What a lofty and resonant idea! It may also be one of the greatest ass-saving constructs in the history of movies—a faux-grand concept that dazzles people enough to keep them from catching on to how completely self-indulgent *Adaptation* is.[34]

Kaufman had already assumed that part of an audience would call the writing self-indulgent. He had already beaten the critics to the punch when in the film his character variously refers to himself as not just self-indulgent but also narcissistic, insane, solipsistic, and pathetic. Regarding both the praise as well as the reproach, Kaufman admitted that in lieu of all the hair-pulling trouble he had with the writing assignment itself, he was just happy that the movie materialized at all. "I honestly did not think this movie would ever see the light of day. I didn't think this movie was going to get made. Putting myself in the script was a really hard thing to do. I wouldn't have done it if I had some distance from it and I wouldn't have set out to do it." He added thoughtfully, "And I don't think I would have been able to do it if I thought it was going to get made."[35] Above and beyond the critics, Kaufman was concerned with what the book author, Susan Orlean, would think. Robert McKee told the screenwriter that the movie was funny and fair. John Laroche, who Kaufman noted was professorial looking in real life, was pleased with the mention of two percent of something in his contract and the clause that included a possible action figure. But what about the author of the source material itself? In her introduction to the published shooting script for *Adaptation,* she acknowledged,

> I didn't meet Charlie until I spent a day on the *Adaptation* set towards the end of the shoot. I was too embarrassed to say much to him, and he seemed too embarrassed to say much to me. What I would have said was that strangely, marvelously, hilariously, his screenplay has ended up not being a literal adaptation of my book, but a spiritual one, something that has captured (and expanded on) the essential character of what the book, I hope, was about: the process of trying to figure out one's self, and life, and love, and the wonders of the world; and the ongoing, exasperating battle between doing what's easy and doing what's good; and the ongoing exasperating battle between looking at the world ironically and looking at it sentimentally. Oh and orchids.[36]

When Meryl Streep apologized to Orlean in advance of the film, Orlean remarked, "Oh, I've seen it. I wish I were Susan Orlean."[37] If Kaufman still had any reservations about his adaptation of her work, he was forgiven.

When Kaufman is pressed to explain what a certain film is really about, he usually demurs, relaying that he would rather not impose his meanings on an audience. He wants them to have their own experience of what is true for them as individuals without being led. He feels he has done his job if moviegoers can experience his film in their own ways at different times in their lives. Specifically to *Adaptation,* there are many aspects one might experience of the film, including what writers do to their subjects, how Charles was able to personally and professionally adapt to succeed in his own life by incorporating his brother's worldview, how a deeply passionate man like John Laroche can also cultivate change in order to prevail. It is no surprise that by the end of the story Laroche has embraced the Internet (with all its advances and flaws) as a way to make a living. Although Kaufman and his director had many discussions about how they were going to talk about this film, in the end they decided it was best to let the viewer decide. *Adaptation*'s composer, Carter Burwell, perhaps sums up the question as to what the film is really about best. In his liner notes to the compact disc of the movie's soundtrack he wrote, "Three themes wind through this musical score. 'The Swamp'—the unknowable, the primordial soup of doubt. 'The Ghost'—the unattainable object of desire. 'Creation'—the great process, which is always the unfolding of some earlier creation, suggesting a spinning wheel of recursion. Hopefully these themes are general enough that they can apply simultaneously to the characters in the narrative of the film, and also to the processes of evolution and adaptation which they study and within which they are bound."[38]

On February 11, 2003, Donald Kaufman's name was read aloud by a presenter at the Academy Awards show, which is televised around the world. He and his brother Charlie Kaufman were both nominated for an Oscar for their adapted screenplay. For their hard work, the main actors were also recognized for their contributions. Nicolas Cage and Meryl Streep were nominated for their roles, while Chris Cooper won the Academy Award for Best Actor in a Supporting Role. At the 56th annual British Academy of Film Awards, the equivalent of America's Oscars, the main actors were once again nominated. The main difference in the British Academy Awards was that this time, Donald and Charlie took home the award for Best Adapted Screenplay.

Some say that Donald Kaufman, the man who broke open the secret to adapting the flower essay for his twin brother, is merely a figment of Charlie Kaufman's writing. Kaufman is not the first writer to be accused of making things up and would be in good company if this accusation were true. Hunter S. Thompson, for example, was accused of creating the character of his friend (and attorney) Oscar Acosta. Often applied to Acosta, and what can be used to describe Donald Kaufman as well, is the description, "Too weird to live, too rare to die." As Charlie Kaufman himself might say, talking about anything too much can spoil it. And besides, Donald Kaufman has the wholly unprecedented distinction of being the only fictitious character to be nominated for an Academy Award.

George Clooney's *Confessions* Lead to the *Darkly* Unproduced Philip K. Dick

Know your dealer.

—Charles Freck from *A Scanner Darkly*

"Clooney went on forever about how my *Confessions [of A Dangerous Mind]* screenplay was one of the greatest scripts he'd read," Kaufman sighed. "But if someone truthfully felt that way, then they'd want the person who wrote it to be on board, offering their thoughts and criticisms. But Clooney didn't. And I think it's a silly way to be a director."[1]

When George Clooney was given the green light to direct Kaufman's screenplay *Confessions of A Dangerous Mind,* which had long been hailed as one of the best unproduced scripts in Hollywood, the writer's previous experiences with directors had been inclusive and collegial. Part of the problem Charlie Kaufman ran into with George Clooney was largely due to that fact: his past directors Spike Jonze and Michel Gondry saw the writer as an invaluable team player in the filmmaking process. He had been treated as an integral part of the team and was involved with preproduction, casting, and the postproduction elements of editing and music. During the actual filming process, he was rarely on the sets because he respected the fact that the actual making of the film was the director's territory. If Jonze or Gondry ever needed quick script changes or tweaks, Kaufman was always available to them, but never stepped over the line of his directors who were at the helm. Kaufman also knew that his experiences with Jonze and Gondry were rare indeed, and that more often than not, once the screenplay writer hands in his script, he loses power over controlling his work. He knew that he had been lucky, up until now.

Needless to say, Kaufman's exclusion from the *Confessions of a Dangerous Mind* project, which he had put his heart into, was indeed irksome. He acknowledged, "I can tell you that George Clooney is my LEAST favorite person. He's like this really charming guy who pretends he's your best friend. I had written him a 17-page note (about changes that should be in *Confessions of a Dangerous Mind*). He didn't make the alterations. I was horrified when I saw the film. Someone can change things, as long as I'm involved in making the decisions."[2]

Chuck Barris's autobiography was originally published in 1984 and benefited from heavy promotion because he was so well-known at the time. The premise was that a successful television game show producer and host, who appeared to be a shambling drunk in front of a camera, was moonlighting as a hit man for the CIA. In the late 1980s, when Columbia Pictures bought the film rights to the book *Confessions of a Dangerous Mind: An Unauthorized Autobiography* for director Jim McBride (*The Big Easy*), the project stalled because no actor wanted to play Chuck Barris. McBride wanted Richard Dreyfuss to take on the lead role, but the actor found Barris's reputation so vulgar and distasteful that he wouldn't even consider it.

In 1997, when Warner Bros. bought the production rights to *Confessions of a Dangerous Mind,* Charlie Kaufman was brought on to write the screenplay. On the sheer strength of Kaufman's reputation from the *Being John Malkovich* script, he was offered the assignment of adapting Chuck Barris's book for the big screen. *Being John Malkovich* hadn't even gone into production yet.

Unlike the trouble Kaufman would later have in adapting the book *The Orchid Thief,* Chuck Barris's book seemed like another type of animal entirely. He did not have the same ethical reservations about adapting the fantastical story. Kaufman remembered his thoughts when he accepted the writing assignment, "The only reason I was interested in that, and the only reason I took it, was because I thought he was lying. And I was interested in the notion that, first of all, *he* said it, and he's lying, so it's okay for me to lie. And second of all, I was interested in the notion that he was lying. I was like, why is this guy—is he making this up, which I think he is—why is this his fantasy? You know? Which is basically a 10-year-old's fantasy, written by a 50-year-old. And he wasn't winking. He wasn't making fun of himself. It was like, no, this is clearly what made him feel like, if he said this, his life would be more valuable, more valid."[3]

Kaufman has always been interested in psychology and is attracted to reading about the ways in which the mind can be pushed over into psychosis. In accepting the writing assignment he was in no way judging Chuck Barris, but was interested in the book as a form of delusional biography. He was attracted to the project because he wanted to delve into the psyche that would create such an elaborate fantasy. By many societal standards, Chuck Barris had already achieved a great deal in his life before he wrote that book. He had succeeded in the two most relentlessly difficult, cutthroat industries in America: show business and the music business. Barris had written a hit song called "Palisades Park," which rose to number 3 on the Billboard Top 100 list in 1962; had worked on the beloved television show *American Bandstand;* became the head of the ABC network's daytime programming; and was the prolific creator and producer of wildly successful television game shows such as *The Dating Game, The Newlywed Game,* and *The Gong Show.*

As the screenplay writer of Barris's autobiography, Charlie Kaufman wanted to illuminate why someone so seemingly accomplished to the outside world needed to create an alter ego for himself. Despite Barris's already storied career, his delusional autobiography in which he claimed he was a secret assassin for the CIA seemed to prove that his successes in the entertainment industry only underscored his inherent emptiness. Perhaps the assassin part was a way for Barris to reconcile the fact that he infused the then relatively new and serious medium of American television with his fast and cheap game shows, which ushered in the reality show phenomenon of the current culture. Barris, a Drexel University graduate who had a penchant for quoting philosopher Thomas Carlyle, was probably not fond of his ugly reputation as the main man of trash TV. A CIA hit man, on the other hand, was someone people could respect or at least fear. Maybe more importantly, the role as hit man was someone Barris himself could respect. In writing *Confessions of a Dangerous Mind,* Barris revealed, "The book would hopefully act as a catharsis, exorcising from my mind and body the agonizing frustration, anger, and bitterness that had been brewing there for too long a time. Perhaps, upon completing *Confessions,* I would understand why some of my peers had been nailing me with such fury to the cross for trying to make people laugh."[4]

Charlie Kaufman agreed to take on the adaptation of the book in June of 1997 and when he turned in his first draft of the screenplay toward the end of that year, director Curtis Hanson immediately voiced his wish to helm the movie. The subject of the film himself liked the draft and Kaufman's name on the project attracted A-list talent such as Sean Penn (to play Barris), along with George Clooney in a smaller role. In addition to Curtis Hanson, director David Fincher had also read Kaufman's script while at Propaganda Films, and enjoyed it so thoroughly that he too wanted to direct it. Many other directors and actors were also attracted to the project. Respected industry names such as David O. Russell, Sam Mendes, Darren Aronofsky, Brian De Palma, and Bryan Singer voiced their interest. For a time the winner looked to be Bryan Singer with Johnny Depp agreeing to play Chuck Barris; however, although Singer had gone so far into preproduction as to build sets in Canada for the film, the production never came to fruition and the director had to bow out to fulfill his contract for the already slated work schedule for what would eventually become, in 2003, the blockbuster movie *X2.* Several months after the news of Singer's departure from the project, *Variety* announced that Nicole Kidman was to star in *Confessions of a Dangerous Mind* to be directed by George Clooney. Other than looking for a vehicle to direct, Clooney was also attracted to the project because his father, Nick, had been the host of the ABC game show called *The Money Maze* in 1974. The studio's set had a powerful connection to the actor's childhood. In a similar sense to Kaufman, Clooney was interested in Chuck Barris's psychological profile, but he admitted that the nostalgia factor was the biggest part of the project's draw for him. "It was a huge part of it. I grew up on game show sets. I was on the back of those sets in the 70s, so I knew what they looked like and what they felt like. I certainly had an understanding of fame and some of those trappings, and of waking up and having other people's perceptions of you being much different from your own perception. So, the reason I felt that I could direct, was that I felt this was a screenplay I knew how to tell the story of."[5] Specific to Charlie Kaufman's writing, Clooney added, "I didn't wake up and say I wanted to be a director. I wanted to be involved in getting the movie made, because I thought the script was that good. And it was starting to look as though it wasn't going to happen. I also felt, if I was ever going to direct, it had better be with the best screenplay I'd ever read."[6]

The casting of the role of Chuck Barris, which had made the rounds from Depp to Mike Myers, Russell Crowe, Kevin Spacey, Ed Norton, and Ben Stiller, finally found a match in the incredibly versatile and underrated actor Sam Rockwell. To Clooney's credit, he fought for the casting of Rockwell. Miramax, who would eventually green light the film, would not even consider casting Rockwell until Clooney's friend, Julia Roberts, signed on to be in the movie. Even still, Miramax executives continued to push for more popular actors such as Robert Downey, Jr., or Ben Stiller to play the titular character of Chuck Barris. It wasn't until George Clooney agreed to make a cameo in Miramax's movie *Spy Kids 2,* as well as offer them first-look deals from his production company with Steven Soderbergh, that the studio finally relented.

Originally, Charlie Kaufman had wanted the real Chuck Barris to serve as the narrator throughout the film as the book is told in first person. Barris's "unauthorized" autobiography begins with a naked, bedraggled, 50-year-old burned-out game show producer examining his landslide of a body, in a full-length mirror in his small, cluttered apartment in Beverly Hills. He reminds himself that he is a celebrity and shouldn't be so depressed. He finds comfort or amusement that his family, back home in Philadelphia, is endlessly impressed with his Beverly Hills address. The successful producer and paranoid narcissist has been holed up watching television and attempting to write his autobiography. He calls his secretary at his production company and tells her he'll be away for awhile: she can take care of business as usual. Barris is tired and has been thinking about resigning from his public life, but wonders what he would do next. He quotes Lawrence Durrell: "The sick men, the solitaries, the prophets, are all those who have been wounded."[7]

The story then backtracks to his younger days as a 33-year-old man in 1963. He answers a classified ad from a college newspaper and interviews for a job with the CIA. Although the staid interviewer only perks up when he and Barris broach the subject of music, the CIA recruiter has never heard of Barris's hit pop song "Palisades Park," and the conversation wanes. The scene exemplifies how Barris's accomplishments were never enough. Maybe rewriting his life to incorporate a hit man scenario would fill the void. Although Barris doesn't pretend he is heroic in the book, the notion of being a killer for hire does offer him something his personality needs. "The entire proposition of being an accomplished killer seemed to instill in me, perhaps inappropriately, omnipotent powers, outrageous confidence, and a superhuman ego. I was larger than life, bigger than the biggest man. If I didn't like you, I could actually kill you, with anonymity and impunity. If not now, then later. At least, that's what I led myself to believe."[8]

The next chapter finds Chuck Barris in Montgomery, Alabama, in 1965, carpooling with Reverend Jesse Jackson en route to the historic civil rights march with Dr. Martin Luther King. Barris, dressed in a rumpled Brooks Brothers suit, would never be pegged as a CIA spy marching into Montgomery. As Barris explained it, the CIA believed that anyone dressed like Cary Grant in Hitchcock's *North by Northwest* would slip right by the Black Panthers. When the demonstration was over, Barris boarded a plane to Washington DC where he handed over his surveillance report to his supervisor Jim Byrd. Perhaps most tellingly, Barris frames his fantasies in phrases that lift him out of his legacy as a trash TV salesman. He writes that one of the organizers in Montgomery tells him, "We've been keeping you for something special. For bigger and better things than the shit you've been volunteering to do." By placing himself in such a historic, important setting in America's history, he counters his other, regrettable choices in life. He wraps up the march on Montgomery chapter by saying, "There was a tremendous feeling of being a part of something enormous: something bigger than life, something that would eventually mean something—though exactly what, no one was particularly sure."[9]

Charlie Kaufman's adaptation of Barris's book begins with ominous orchestral music as the accompaniment to a scene showing a speeding New York City cab hurtling through rain. It's the fall of 1981. The cab driver glimpses his passenger, a sweaty young man in a gold blazer, clutching a shopping list that includes a double-coated waterproof fuse (500 feet), .38 ammo (hollowpoint configuration), and potato chips (Lays). The script then cuts to the set of *The Gong Show* in which a heavy man recites *Hamlet* with loud belching sounds. The audience is happily booing as the contestant gets "gonged." The 50-year-old Chuck Barris pulls his hat over his eyes and ambles out to the stage to comfort the agitated performer. Barris asks his celebrity panel why they gonged this guy and Barris's friend, the lively, smoky-voiced Jaye P. Morgan, replies, "Not to be. That is the answer." The studio audience laughs.

Kaufman's script then cuts back to the rain-soaked taxi stopped in front of a liquor store waiting for Barris as he runs through the storm. The scene cuts back to the older Barris doing a shuffle dance with his friend Gene Gene the Dancing Machine on *The Gong Show*. Barris takes the show to a commercial break with his usual segue, "We'll be right back with more stuff." As the scene cuts to the rain-soaked cab of the 1980s once again, the younger Barris and the cabbie exchange a mysterious, small package for money. When the scene moves back to *The Gong Show* for the last time in Kaufman's sequence, the video image explodes as we watch a large dog sniff Barris's crotch. The camera pulls back to find the older Barris, now crouched and naked, holed up in a hotel room, where he has just shot his television. Kaufman calls for the camera to pan across the hotel room walls where we see yellowed newspaper clippings that read: "*Gong Show* a New Low in Television," "The Dumbing of America," and "Chuck Barris Is the Decline of Western Civilization." Barris was indeed the king of crap TV. The writer Peter Andrews may have summed it up best when he noted that Barris's output was "unremittingly witless, tasteless, illiterate, and stupid."[10]

In Charlie Kaufman's script, he calls for the actual Chuck Barris to be interviewed in a documentary type, raw, vérité style that is much different from Clooney's version in the film. The script called for the real Chuck Barris to tell the interviewer: "When you're young, your potential is infinite. You might do anything, really. You might be great. You might be Goethe. Then you get to an age where what you might be gives way to what you have been. You weren't Einstein. You weren't anything. That's a bad moment."[11] In the film version, Clooney chose to change the reference from Goethe to Joe DiMaggio, and does not use footage of the real Chuck Barris's interviews until the very last scene in the movie. Clooney did decide to use vérité, interstitial interview clips of Barris's colleagues and jilted girlfriends in the movie, but does not include the real Barris until the end, because he believed the real-life comparison would be unfair to actor Sam Rockwell.

In Barris's book, when his girlfriend Georgia becomes pregnant, he stops into a church to rant at god and reveal his true feelings about the predicament: "Take this two-faced cunt I'm living with, God; this nice little Catholic girl with the big kazoos who's spent her whole life learning about rhythm fucking—this sleazebag is telling me she's pregnant! Now I ask you God, what am I supposed to do? Never in the history of my religion has a Jewish boy left a girl when she was pregnant. So what am I supposed to do."[12] In Kaufman's screenplay version, Barris sits at a bar and tells a nearby patron that he is going to skip town. He tells the barfly that he intends to be important and that he can't be saddled with this. But then he remembered something Thomas Carlyle said: "Do the duty which lies nearest thee." Luckily for Georgia, she finds she is not pregnant and Barris leaves her immediately after her good news. Kaufman's script and the movie version features a vérité interview with the real, middle-aged Georgia. She tells the interviewer that when she woke up, Barris was gone.

By the time Chuck Barris had turned 30 years old, he was working as an executive at ABC. Kaufman's script calls for a close shot of a copy of the *New York Herald Tribune* in which the headline refers to Dick Clark testifying before the "Payola" Committee. The 1961 payola music scandal at the time refers to the words *pay* and *Victrola*. Since the advent of radio, DJs were offered money or gifts in exchange for airplay for songs. When the powers that be realized that Dick Clark had investments in both publishing and record companies during the height of the success of his popular television show *American Bandstand,* his business practices came under fire. Although Clark was innocent, he did have to relinquish his stocks as this was seen as a conflict of interest. Some news accounts reveal that Chuck Barris was Dick Clark's assistant at the time: Charlie Kaufman's adaptation reads that ABC *assigned* Barris to the unique position of keeping an eye on Clark's *American Bandstand* tapings in Philadelphia. Kaufman was laying the groundwork for Barris to consider himself a spy even then, as he was playing both sides of the fence, collecting a paycheck from ABC and enjoying making Dick Clark nervous, while using his "friendship" with him to produce a treacly, pop song called "Palisades Park." The inspiration for the song stems from 30-year-old Barris trolling amusement parks on weekends because, as he says, "That's where the young girls were." Kaufman includes Barris's lyrics in his script, which start with "I took a ride on the shoop de shoop / that girl I sat beside was awful cute."[13] To bed women, Barris plays up his pop song fame by literally carrying a music magazine clipping on him to prove his accomplishment. Kaufman makes an allusion to a similar thought in his directorial debut, *Synecdoche, New York,* as his character Caden (Philip Seymour Hoffman) tells his psychiatrist that he could use the fact that he is a screenwriter to bed women, but wants them to like him for him.

In the *Confessions of a Dangerous Mind* screenplay, Kaufman writes a funny interstitial interview showing Dick Clark speaking to an off-camera interviewer. Clark responds to the interviewer's question with the response, "Chuck Barris? He spooked me. I tried to keep on his good side because he was sort of … spooky … there was something in his eyes. Something dark, like unbridled ambition, maybe. Or an inarticulate rage."[14]

Other important points in the screenplay that were not used in the final movie include insights into Barris's fictitious childhood. Kaufman wrote a scene in which a baby doll is set afire while young Barris dances around it. As the adult Barris remembers this, Kaufman calls for Barris to recall in voice-over the sickly sweet smell of a burning doll on a crisp fall day. Other unused childhood scenes include Barris's mother dressing him in velvet, as she clearly wanted a female child. When as a toddler she undresses in front of him, she says that "Chuckie likes the way mommie looks" and that he would like to be a mommy some day too. The toddler Barris agrees.

In the film, Clooney does include the childhood scene in Barris's auto-biography and Kaufman's screenplay in which a 16-year-old Chuck Barris pulls his penis out in front of his sister's 13-year-old friend Tuvia and convinces her to lick it "because it tastes like a strawberry lollipop." Barris lazily tosses a football on the couch while his sister practices playing scales on a violin. Absent from the film, however, is the young Barris saying to Tuvia that his sister Phoebe is no Walter Page. When Tuvia replies that she doesn't know who that is, Barris replies that of course she doesn't. Walter Page was the jazz bassist in the legendary Count Basie orchestra, but more importantly, it is here where Kaufman begins to give the audience insight into Barris's bullying nature and his view of women (and all people) as intellectually inferior to him.

When as an adult Barris impresses Debbie (Maggie Gyllenhaal), a young woman working at ABC, with the tedious line that he wrote a hit pop song, they have mechanical, joyless sex, while in voice-over they discuss the future of TV game shows. It is at this point that Barris goes to the refrigerator in Debbie's house and meets Penny, her roommate. Barris is immediately intrigued by Penny, who has been collecting men with different ethnic backgrounds with which to have sex. The actor Sam Rockwell plays this scene with an awkward sweetness and throughout the movie infuses the Barris character with much more humanity than found in Barris's own characterization of himself in his book. Though Barris never pretends to be admirable, Sam Rockwell gives him a soul. When Penny mentions that she knows him from his "Palisades Park" song, of which he is so proud, she seems to see past his faux charm and tells him with honest enthusiasm, "I love that song. It's such sentimental bullshit."[15]

This perhaps sums up Barris's life work and mirrors his vague unhappiness for having produced nothing of value. Kaufman's script begs the question, Was Barris just a common variety sociopath who was savvy enough to give the people what they wanted? He godfathered modern television's dumbing-down of America, but he was both puppet master and puppet. The audience was and is complicit in buying into humiliating a person on national television (e.g., the success of reality TV). Barris once told the host of *The Newlywed Game* that "a good show review is the kiss of death. If for some strange reason the critics liked it, the public won't. A really bad review means the show will be on for years."[16]

Although in Barris's book Penny's prescient comment about his famous song being sentimental bull seemed to hurt him, he is soon inspired with another TV game show idea—*The Dating Game*. In voice-over in the script, the real Barris says that all he had to do was get the pilot made and he would be a millionaire, and then everyone would love him. Kaufman wrote the insightful line for Barris to utter: "Was anyone ever so young?"

In a scene in the movie that is played out over the phone, Kaufman's script calls for the audience to actually see the 30-year-old Barris on his childhood bed and his aged dog Albert on the floor. His sister Phoebe enters the room and Chuck tells her that Albert is dead. They both agree that the dog had a long life, and Phoebe angrily tells Chuck that he is 32 years old, has been staring out the window of their mother's house for six months now, and is breaking their mother's heart. Though absent from the film, the scene as written calls for Barris to look out at his emaciated, wheelchair-bound mother in the yard, staring off into space. Barris says that somehow his being born broke their mom's heart.

While in Barris's book, he claims that he was hired as a CIA hit man by answering a newspaper ad, Charlie Kaufman plays up Barris's bar fight scenes (he is often drunk and constantly starting fights) and writes that a CIA supervisor, Jim Byrd, had noticed him in the bar and eyed him as a possible recruit. Kaufman's version plays into Barris's egomaniacal need to be more important than he is. If the CIA noticed him and wants him, he must be pretty valuable. Kaufman's mode of introduction to Jim Byrd also implies that Byrd only exists in Barris's mind. He is the fairy godfather of Barris's imagination. At first, Barris tells the mysterious CIA recruiter that he can't work for him, because his future is in television. Byrd then reiterates what Barris's scolding sister said: "Oh good. Why don't you spend another six months developing 'em while staring out the window at mommy's house next to poor dead Albert the dog."[17] This funny line written by Kaufman convinces Barris that his life is important enough to be studied by the CIA. They seem to know an awful lot about his personal life.

He then begins a training course that involves being schooled in all facets of the art of war, including weaponry, combat, and chemistry. It is portrayed as an over-the-top, fun, intensive training course, similar in pace to quick hit language immersion classes. Although the scene is not in Kaufman's original script, George Clooney commented on the DVD extras that at the last minute, as a prank, he added that Barris had been trained with Lee Harvey Oswald and Jack Ruby. Barris is seen shooting his rifle between two recruits whose name tags read Oswald and Ruby.

In Barris's memoir, after taking part in the historic march in Montgomery, Alabama, his next CIA assignment was to help kill the fictitious Salvador Panagra Renda, whom he describes as the mysterious, silent partner of the very real Ernesto "Che" Guevara. Barris's all-knowing mentor, Jim Byrd, was the team leader assigned to kill Renda and the dream of a communist South America led by Fidel Castro. In the book version, Barris only watches Renda's killing, but is thrilled to "help murder an enemy of the United States of America." He added, "but I couldn't tell a living soul, and it was agony."[18] In Kaufman's version and on screen, Renda pleads with Barris to spare his life, telling him (in Spanish) that he has three children. Looking directly into the frightened man's eyes, Barris hesitates and attempts to quickly and comically consult a Spanish-to-English dictionary, so that he might understand the man. However, Barris's gun goes off accidentally and Renda is killed. Regardless of the incompetence, Barris completed his mission. Barris's autobiographical version is full of pride and accomplishment, while Kaufman's script calls for Barris to question Jim Byrd and himself about the murder. When Byrd offhandedly assures Barris that Renda was one of the bad guys, Kaufman's version of Chuck Barris asks, "Bad for the U.S. right, Jim? Not bad in an absolute sense, just bad for the U.S."[19] Kaufman's dialogue instills Barris's character with an interior life and depth.

Meanwhile, back in Hollywood, as Penny bathes and Barris cooks dinner, Charlie Kaufman sneaks an ape reference into the dialogue. Penny tells Barris about a dream and says, "...so this ape and I were looking at each other. It was like, across time and evolution. Then he began to talk, but it was a language I didn't understand..."[20] From Penny's dream involving a lack of communication and evolution, Barris is inspired to create the television black hole called *The Dating Game*. His new show was an immediate hit with audiences although Kaufman depicts Barris as being embarrassed by the crude bachelors and bachelorettes. The studio executives tell Barris that the show is unairable because of its lewd dialogue and sexual innuendos. Barris explains that the unscripted frankness is part of the show's charm. He makes a valid point when he tells network executive Leonard Goldberg that nobody is indifferent to these shows and show business must avoid indifference at all costs. Barris deals with the problem by hiring his old training camp instructor Jenks to pose as a representative from the Federal Communications Commission. Jenks scares the "charm" right out of the bawdy contestants before a show taping with one of Kaufman's funniest speeches to date. The severe-looking Jenks addresses the on-stage contestants, "I don't know if any of you are aware of this, but it's a federal offense to make licentious remarks on a network television broadcast. The penalty for this disgusting, un-American behavior is one year in prison or a ten thousand dollar fine or both. Anyone making a sick, suggestive remark tonight will be arrested immediately." The contestants are appropriately paralyzed with fear as the increasingly angry instructor continues, "I will then personally escort the offender to federal prison for booking under edict 1963. And it's a long drive to that prison. Just you and me. No other witnesses—." The charming Chuck Barris then jumps in to cut Jenks's speech off with, "Any questions?"[21]

The screenplay then takes us to the site of Barris Productions circa 1967. Kaufman wrote that the 36-year-old game show creator was now the new Barris: confident, hip, relaxed, and slovenly. Outside in the bullpen area we hear the hustle and bustle, laughing and screaming of a busy but casual office. The studio executives want to take *The Dating Game* to prime time and the ringleader is tasked with making the program more exciting for a nighttime audience. While he paces the darkened set and thinks, the mysterious

Jim Byrd appears out of the darkness and locks his arm around Barris's neck. Barris struggles to breathe and Byrd releases him before he chokes.

Over lunch, Byrd entices him to join in another murder/spy/fantasy assignment. When Barris balks because he has more important things to do now, Byrd gives him the idea to take *The Dating Game* to international waters in order to liven it up a bit. Barris can chaperone contestants while he is on a spy mission.

On a game show trip to London in 1967, Barris seeks out his female contact in a pub. Patricia (Julia Roberts) hands him an envelope and makes leave of him while Barris, intoxicated once again by a female asks her what he should call her. He whines, "At least give me a made-up name. Something for me to cry out during those dark nights of the soul." Patricia makes a reference to Shakespeare's play *Twelfth Night* and tells him to call out the name Olivia! Similarly to Jim Byrd, Patricia may also be a figment of Barris's writing. Just as Byrd may symbolize the untrustworthy, father-figure mentor, Patricia is emblematic of the beautiful, traitorous female. Barris, the self-styled literary name-dropper, is enthralled by Patricia's quick wit. As the two sip champagne, Barris oozes, "All the information I have about myself is from forged documents."[22] Patricia matches his wit and replies that she knows he is referencing Nabokov. Kaufman's quote from Vladimir Nabokov's novel *Despair* is apropos for the character of Barris on many levels. Nabokov's protagonist Hermann lies about his background and believes he has a twin, who in reality looks nothing like him. Just as Barris creates an alter ego for him to earn respectability by being a spy, Kaufman created an alter ego for himself in *Adaptation* to learn his own truth. The specter of Nabokov has reared its head before in Kaufman's career. In 1995, while serving as a writer and coproducer on the short-lived television sitcom *Misery Loves Company,* one of the episodes was entitled "That Book by Nabokov."

Just as Hermann's state of mind is questionable, the Chuck Barris character grows increasingly deluded and paranoid. When Barris returns to Los Angeles after his meeting with Patricia, his assistant greets him and mentions that he is the hit man. In Barris's degraded state, he thinks that his assistant must know he is also a murderer (of more than the medium of television). His office workers start to chant the word *hit man* and while he struggles with what may become a confrontation, his assistant finally informs him that ABC is going to pickup *The Newlywed Game.* Hit man indeed. Kaufman wrote for the Barris character to say that *The Newlywed Game* was based on his theory that almost any American would sell out their spouse for a washer–dryer or a lawnmower you can ride. "Such was my respect for that most holy of unions. I must've been on to something, because the show aired for thirteen years."[23]

In a funny scene absent from the final film, Barris interrupts a quiet night at home playing Scrabble with Penny to make a trip to the liquor store and pick up a teenage girl named Monica. When Monica takes him to her apartment she introduces him to her equally teenage roommate, Mindy. Barris eyes them both and clearly thinks he is in for a more interesting night than Scrabble could offer. Just as Barris relaxes on the girls' couch, Monica asks him if he has accepted the Lord Jesus Christ as his savior. The next vérité interview with the real Barris calls for him to remember Monica (her first name at least) as he tells the camera operator about her genitalia. Monica then appears at his production studio crying that she is pregnant and that she can't get an abortion. This scene is reminiscent of Barris's first pregnancy scare when he was younger. However, this time, the girl truly is pregnant. Barris solves his problem by convincing Monica to have an abortion in Mexico. He walks the crying teenager down a garbage-strewn alley to the doctor's office. The next scene, as Kaufman wrote it, cuts to Barris and Penny walking through a garden at UCLA. Penny sadly sums up by saying, "What a waste," while Barris replies, "Tell me about it. I figure over the years I must've spent close to twenty grand on these abortions: airfare, hotels, doctors, gifts, etc."[24] Kaufman's words are very close to what Barris says in this scene in his book as well. They are equally harsh. The script then cuts to a series of vérité interview shots with middle-aged women in different locations addressing the camera. Nine women are interviewed and most of them say, yes, they were pregnant with Barris's baby. One of the women says she just needed someone to pay for it.

Conversely, Barris speaks of his TV shows being the only babies that truly matter to him. After an executive tells him that all four of his currently running television shows are going to be canceled, he fantasizes that the contestants on the set and the audience members are violently murdered, soaked in blood. He drunkenly tells a bartender that the suits killed his babies. He claimed that he pushed them into the world through the birth canal of his imagination. In the DVD commentary to the film, Clooney said that it was the American audience that Chuck really murdered.

After Penny finds Barris having sex with a woman in his house, she attempts suicide. She fails and soon Barris is off to West Berlin chaperoning a *Dating Game* couple while in town for his next assassination. He crawls through a tunnel that leads to the other side of the Berlin Wall where he meets Keeler (Rutger Hauer), a fellow CIA agent. For two days they lay in wait in a car, in order to kill their next target, a man named Colbert. In a very funny scene that is equally well acted, Keeler throws Colbert in the back seat of the car and calmly asks the flustered Barris to take a picture of him as he squeezes the life out of the bulging-eyed Colbert.

In a scene Kaufman penned but was absent from the final film, Barris manages to escape the KBG as a kind Frenchman (also some sort of rogue agent) whisks him away in a speeding car in order to give him the one-person plane he has been stowing in the trunk. Barris flies the fully inflated rubber plane over the Berlin Wall and is shot down by a soldier.

Back at the television studio, Barris and the executives sit through a tortuous round of auditions for *The Gong Show*. Barris realizes that the show should be based on bad singers and performances instead of good ones. Celebrity judges can ring a bell to end the act, in a way killing the contestants. The original host of the show is too agitated by the callous celebrity criticisms, and the executives ask Barris himself to serve as host. He is reticent at first until he is offered cocaine to lift his reserves of confidence. Although Kaufman paints a realistic portrait of a 1970s-era game show host, Barris asked Clooney to remove the drug-related scenes. Barris claims that he has never taken drugs and simply did not want the audience to be misinformed.

Interestingly, Thomas Carlyle, one of Barris's heroes, said that a well-written life is almost as rare as a well-spent one. Specific to Barris, the well-lived life would come in the form of the rewriting of his life. In his book, his revisionist approach to history anchors him in such transformative world events as Dr. Martin Luther King's march to Montgomery, Alabama in 1965.

In the story, when Barris meets Keeler for dinner, they wax lyrical about how once you acquire a taste for killing, you cannot replace that kind of exhilaration. Keeler quotes Ecclesiastes but Barris, whose God is Carlyle, attributes the quote to the latter: "Whatsoever thy hand findeth to do, do it with thy whole might. Work wile it is called, for the night cometh wherein no man can work."[25] Soon thereafter, Barris is informed that Keeler committed suicide.

No matter. *The Gong Show* is a giant hit and Barris is now the Game Show King. Sex, drugs, and alcohol flood the scene as he now has everything he ever hoped for. However, the newspaper headlines read, "Chuck Barris *Is* the Decline of Western Civilization." In a very funny and dramatic scene Kaufman wrote that did not make it to the final film version, Chuck Barris is invited to the Emmy Awards. Jim Brooks, the producer of the TV show *Taxi* wins the Emmy and thanks the Academy for their support of high-quality television. Later in the bathroom, an agitated Barris pulls as gun on James L. Brooks and aims it at his back. Just then he realizes he can't kill the man responsible for *Mary Tyler Moore, Rhoda, Cindy, Phyllis,* and episodes of *My Friend Tony*. Barris then turns the gun on himself, but can't go through with the act. Finally, he manages to composes himself and congratulates Brooks on his Emmy win. Brooks is very gracious and tells him he appreciates the sentiment. Kaufman then cuts to a vérité scene where the actual Jim Brooks is being interviewed. The real Brooks says that he doesn't actually remember ever meeting Barris, but kindly adds that it could have happened. He ends with saying that it just doesn't seem like much of an anecdote: for him it was just a fleeting bathroom greeting.

When Barris is at the height of his celebrity, Kaufman's script calls for him to be welcomed at parties at famous haunts such as the Chateau Marmont in Hollywood. He is surrounded by late-1970s celebrities such as Alan Alda,

Burt Reynolds, and Farrah Fawcett Majors. The mood changes to what looks like the location of the Playboy Mansion grotto as Barris watches a beautiful woman in the pool. He follows her into the cave-like part of a grotto where Kaufman has the pretty woman deliver the emasculating speech that sums up Barris's life. Director George Clooney cast his then girlfriend in the role (Krista Allen) and the dialogue is delivered nearly word for word from Kaufman's original script. The pretty woman tells Barris in her sweet, honey-dripping voice, "I'm glad to meet you because I wanted to tell you that I've seen *The Gong Show* and I think you are the most insidious and despicable force in entertainment today . . . How dare you subject the rest of the world to your loathsome view of humanity." When the emasculated Barris tries to defend himself, she continues to slide the knife in with, "What is it then? To mock some poor, lonely people who just crave a little attention in their lives. To destroy them. So everybody's not brilliantly talented. They're still people. They deserve respect and compassion. I mean, who the hell are you? What the fuck have you ever done that elevates you above the pathetic masses? Oh I forgot, you created *The Dating Game*. Wow, right up there with the Sistine Chapel."[26] Before she can finish, however, Barris flees the scene. As he makes his way out the door and down the street amidst fans yelling "Chuckie baby!," he smiles and nods, but starts hallucinating. Now he thinks he sees the bachelor he killed in London. He sees the bullet hole in the man's head as he begins to spot the corpses he has murdered.

In an attempt to give Barris a reason for his psychotic, or at least disordered personality problems, Charlie Kaufman invented a backstory that involves Barris having a twin sister who was strangled by their umbilical cord in the womb. His mother has always blamed Chuck for her death and is the reason why he was raised as a girl. The real Barris liked Kaufman's touch, but says that this is not true about his real life. Barris also liked the parts of the script that didn't make it to the screen in which Kaufman wrote that Barris's biological father was a serial killer. Barris's mother didn't know this about him when she slept with the monster also known as the Tarrytown Troll.

Towards the end of the film, when Barris visits Patricia, he seems to genuinely open up about himself and tells her that like his philosophical and literary heroes, he wanted to write something that a lesser person would quote. He wants to be viewed or thought of the way he himself thinks of Carlyle. In a poignant moment, he realizes that he is that lesser person and also disposable.

Barris says he hates himself, to which Patricia replies with a quote from Nietzsche, "Whoever despises oneself still respects oneself as one who despises." They discuss moving to Boston and starting a legitimate life selling insurance. Just before Patricia (who has been the mole in the CIA the whole story) can reach for her gun, Barris quickly shoots her twice in the head and once in the heart. George Clooney thought this death scene, as written, was too abrupt and wanted to draw it out. On the director's commentary on the

DVD's special features, Clooney explained, "In the original draft he walks in and shoots her point blank and I thought, well, that's not that fun, so we basically sort of made it the *Princess Bride* [a game of switching poisoned drinks]."[27] In *Entertainment Weekly,* Clooney went on to explain that he designed one scene "directly from John Frankenheimer's TV production of *The Snows of Kilimanjaro* in 1960. I had Sam [Rockwell] look directly into the camera while we spun the set and he changes his clothes—all while he did a two-page monologue." He goes on to admit, "[As an actor] I don't know how open I would have been to that."[28]

To add insult to injury, Clooney deferred to Chuck Barris instead of the screenwriter when it came to content. The real Barris had been smart enough to hang around for the 10 years that his book changed hands in the studio system, and he made his presence known to the bitter end. Barris said of the process, "[George Clooney asked me,] 'If there's anything you don't want in the film, let me know. I'll take it out.' I asked him if he would take out the bits that I was on drugs. Because Charlie originally wrote me as a pretty good druggie. And he did. There were other things in the script that I would have liked to have seen go, but I thought I asked for enough."[29]

At the end of Chuck Barris's book, he marries the long-suffering Penny and believes he is being persecuted as they make their way through the well-wishers to the waiting limousine outside the chapel. He believes he sees a hand holding a gun and thinks to himself, "Who could it have been? Who was the killer? Was he CIA? Had they put a contract out on me because of my book? The Company knew I was writing *Confessions of A Dangerous Mind.* They had warned me not to write it. Even threatened me on one or two occasions."[30] The scene illustrates how Barris's paranoia has come to full tilt. In the last scene of Kaufman's screenplay as well as Clooney's movie, the real Chuck Barris finally makes an appearance. He is broken, bloated, and looks as if he has turned to cracked dough. He delivers the line: "I came up with a new game show idea recently. It's called *The Old Game.* You got three old guys with loaded guns onstage. They look back at their lives, see who they were, what they accomplished, how close they came to realizing their dreams. The winner is the one who doesn't blow his brains out. He gets a refrigerator."[31] The monologue is pure Kaufman serving the voice of the story, and Chuck Barris was thrilled with it. The game show host told *Time* magazine, "I was just so happy that people might think I wrote that line."[32]

To this day, Charlie Kaufman has never met Chuck Barris, yet a common question he is still asked by fans is whether Barris's claims of being an assassin are true. Kaufman asserts that he doesn't know the answer, and that he is more interested in the question. As for Barris's reaction to Kaufman's adaptation of his book, *The Gong Show* creator said, "He wrote stuff out of nowhere. My mother never dressed me like a girl. I was never on drugs. The part about my father being a serial killer? That's Charlie. He writes such good stuff."[33]

Still, despite the sound bites, Kaufman was irked by the fact that Clooney did not want his involvement during production and that the director was more interested in the angle that Chuck Barris was a game show host by day and a CIA agent by night, rather than the complexity of the character. Kaufman believed these elements to be secondary and wanted to focus on the psyche that would create such a fantasy. Without that inroad, Kaufman thought the movie had no power or truth. However, he does emphatically say that Sam Rockwell was wonderful in the film, and that it was some of Drew Barrymore's best work to date.

Kaufman explained in *Arena* magazine in 2004: "I was upset by the fact that he took the movie from me and then cut me out after that. I'm unhappy with the end result. And I'm unhappy with George Clooney. I had a movie that I wrote and that wasn't it."[34] Although much of Kaufman's actual dialogue remains in the final version of the film, the execution of the scenes varies wildly. While Kaufman prefers the photography to be organic to the story, and true to each character's experience, George Clooney admittedly relied on well-known shots from famous films. In the DVD commentary to *Confessions of a Dangerous Mind,* Clooney mentions that he employed camera set-ups from movies such as *A Place in the Sun* (for the kitchen scene where Barris first meets Penny), *The Verdict* (when Barris introduces the drill instructor to prep the game show contestants), and *The Parallax View* (to reveal Keeler on a slab). Clooney also mentions paying homage to *Three Days of the Condor* and *Carnal Knowledge* (the latter of which he cites twice). While all of George Clooney's filmic inspirations are indeed influential classics, Charlie Kaufman is not one to force an audience to evoke emotions based on former cinematic moments and experiences. To this end, Jim Carrey (who lobbied for his role in *Eternal Sunshine* and happily cut his acting fee to scale) has said, "If any of his films looks anything at all similar to anything else that's already been done, it's because of someone like me, with way too much power, comes along and screwed it up."[35]

When the film was released early in 2003, it was received with mixed reviews. And it was inevitable that Clooney's choices would be compared to what Spike Jonze and Michel Gondry had done with Kaufman's previous scripts. *LA Weekly*'s John Powers noted,

> For all their whirring ingenuity, Kaufman's scripts require a director who will tether his cleverness to reality. Spike Jonze has done this for *Being John Malkovich* and *Adaptation,* whose wildest conceits come off because they are played straight. But like director Michel Gondry in *Human Nature,* Clooney mistakenly ratchets up what's already over-the-top. Neither the filmmakers nor the audience actually believes Barris's guff about the CIA, but for the story to grip us, we must believe that Barris believes it. For all its inspirational hokum, *A Beautiful Mind* took care to make us see what John Nash saw—we understood what was flipping him out. Not so in *Confessions,* whose bloody CIA fantasies carry no emotional weight because they keep descending into theatrical black

comedy (not least in Julia Roberts's mirthless foundering as a Cold War Mata Hari). We simply don't care what happens.[36]

The fact that the film premiered in January certainly didn't give the impression that the distributors felt they had an award contender on their hands. Similar to how the marketing of *Human Nature* did not help that specific film, audiences and critics were also confused as to what kind of movie the distributors of *Confessions of a Dangerous Mind* wanted it to be. The always hysterically funny and spot-on writers at *The Onion* mock-reported that the movie was being marketed as six different genres. Their "source" said: "'So far, I've seen TV ads making it look like a romantic comedy, a spy thriller, a Hollywood satire, a straightforward biopic, and a strange, *Being John Malkovich*-esque mind-bender.'"[37]

For Kaufman's part, the National Board of Review awarded him the Best Screenplay of the Year. While speaking to the BBC approximately a year after the film was released, Kaufman was able to get more perspective on that time in his life, but remained true to his original feelings about the whole affair. He summed up his experience with *Confessions of a Dangerous Mind* and George Clooney thusly: "I spent a lot of time working on the script, but I don't think he was interested in the things I was interested in. I've moved on and don't have any animosity towards Clooney, but it's a movie I don't really relate to."[38] As far as Kaufman was concerned, the movie he had written would now never be made.

At the end of the film, Clooney used his Aunt Rosemary's famous song "There's No Business Like Show Business" to play over the final credits. There is no better approximation for Kaufman's experience on the project. When the press had finally cooled and all involved had moved on to new assignments and the next stages of their lives, Kaufman may have thought he was through with George Clooney, but Clooney would not be through with him.

Back in 1997 after the critical success of *Being John Malkovich,* the production company Jersey Films offered Charlie Kaufman the assignment to adapt novelist Philip K. Dick's opus, *A Scanner Darkly.* At the time, the Australian director Emma-Kate Croghan (*Strange Planet*) was attached to the project. However, Jersey Films ultimately lost interest in their version of the story and years later the book rights were picked up again by someone else. The project passed through several hands, including the idiosyncratic director Terry Gilliam. Ultimately, director Richard Linklater adapted his own version of the book and released the movie in 2006. Instead of a strictly live-action film, he employed the same rotoscoping technique he had used in his previous film *Waking Life.*

The novel's name, *A Scanner Darkly,* is a reference to a letter the Apostle Paul wrote to the Corinthians: "When I was a child, I spake as a child, I understood as a child, I thought as a child: but when I became a man, I put away childish things. For now we see through a glass, darkly, but then face to face: now I know in part; but then shall I know even as also I am known."[39] The author has said that his reference to the Apostle Paul's letter was borne of his opinion that he and his adult friends were like children running into traffic. He asserts that each of them knew how dangerous drugs could be to their bodies and sanity, but perhaps only from the distance of an adult looking back on one's own childish decisions. The prolific writer does not ask for empathy, but acknowledges that even as an adult, he did not put away childish things—in this specific case, the loaded gun of choosing to use drugs.

Although it was Richard Linklater's clear intent to stay true to the original story, much of the raw emotion inherent in the book and Charlie Kaufman's adaptation is gone. Dick's novel is full of comedic moments and tragic events, which Linklater has said he admires, but the director leans closer to the characters' weed-soaked ponderings and rants rather than the sheer wastefulness of their lives. Kaufman's screenplay remains true to the story as well, but doesn't shy away from the true hell that comes with drug withdrawal. And although Kaufman's screenplay was not filmed, it is a significant entry in his body of work as a writer. Additionally, an assessment of his choices to include certain aspects of the book in adapting the novel he so loved, speaks to understanding his overall sensibility.

Originally written in 1977, Dick's novel, set in Anaheim, California, depicts the then future 1994. While friends and critics say that *A Scanner Darkly* is Philip K. Dick's most autobiographical work, his character Bob Arctor also serves as Dick's alter ego as Bob is a divorced undercover narcotics agent, living with bachelor friends he is also investigating. Once a married man with small children, Dick gave up his suburban lifestyle to live with friends who became escalating drug users.

The novel begins with the character Jerry Fabin (a real friend of Dick's who killed himself while Dick was writing the novel), whose mind is so shattered that he spends his time taking eight-hour showers in an attempt to wash off the invisible aphids he believes to be constantly biting him. His friend Charles Freck (who serves as a composite character for both Fabin and Freck in Kaufman's screenplay as well as Linklater's film) initially fails to see said aphids, but helps Fabin collect them in jars nonetheless. Fabin's paranoia, brought on by the drug Substance D., causes him to prowl his home with a shotgun and eventually barricade himself in a room until his friends are forced to call medics at New-Path, a rehabilitation center, to cart him away.

While Linklater's version begins with Charles Freck (Rory Cochrane) scrubbing himself raw in the shower, Kaufman's script begins with Bob Arctor's voice-over in which he says that lately Jerry Fabin stands all day shaking bugs from his hair. His script direction calls for the sound of fingers scratching a scalp, growing louder and louder over a montage of Coca Cola planes setting out from loading docks, a bird's-eye view of Coke trucks spreading out through the city, pulling into the 7-Eleven chain stores, and a uniformed delivery man hauling cases of Coca Cola into a McDonald's. Deleted from Linklater's version, Philip K. Dick's novel paints a picture of these chain store conglomerates as an oppressive character that plays into a corporate conspiracy of mind control, including the very harvesting of the dangerous illicit drug Substance D. Wishing to delay a work meeting while driving aimlessly in his car, Bob Arctor notes, "In Southern California it didn't make any difference anyhow where you went; there was always the same McDonald burger place over and over, like a circular strip that turned past you as you pretended to go somewhere. And when finally you got hungry and went to the McDonald burger place and bought a McDonald's hamburger, it was the one they sold you last time and the time before that and so forth, back to before you were born."[40] However, because Linklater (possibly because of studio involvement) changed the name of McDonald's to General Burger and removed the Coca Cola references in the movie altogether, Dick's through line of corporate conspiracy is lost.

Indeed, corporate identity as the ultimate power versus the question of individual persona serves as a source of paranoia in the novel as well as Kaufman's script. Always interested in identity and duality (for example, the twin brothers in *Adaptation*), much of Kaufman's work reflects Dick's own sensibility. In the novel, when Arctor finds himself roaming aimlessly on a street, "he always had a strange feeling as to who he was ... he looked like a doper; those around him now no doubt took him to be a doper and reacted accordingly. Other dopers—see there, he thought; 'other,' for instance—gave him a 'peace brother' look, and the straights didn't. You put on a bishop's robe and miter, he pondered, and walk around in that, and people bow and genuflect and like that, and try to kiss your ring, if not your ass, and pretty soon you're a bishop. So to speak. What is identity? he asked himself. Where does the act end?"[41]

That act comes into full view in the film when the audience hears pronounced breathing and then sees an ever-shifting nebulous blur of a man representing himself as Fred (Keanu Reeves in the dual role of Fred and Bob Arctor). The continually changing suit and facial features is indeed a Scramble Suit used for undercover police work. The suit makes the real person's identity unrecognizable to his colleagues and perhaps himself. Fred, the undercover narcotics agent from Orange County (who inside the suit is 30-year-old Everyman, Bob Arctor), addresses the crowd at the Anaheim Lions Club (although Linklater changed the name to the fictitious Brown Bear Lodge). He delivers a speech intended to incite the concerned citizens to stamp out the drug trade that is infecting their children. He relates that he too has small daughters and aims to protect them from the dealers who prey on the young. However, in the middle of his prepared speech, Fred experiences thoughts of the real Bob Arctor who is seeping through, and loses his train of thought. After a thoughtful pause, which is lost on the audience, he improvises and compares a diabetic to a drug addict. "Would you steal to get the money for your insulin or just die?" he says. Suddenly, a voice coming from the tiny prompter in his earpiece strongly suggests that he return to the script. Although Fred had successfully made his presentation in many previous lectures, Arctor is now blocking the contrived rhetoric. Fred/Arctor disdainfully tells his phone advisor that he believes he is blocking the speech because this soulless, ineffectual, prepared text is what gets people on dope in the first place.

It is Arctor's lot to live with and do surveillance on his similarly disaffected friends, Ernie Luckman (Woody Harrelson), an affable enough slacker, and the devious, drug-addled Jim Barris (Robert Downey Jr.). Donna Hawthorne (Winona Ryder), Arctor's friend for whom he has genuine feelings, is a small-time drug dealer, thief, and cocaine enthusiast. When Arctor finds that his valuable cephalochromoscrope is broken, he assumes that the wily Barris has sabotaged it. Dick defines a *cephascope* as a gadget equipped with a screen upon which graphic, colored representations of the user's thoughts are displayed. It is an expensive household item intended to relax the user and induce a peaceful state of mind.

This seemingly innocuous event gives the audience insight into Arctor's dynamic with Jim Barris as Arctor believes that Barris broke his favorite source of comfort (without the use of drugs), while Barris believes that Arctor broke it himself, but is so deluded by Substance D. that he has no memory of doing so. Jim Barris's personality is also further illuminated as he offers another theory on the broken cephascope, in which he may have broken it because he was hired by secret forces. In the Dick novel, Barris is a veteran suffering from burnout, while in the movie his character is merely a spiteful, toxic, unreliable megalomaniac (suffering from burnout). At this point in the story, Kaufman's version relates back to his opening shot of Arctor reading his journal entry. In voice-over, Arctor reveals that a drug dealer named Spade Weeks has lost himself inside the New-Path rehab center, as the supervisors assign a patient a new name as part of the identity rebuilding process. Although Arctor sees New-Path as a perfect potential hiding place, the loss of one's name and personality symbolizes yet another form of mind control by a franchise corporation.

Over lunch at a diner, Charles Freck tells his friend Barris that he can no longer handle the never ending chase of having enough Substance D., and is considering turning himself into New-Path for rehabilitation. Barris, friend that he is and perhaps not wanting to lose a complicit drug mate, ostensibly convinces him that the ordeal is beyond human pain and not worth the trauma. In any case, Barris claims he can show Freck a way to coerce Donna into lowering her selling price for Substance D. by plying her with home-made cocaine, Donna's drug of choice.

Although both Linklater's and Kaufman's adaptations are intensely faithful to Philip K. Dick's tone, one of the major differences in their scripts can be found in the way in which the story ends. In Linklater's filmed version, when Donna brings Bob Arctor into the rehabilitation center, Arctor falls to the floor and vomits. He looks to be suffering, but in no more pain than what a bad stomach flu forces on you. Philip K. Dick's original sequence called for the true breakdown of the body: "The two New-Path staff members stood surveying the thing on their floor that lay puking and shivering and fouling itself, its arms hugging itself, embracing its own body as if to stop itself against the cold that made it tremble so violently."[42] Dick's description of Bob Arctor's collapse depicts him as a dying animal. His mind, body, and spirit are so broken that the New-Path employees only refer to him as "it." Not one to shy away from the reality of bodily fluids, and the way the body betrays our wishes, Kaufman's script described the scene thusly: "Arctor lies on the floor, curled up and shivering. Dried vomit flecks his face. The stain on his pants is bigger now. Two New-Path staff members stand surveying the trembling Arctor."[43]

From here, Richard Linklater shows the audience that Arctor is now a custodian at New-Path and is then transferred to a farming area where he can work outside. In the novel however, Philip K. Dick spent a great deal of time showing us how Arctor was humiliated, belittled, and surrounded by a constant barrage of screaming, shrill, hateful patients shrieking obscenities at him during group therapy. The executive director of New-Path encourages this course of treatment, calling Arctor, "You turd prick, you weakling. You puke. You suck-off."[44] Although these scenes are absent from Linklater's film, Kaufman included them in his screenplay, nearly word for word, allowing the horror of Bob Arctor's situation to reach the audience.

One of the highlights of Linklater's version, which is not found in Kaufman's script, is the fractured conversation in which the boys argue about bicycle gears. On film, it reads as a fun, lively scene, but Dick's original intention in the story was to illustrate how their minds can no longer even grasp the simple concept of bike gears. And although we are to believe that Arctor's friends encompass his current family, Charles Freck overdoses without much notice from his friends while Arctor's roommates are played as transients. Ernie Luckman is at least concerned about their pets (when they are discussing a possible break in to the home), but he is the only character who seems to give a thought to anything other than his own lot in the world. On screen, Arctor's relationship with Donna appears to be wistful yet superficial. Donna shows real concern for him at the end of the film, while it is harder to assess Arctor's feelings. His opaqueness may be by design, due to his brain damage from drug addiction, but the movie may have benefited from Dick's revealing passage about how Arctor feels about Donna: "She took his hand, squeezed it, held it, and then, all at once, let it drop. But the actual touch of her lingered, inside his heart. That remained. In all the years of his life ahead, the long years without her, with never seeing her or hearing from her or knowing anything about her, if she was alive or happy or dead or what, that touched stayed locked within him, sealed in himself, and never went away. That one touch of her hand."[45]

Another subplot included in the novel as well as Kaufman's adaptation is the scene in which Arctor visits his friend Kimberly, who is living with an abusive man. The scene further illustrates Arctor's empathy as he wants to protect her as well as her frightened neighbors. This scene would have been useful in Linklater's movie. However, the most crucial difference from the novel (and Kaufman's version) is Linklater's addition of a "gotcha" ending often used in the mystery and thriller genres. In Linklater's movie's case, the character Hank pulls off his Scramble Suit in Scooby Doo fashion to reveal Winona Ryder (Donna) stepping out of the costume. Philip K. Dick does *not*, however, explicitly reveal Hank's identity in the novel, nor does Kaufman in his adaptation. Like the novelist, Kaufman believes that the messy reality of relationships, and in fact, the truth of real life is not magically tied up in a neat package with a bow on top to be delivered in the third act.

Just as Kaufman has been asked if his characters are really playing him in his films, fans of Philip K. Dick infer that Bob Arctor serves as his alter ego in the novel. In the author's note that follows *A Scanner Darkly*, Dick asserted, "I myself, I am not a character in this novel; I am the novel. So though, was our entire nation at this time."[46] Similarly, film critics have implied that most of Kaufman's lead characters, from Joel Barrish in *Eternal Sunshine of the Spotless Mind* to the frustrated writer named Charles Kaufman in *Adaptation* to Caden Cotard in *Synecdoche, New York,* have served as alter egos. Although inserting himself and his plight as a writer in attempting to adapt Susan Orlean's book in the film *Adaptation* leads an audience to understandably link the real Charlie Kaufman to his namesake, Kaufman denies that his lead characters are versions of himself: "I am not ever writing a movie full of Charlie Kaufmans, even if a character is named Charlie Kaufman. It's not me. It's a character. That's very serious and important to me."[47] Furthermore, of *Synecdoche, New York,* specifically, Kaufman has said that he is not a character in the film, but rather, the film itself.

As the final credits roll on Linklater's movie, he reveals the list of names at the end of the novel, for whom Dick dedicated his book. In the book, the list reads as a tragic testament to the loss of his dear friends. However, adding the list of Dick's lost loved ones to the end of Linklater's film feels tacked on and superimposed. It seems that a backstory or a working knowledge of the well-respected author would do well to flesh out the gravity of the novel for the screen. Knowledge of Dick's dissolution of his marriage and young family in real life makes Arctor's past more poignant. Although it isn't mentioned in the novel or in the adaptations, it would lend weight to the film's ending to know that one of the people on the list in drugs' aftermath is Dick's ex-wife. Dick's own name appears on the list as well. Moreover, Linklater's languid style of working with his actors (which works well for his own material) didn't merit the sense of urgency so prevalent in

Philip K. Dick's novel of a dystopian future. The final version on the screen lacks Dick's inherent gravitas.

Regarding Richard Linklater's interpretation of *A Scanner Darkly* compared to his own adaptation, Charlie Kaufman was surprised that the director chose the rotoscope animation technique over live-action to make the film. However, in his usual humble manner, Kaufman noted, "Certainly my version doesn't offer anything that the book doesn't. At the time, I felt like I was trying to do something that was respectful of the Dick book. I felt like the movies coming out based on his books had nothing to do with his books … I was a big admirer of his stuff so I wanted to do the movie version of that book—but you might as well read the book."[48] If Linklater's added bit of irony to end the story seemed contrived, the final bookend to Charlie Kaufman's real-life experiences of seeing *two* of his heart-felt book adaptations swept to the side was not. In the final credits of Richard Linklater's film version of *A Scanner Darkly,* a familiar name scrolled down the reel in the darkness of the theater. It plainly read, executive producer, George Clooney.

6

Eternal Sunshine of the Academy Award

Do you think you can drink like this and remember names?

—Anne Bancroft as Mrs. Kennsinger in *Malice*

"It was miserable ... I was in this terrible pain," Kaufman recalled of pitching the story for a film concerning memory erasure.[1] He may have been referring to the gnawing toothache he had at the time. However, it also spoke to his feelings of doubt and exasperation, having never pitched anything before in his life, let alone an idea that didn't originate in his own fertile brain. Just the idea of pitching made him cringe, but he was accompanied by his friend and colleague Michel Gondry, who had approached him with a story idea after a conversation with a visual artist named Pierre Bismuth. Bismuth, Gondry's friend, had fantasized about a hypothetical situation, conceived as performance art, in which a person sends a card to someone, such as an ex-lover, to inform them that they've been erased from their ex's memory. That was where Bismuth's involvement in the project ended: as far as an actual story was concerned, that was up to Kaufman. Gondry was so excited that he began to schedule Hollywood pitch meetings for the pair, although Kaufman had little expectations for a sketchy idea about memory erasure. In addition, the week before the pitch meetings, he had just gotten the job to write *Adaptation*. The last thing he needed at the time was another complicated screenplay. To his ultimate surprise, and despite his throbbing head pain, the pitch sessions went incredibly well and even resulted in a bidding war. How ironic that the one project he assumed would go nowhere would become the most commercially successful of any of his films to date. After years of working in the film industry and a handful of nominations, it would be *Eternal Sunshine of the Spotless Mind* that would win the Oscar for Best Writing for Original Screenplay.

The pitch, however, was the easy part. Now Kaufman had to go away by himself and write about a man who finds out that his girlfriend had her memory of him erased. The man doesn't want to be alone with the memory of their relationship, so he decides to have the procedure done too.

In his original draft of the screenplay, the story begins with a sickly, hollow-eyed, elderly woman in the reception area of a grandly modern publishing house called Random House-Knopf-Taschen. She walks in clutching a giant manuscript, possibly over a thousand pages long, and is greeted by a young receptionist dressed in a shiny, stretchy, one-piece pantsuit. The old woman asks to see a man who we assume is an executive but the receptionist interrupts the old woman and tells her the man is in a conference. However, the old woman insists, begging the receptionist to at least try to reach him. The old woman sits down with the bulky manuscript on her lap while directly in front of her the receptionist speaks quietly into her headset with her boss, who is of course available, but wishes to ignore the old woman, who has apparently been here many times before. Her noble attempt denied, the sympathetic receptionist apologizes to the old woman, using the excuse that it's a crazy time of year while gesturing to the Christmas tree in the corner decorated with holographic ornaments. After once again being rebuffed, the old woman desperately pleads her case by saying that it is essential people read her book, because it is the truth: the truth as only *she* knows it. "Maybe after the holidays then," is all she gets in response.

She then departs via an Arthur C. Clarke–like futuristic subway transport system, and it is revealed that the title page of her manuscript reads: *Eternal Sunshine of The Spotless Mind*.

With this quiet yet dramatic opening sequence, Charlie Kaufman demonstrates his innate storytelling brilliance. In what would be perfectly comfortable in the opening of a novel by Philip K. Dick or Kurt Vonnegut, we are introduced to a world like ours, but strangely altered with little details that speak to a more modern age. Holographic ornaments, a publishing company that seems to represent a mass merger of industry power houses, and a streamlined tubular über-train, are all indications that this isn't *our* reality. Without saying it directly, Kaufman deftly places us 50 years in the future, with a mysterious old woman whose all-important story of truth as "only she can tell it" includes the tragic tale of two doomed lovers who strive to forget one another through very drastic measures. The old woman is Mary Svevo, a character we will come to know as the wide-eyed, young receptionist of Lacuna Ltd., a company that provides a very particular and unique service.

Fifty years prior to that fateful scene in the publishing house, a young Mary Svevo sits behind the counter in Lacuna's run-of-the-mill medical office as a 30-something, electric-blue coiffed, funky woman named Clementine waits for a consultation. She considers herself the perfect candidate for the "unique" service they provide; surgically erasing a painful relationship from her memory, because it failed to live up to her own unrealistic standards. She explains as much to Dr. Howard Mierzwiak in their first meeting: "I think maybe I'm just a victim of movies, y'know? That I have some completely unrealistic notion of what a relationship can be."[2] Charlie Kaufman reiterated this very feeling in an interview with Charlie Rose when he said that for him, "Hollywood romances have been very damaging. That depressed me. But I realized that real life is more interesting." With this script especially, he wanted to "not put more damaging stuff into the world."[3]

The headquarters of the company Clementine employed for this service, for all its astounding technological advancement, is physically a shabby-gentile, dated office space with 1970s basement rec room paneling and a woefully retro filing system. Kaufman's choice of name for the company, Lacuna, is significant because *lacuna* is defined as a "gap, especially a missing portion in a text." In reference to psychology, lacuna is also used to describe amnesia about a specific event.

In the final shooting script and the story that unfolded on the big screen, the science fiction element so evident in his original draft is played down and the Lacuna company is shown as realistically and mundanely as possible. Kaufman wanted the story to focus on the relationship aspect rather than the technological angle, which was less interesting to him.

In the final filmed version, the story opens on the snowy exterior of a Long Island train platform, with 30-year-old sad sack Joel Barish (Jim Carrey) hunched over a pay phone, calling in sick to work. The name *Barish* alludes to this character being bare, unprotected, or in a raw condition. The film that made it to the screen has a similar opening with Joel waking up in his austere little apartment. Upon leaving for work, he finds that his car has been dented and assumes the upstairs neighbor is to blame. The audience will later come to realize that Clementine (Kate Winslet), in fact, dented his car, but Joel's memory has been conveniently erased of this incident. On screen, Joel slumps through his work-a-day life like a zombie. He sleepwalks through the daily mind-numbing process of cueing up like cattle in order to board the commuter train. However, when he finds himself on the train platform *this* day, he impetuously decides to take a different train and at the last minute travels to the quaint seaside community of Montauk instead. This sudden change of plans, especially on a work day, is uncharacteristic of him, and he makes a point of saying he is not an impulsive person. He behaves as if he is being led.

While in wintry Montauk, he attempts to read his journal, which is full of his doodlings (actually provided by the artist Paul Proch, Charlie Kaufman's former writing partner), but finds that pages are missing and that he hasn't made an entry in two years. He sees an interesting-looking woman in an orange sweatshirt on the beach but resigns himself to the fact that he will probably stay with his lukewarm live-in relationship with his current girlfriend, as he can barely make eye contact with other women. This glimpse of Clementine is reminiscent of a scene in Chris Marker's experimental film

Sans Soleil, when a lone figure in a red shirt stands at the shore of a cold, lonely, but lovely beach. The narrator in *Sans Soleil* remarks, "After so many stories of men who had lost their memory, here is the story of one who has lost forgetting."[4] When Joel begins to write in his diary, he realizes he has nothing interesting to document. Due to the fact that Clementine was his focal point for the past two years, without knowing *her* past, he has no reference to his own. She served as his grand obsession and without her he is literally blank. Who are we if not a repository of our entire lives? Just as pages of Joel's diary are missing, so too is a part of his identity. When he eyes the woman on the beach, he believes this is the first time he has ever seen her.

In Marker's *Sans Soleil,* the filmmaker explores his obsession with Alfred Hitchcock's spiraling mystery *Vertigo.* Jimmy Stewart's character, Scottie, is obsessed with recreating memories of Madeleine, his lost love. Her namesake is perhaps a nod to Marcel Proust's beloved Madeleine cookie, an image of comfort and love that Proust employs to represent memory and loss. Just as Scottie has a haunted quality, Kaufman's Joel Barish is bedogged by the past as well. *Eternal Sunshine of the Spotless Mind* also has parallels to another of Chris Marker's great works, the short film *La Jetee* (1962). In this postapocalyptic montage of a story, the main character is subjected to cruel experiments not unlike electroshock therapy or what is now referred to as electroconvulsive therapy. In the short film, the protagonist is blindfolded and hooked up to a head apparatus with wires (calling to mind the headgear Lacuna uses in their memory erasure process). Somehow, Marker's main character is able to break through time and space and travel back before World War I, also called, the War to End All Wars. While being restrained in a bed, just as Joel has been restrained by being anesthetized, Marker's protagonist is able to live for a time in his memory. He remembers a woman he loves or even affects an entire memory of her, creating a new personal reality.

In Kaufman's script, after Joel sees the intriguing woman on the beach at Montauk, he sees her again in a diner and yet again on the train home when she starts up a conversation with him. Although they are seemingly strangers, remember that we are in Kaufman territory, and this second meeting for the couple (they feel as if they are meeting for the first time) may be the 7th or even 77th time. In the original draft of the screenplay, in the diner scene, Joel notices Clementine reading Stephen Dixon's book *The Play and Other Stories.* In the eponymous story in the collection, Dixon writes about a middle-aged playwright struggling to come up with his next big hit. With the money from his last success, he and his young family have been living comfortably for the last seven years, but now he needs another windfall. The story plays out as a stream of conscious rant with the author attempting to avoid distractions, such as neighbors and family, and get back to work. What he fails to notice is that his seemingly annoying neighbor is offering him perfect fodder for a new story.

In one of Dixon's short stories in the book called "The Last Resort," a couple struggle to permanently separate yet always seem to return to each other with the same troubles they had in the previous stage of their relationship. Much like Joel and Clementine, the husband and wife characters in "The Last Resort" wish to be rid of each other at different times in their turbulent history. As a final effort (the last resort), the wife gives her sullen husband what she refers to as a love potion. Although he thinks she is being silly, he indulges her and drinks the serum. The next day, and for the next three years of their lives, they enjoy an idyllic marriage until the wife's untimely death. Dixon's story recalls the scene in *Eternal Sunshine of the Spotless Mind* in which Clementine is furiously stomping around Joel's apartment looking for her boots so that she may leave for the night. Joel is watching an episode of the beloved television show *The Munsters,* in which Grandpa (Al Lewis) or a voice out of frame shouts, "Why are you showing me poisons?" to which someone else replies, "Potions, I said potions. Love potion please."[5] Although the Stephen Dixon book reference did not make it to the final version on the screen, the love potion line does.

In the shooting script, Clementine is reading *The Red Right Hand,* by Joel Townsley Rogers. Joel Barish tells her, that the author is one of his favorites and mentions that the story is one of the oddest locked-room mysteries. The crime novel *The Red Right Hand* is a surreal, pulpy, multilayered mystery with all the usual suspects and yet it qualifies as a locked-room mystery too unbelievable to fathom. Its Felliniesque characters take the reader down one false path after another. One is reminded of the scene in Terry Gilliam's *Twelve Monkeys* when Cole, the main character, is strapped down to a bed in a cell and is later found to have vanished. How does a grown man strapped to a gurney in a windowless cell disappear into thin air? Clementine makes reference to an unknowable solution such as this when she and Joel are in bed and she is attempting to get him to open up to her. She implores him to communicate with her, saying she wants to know him and that by talking and sharing, people get to know each other. Joel replies by saying that he just doesn't have anything that interesting to say. When Clementine presses him on the subject, he purposely hurts her by saying that constantly talking isn't necessarily communicating. Referring back to *The Red Right Hand,* although the dialogue is absent from the final film, Kaufman's shooting script calls for Clementine to react by saying, "Joel, you're a liar. You're like one of those locked-room mysteries."[6] Another crucial reference in the Townsley Rogers's book is that on page six of the novel appears an all-important Charlie Kaufman word: *lacuna.*

When Clementine finally introduces herself to Joel on the train, she tells him not to make jokes about her name. He replies that he doesn't *know* any jokes about her name. Clementine wonders how anyone from her generation could not have heard of Huckleberry Hound, but Joel doesn't know the common childhood reference. She finds it astonishing and sings him the

"Oh my darlin' Clementine" song in an attempt to jog his memory. What neither Clementine nor Joel know is that Joel's former self did indeed know of Huckleberry Hound, but since it was associated with his painful relationship with Clementine, that memory was erased.

The first time Joel and Clementine met (chronologically), Joel had reluctantly agreed to go to his friends Rob and Carrie's party at the beach. Joel was living with a woman named Naomi at the time but she was busy so he went alone. He noticed Clementine on the beach in her ubiquitous orange sweatshirt, which he would come to know so well and even hate eventually. Clementine was the aggressor and introduced herself while he was eating. When she is surprised that he has no jokes about her name, Joel replied by singing the Huckleberry Hound song and intoned wistfully that he has no jokes about it because, "My favorite thing when I was a kid was my Huckleberry Hound doll. I think your name is magical."[7] In undergoing the memory erasing procedure, not only was their relationship erased, but so was one of Joel's happiest recollections from childhood. Heartbreakingly, Joel has lost part of his true self. The Lacuna company did indeed erase the painful parts of who he has become, but he lost the lovely bits as well.

In their meeting on the train, the length of the dialogue is cut considerably from the screenplay. Also apparent is that contrary to modern cinematic structure, the music in the scene plays only while Joel and Clementine are talking to each other. Instead of filling the potentially awkward silences with comforting music, composer Jon Brion and the filmmakers allow us to witness the reality of the natural awkwardness true of most first meetings.

In both the original draft and the shooting script, however, Joel mentions Tom Waits's album *Rain Dogs*. He says that he can't remember the album very well, but remembers liking it (leading us to believe that this memory was already modified by Lacuna). Clementine recites the lyrics from the song "9th & Hennepin," in which Waits sings of someone being full of bitters and the drink, blue ruin "and you spill out / over the side to anyone who'll listen."[8] The lyrics are significant because Clementine makes Joel a gin and tonic drink called a "blue ruin" when she invites him up to her apartment. It is also the name of one of her hair colors (one of the ways she expresses herself). In addition, the line about someone who brims over to the point of spilling out to anyone who will listen to them, applies to Clementine because her aggressive behavior towards Joel leads the audience to believe that she may act this way with simply anyone who will pay attention to her. Joel feels special and alive in her presence, but he wonders if he can trust that they share an intimate dynamic or if her boisterous personality applies to everyone she meets. The name of the song itself is meaningful to Charlie Kaufman as well, as 9th and Hennepin is a street corner in Minneapolis, Minnesota, where he lived for many years after college.

While in her apartment, in both versions of the script, but not on the screen, Clementine waxes nostalgic for grade school and tells Joel that she

would like to have been from the 1940s. She seems to ostensibly be yearning for any time but her immediate present. In Clementine's version of the
1940s, "everyone wore hats." However, it is easy to idealize an era in which
one hasn't lived. A 30-year-old, single woman in that decade in American
history would have been labeled a spinster and have had very few options
for gainful employment. A free-spirited, young woman like Ms. Kruczynski
would have been ostracized. Plus, she seems to forget that the 40s was the
time of Hitler and the horrors of World War II. When Clementine mentions her affinity for Norman Rockwell she seems almost apologetic, the way
people do when they admit they like J. K. Rowling. Clementine qualifies her
fondness for liking Rockwell's sensibility by dismissing it as strictly a grade
school type of thing. In a recent interview, Kaufman addressed the question
of why certain artists have a stigma attached to them. "I was thinking about
that whole thing about being embarrassed to read things. It's such an important thing to get over. Where does it come from? Something about my age
and where I came from, there was this guy, Rod McKuen ... as a little kid I
knew somehow from my family that this guy was a joke as a poet. But I didn't
know why—and I don't know if I ever really read him—I just thought, well
I can't like this guy, I have to be really careful about who I do like so that I
don't embarrass myself."[9]

As Joel and Clementine continue to get to know each other over drinks,
Clementine mentions the subject of truth, which is one of Kaufman's over-
arching themes throughout his body of work. Most of his main characters are
in pursuit of the truth of their essence, no matter how painful the truth is.
Clementine says, "My feeling is that's how you die, because you stop listening to what is true, and what is true is always changing."[10] When interviewed
by Charlie Rose, Kaufman said that the naturalistic dialogue he wrote for
Eternal Sunshine of the Spotless Mind is what is true to him. He can only be
sure of his own truth and as a writer, this is what he has to offer.

The scene at the frozen Charles River does much to illustrate both Joel
and Clementine's personalities. The way they behave in this situation speaks
to their respective individual natures as Joel is reticent to even venture out
onto the possibly weak ice, while Clementine rushes headlong out on to the
frozen river. In her haste, she falls and bruises herself, a foreshadowing of the
pain she will feel later in their relationship. However, her willingness to possibly fall and her subsequent pain proves that unlike Joel, she embraces life
with all its bumps.

Approximately 18 minutes into the film, the opening credits roll. In the
extras package accompanying the movie, Kaufman explained that because
the scene is so dramatically different in tone from all that has come before,
rolling the credits at this juncture made sense. While driving, Joel is crying and distraught. Obviously, he is traumatized, but the audience remains
in the dark as to why. When Joel goes into his apartment and runs into a
neighbor while getting his mail, we see he has what looks like a pen mark or

a magic marker smudge in the shape of a dot near his temple: he has already undergone the memory erasure process. When Joel visits Clementine at her work, the bookstore, she greets him as she would a stranger. Her words, May I help you sir? and her business-like stance cut Joel to the bone. He is agape as he watches her kiss a strange boy and then she basically ignores him as if he were just another annoying customer getting in the way of her real life. Joel doesn't get a clear look at her love interest, but can surmise he is a boy and not yet a man. After this bizarrely cold encounter, he goes to his friends' house (Rob and Carrie) in search of clarity and some comfort. Unbeknownst to Joel, his friends recently received a letter that read: "Dear Rob and Carrie Eakin, Clementine Kruczynski has had Joel Barish erased from her memory. Please never mention their relationship to her again. Thank you. Lacuna, Ltd."[11]

Joel doesn't understand why Clementine is rejecting him so absolutely and tells his friends that she must be punishing him. This statement recalls the pain the husband feels in the film *Away From Her* (2006), based on the short story "The Bear Came Over the Mountain" by Alice Munro, in which a man's wife of 50 years is possibly suffering from Alzheimer's disease. The husband questions whether his wife's mind is really degenerating or if she is just punishing him for past hurts in their marriage. The comparison is relevant to Kaufman's excruciatingly personal writing, in that just as Clementine treats Joel with a distant yet professionally courteous air in the bookstore, so too does the wife regard her husband when he visits her at the nursing home. He finds his wife Fiona in the common room playing cards with a stranger and yet she and an older man (who is also a resident at the nursing home) behave as though they have been intimates for years. When Fiona first sees her husband Grant, she offers a smile and greets him; however, she treats him as though she is the welcoming committee and he a new resident at the home. She is kind and gracious, but only as so far as courtesy and good breeding allows. Her husband doesn't know if she is playing a game or trick on him (a trick not unlike the Lacuna calling card), or if she truly doesn't remember him. Grant tells a nurse at the resting home, "She could have been pulling a joke. It would not be unlike her."[12] Similarly, Joel doesn't know if Clementine's behavior at the bookstore is a cruel joke, because he doesn't know what else could explain her demeanor. Her treatment of him is so severe, it is as if he is a completely different person. He is unrecognizable to her and feels like he might not even exist in the way he thought was real just a short while ago. Charlie Kaufman recalled a time in his life when he was much younger when he felt very similar to Joel in this respect. "I had a relationship with somebody for years, which was this kind of unspoken, intense love between us." He remembered that they were on a subway platform when he finally told his friend that he loved her. He was "expecting to have that expressed back to me. And she turned off, and she got on the subway . . . One of the things we shared was sort of a disdain for a lot of other people.

Then I called her from a pay phone and heard her talking to me like I was one of those people."[13] He said it was like a switch had turned off. Just like that.

Another meaningful Kaufman reference can be seen at the Lacuna office, as the receptionist's desk plate reads Mary Svevo: a nod to the Italian novelist Italo Svevo, one of Kaufman's literary influences, who is considered a forefather of experimental modernist writing. One of Svevo's novels, *As a Man Grows Older* (*Senilità* in Italian), is about a 35-year-old man, Emilio Brentani, who is obsessed with a younger, beautiful Italian girl. The girl, Angiolina, is thoughtless, vain, and cruel as she collects boyfriends and creates a web of lies that Emilio is well aware of and yet he can not clear his mind of her. After suffering a certain amount of indignities, he makes up his mind to leave her and does so, but thereafter continues to seek her out. She is affectionate with him but insensitive to his feelings as she consistently talks of other boys and men. However, one wonders why Brentani did not marry her in the beginning of the story. It is implied that she was not worthy of him, because she had such a bad reputation and yet he contributed to this very reputation; they were both complicit in the game.

The obsessed Emilio in *As a Man Grows Older* can be compared to Charlie Kaufman's character Mary (Kirsten Dunst) of *Eternal Sunshine of the Spotless Mind,* as she is hopelessly in love with her employer, Dr. Howard Mierzwiak. As the story unfolds, we find that Mary has always been in love with Howard and that by the time *we* meet her, she has already undergone the erasure process herself (at first unbeknownst to her). Although Mary's larger subplot only appears in the screenplay, Kaufman attributed a much deeper regret to her than what appears on the screen. Although Mary is clearly in pain and adores Howard, their past relationship went so far as for Mary to find herself pregnant with his child. Despite the fact that Mierzwiak is moved by her and has feelings for her as well, he is married and more than twice her age. In Kaufman's screenplay, he persuades her to have an abortion and then her memory erased.

In Emilio Brentani's case, Angiolina's, slights and betrayals only bond him to her more. Although he is an adult business man, he has the broken heart of a lovesick teenager; nothing or no one else can bring him any comfort. He lives in a constant state of agitation, self-loathing, and suppressed rage. It is not until Angiolina finally runs away with a boy who robbed a bank that Emilio no longer frequents her parents' home. Her physical absence brings him no clarity, however, and as he ages, the memory of her becomes even more of an idealized projection. In his mind, she morphs into an object of worship, as he thinks of her as an angelic statue on an alter, and imbues her with thoughtful qualities she never embodied.

As in Charlie Kaufman's writing, Italo Svevo's work has a dreamlike, visceral quality. In *As a Man Grows Older,* Svevo writes of Emilio: "His pain and his remorse had both become much milder. The elements of which his life was made up remained the same, but they had become attenuated, as if seen through a dark lens which robbed them of light and violence. A great calm, an endless ennui lay like lead upon him."[14] While Emilio's tragic, unrequited love never ceases, there is hope for Kaufman's Mary Svevo. When she finds out the truth about Mierzwiak's betrayal, Mary takes matters into her own hands and decides to get the painful truth out to the patients at Lacuna as well. As it was part of her job duties as the receptionist to mail out the erasure notices, she confiscates the files and alerts all former patients about the procedure and their collective reality. Although the exchange is absent from the screen, a version of the screenplay calls for her coworker Stan to go to her home and tell her that the patients have come back and that the office is full of people who want their memory *re*-erased. Her passionate attempt to help the patients seems to have created a further need for Lacuna's services.

In the final film version, Dr. Howard Mierzwiak (Tom Wilkinson) explains the memory erasure process to Joel and tells him that the good people at Lacuna want to empty his home of mementos and therefore start to clean away his messy life with Clementine. More of Paul Proch's art work can be seen as Joel goes through his portfolio in order to attempt to weed out all things associated with Clementine. What Joel isn't told is that along with losing his memories, he is about to suffer an invasion of privacy and a subsequent loss of identity. When the so-called technicians Stan (Mark Ruffalo) and Patrick (Elijah Wood) come to Joel's house to start the procedure, they treat him and talk about him as if he were a dead man; a nonentity. In the movie's commentary section, Kaufman has said that this is symbolic of the customer service industry and how the employees really want to treat you. This is just a job to get through, not the delicate essence of a man's life they are supervising. They ignore Joel so thoroughly that neither realizes that he murmurs Patrick's name and must at least unconsciously have an idea of what is going on around him in his apartment.

When the boys have trouble with the machine and Patrick hits his head on a table after trying to fix the computer wires, he subsequently bumps the monitor. He is frustrated with all the cords and the audience sees flashes of intense, quick cuts of Joel's memory on the screen. Stan admonishes him and says, "Just take it easy … Let's not roach the guy." This line from the movie isn't found in any of the scripts—even the shooting script—but could be construed as a reference to Franz Kafka's character Gregor Samsa, who undergoes a drastic change (into a giant bug, of course) and is unrecognizable to his family, just as Joel's psyche will be unrecognizable after the procedure. Perhaps the clever Mark Ruffalo knew that Charlie Kaufman was influenced by Kafka's writing or maybe this is just a happy accident of the collective unconscious that occurred on the set.

When "the eraser boys" Stan and Patrick arrive at Joel's house to begin the "operation," one is reminded of Shakespeare's lesser characters such as Rosencrantz and Guildenstern. Although both duos seem to have minor roles, they don't realize how important they are to the larger story and are woefully, comically inept. Like the characters in Tom Stoppard's play *Rosencrantz and Guildenstern Are Dead,* Kaufman's Lacuna technicians don't know what is going on around them and seem strapped to the wheel of fate. Kaufman's character Patrick, specifically, is so self-absorbed and unconcerned about the welfare of his patient Joel that he seduces Clementine by essentially stealing Joel's identity. Patrick begins this emotional rape and pillage by stealing things such as Clementine's underwear, Joel's notebooks, drawings, and a gift intended for Clementine. He clearly exploits the situation when he is entrusted to oversee the technology and serve as a form of caregiver during the erasure operation. He treats Joel as if he were a corpse and consequently has no remorse about the invasion of a dead man's privacy. While the younger and effusive Patrick insinuates himself into Clementine's new life, Joel lies strapped (literally and metaphorically) to his bed, being bled of his history.

Lying prone, as Joel falls into memory, the audience sees him re-living a scene but it grows shadowy and the sound warps. When Clementine stomps off into the night after she and Joel argue after she returns home at 3:00 A.M., a car literally falls from the sky. Joel's memory or his fight to keep his memory is so twisted that the laws of gravity no longer apply. As Clem rushes down the street, her leg disappears: in the director/writer commentary from the film, Michel Gondry reveals that her leg is unintentionally missing from sight. Gondry implies that the invisible leg may be due to a computer graphics oversight, working against a blue screen, but the mistake can also be taken as Clementine's body starting to disappear in the context of the story.

Back at Joel's apartment, Patrick and Stan are busy bungling the erasure process as Patrick reveals to his colleague that he "kinda fell in love" with Clementine the night they were erasing her memory. Stan's reply, "Do you know how unethical that is?" is one of the most comical lines ever uttered in context, considering the nature of their jobs and how they handle the process with the efficiency of fast-food industry clerks.[15] It is a great example of Kaufman's deeply felt sense of humor. As Joel is unconscious on his bed, his mind takes him to a memory of him walking around a flea market with Clementine. They argue when Clementine says she wants to have a baby and Joel tells her they aren't ready. Based on his reaction, he also clearly doesn't want to talk about such an intimate subject in public. Clem yells at him and defends her position. When he mumbles a reply, she strikes out at him with, "I can't hear you! I can never fucking hear what you're saying ... fucking ventriloquist!"[16] This remark has at least a dual meaning in that yes, Joel is mumbling, but he may also just be a puppet. She implies that he makes no choices for himself, has no control in his own life, and exists only to be used by someone or something else. Used by whom or what are the bigger questions. The remark also brings Kaufman's concepts in *Being John Malkovich* to mind. As this scene starts to fade from view, it is a sign that Joel's memory is weakening. Clementine's rant becomes increasingly fuzzy; her voice seems far away and hollow to the ear.

When Mary joins Stan and Patrick at Joel's apartment, she shows momentary compassion for Joel, who is hooked up to the erasure machine, but quickly resumes a flirtation with Stan. Mary makes an appropriate toast and quotes Friedrich Nietzsche: "Blessed are the forgetful, for they get the better even of their blunders." At this juncture in the story, Mary has no idea just how ironic that toast will be in relation to her own personal life. Her character, as well as Kaufman's story as a whole, serves as an example of Nietzsche's philosophy of eternal recurrence. Time is cyclical and Mary will not be able to escape her passions. Similarly, in Kaufman's film *Adaptation,* the Charlie character frustratingly says that he is Ouroboros—the snake eating itself to create the endless circle. In *Human Nature,* the Nathan character is doomed to an afterlife in which he is trapped in an eerily blank room in which he has no choice but to tell his story over and over again, eternally. One of Kaufman's literary influences, Philip K. Dick, also shows the same sensibility: in Kaufman's adaptation of *A Scanner Darkly,* he includes the fate of the suicidal Charles Freck, who on his deathbed is met with a demon, who insists on reading him his sins on an endless loop. In Kaufman's most recent work, the character Caden in *Synecdoche, New York,* will return again and again to recreate the events and circumstances in his life, in order to get at the truth and an understanding of his world.

In *Eternal Sunshine of the Spotless Mind,* Clementine's experience with Patrick, who exploits the eternal return for his own gain, suddenly makes her think she is losing her mind. In an important clue to understanding Kaufman's work, Patrick calls her by the name Tangerine, instead of Clementine. At the same time, Joel, still asleep on the bed, wonders how Patrick knows to call her that name—a new nickname Joel made up during an intimate moment that Patrick could not have been privy to. Something is beginning to click for Joel in the respect that he is no longer merely visiting his past by remembering, but that he is in the process of forgetting.

As Patrick goes to Clementine's apartment, Stan and Mary smoke a joint and free associate while lying on Joel's bed. Mary rhapsodizes about how Howard has given so much to the world with his memory erasure procedure. She muses: "To let people begin again. It's beautiful. You look at a baby, and it's so pure and so free and so clean. And adults are, like, this mess of sadness and phobias. Howard just makes it all go away."[17] What Mary doesn't remember, and in a subplot Kaufman wrote but was left out of the final film, is that Howard convinced her to abort their child. Mary's mention of the word *baby* while she is relaxing with Stan may be part of a ghost memory or the subconscious trying to seep through to her current reality. The dialogue also evokes Kaufman's characterization of Susan Orlean, who utters that she wishes she could be a baby again and just start her life over, in his film *Adaptation.*

When Patrick tries to comfort Tangerine (our Clementine), she is shaking with anxiety as nothing makes sense to her right now. She falls back on a tried-and-true comforting event in her life and tells him they need to go to the Charles River. She feels this might restore order to her reeling mind. Patrick quickly offers her an early Valentine's Day present and because she just recently met him, she is excited but appropriately uncomfortable with this gesture, which may be happening too soon in their new relationship. When she asks what it is and he answers that he doesn't know, but she should open it, he truly doesn't know what it is as he stole the jewelry box from Joel's bag. Joel had thoughtfully picked out this gift for Clementine. When she genuinely likes the gift, she is shocked and tells him that none of her ex-boyfriends knew her taste in jewelry. This compliment is meant for Joel, however, as he is the one who knows her well enough to perceive her likes and dislikes.

In Joel's mind, just as he fully realizes what he has agreed to in signing his memory/identity/life away at Lacuna, the scene takes us to Clementine's apartment where she and Joel are under a blanket on the floor. In the early drafts and the shooting script of the screenplay, Kaufman wrote an eloquent piece of dialogue wherein Clementine tells Joel about her favorite book, *The Velveteen Rabbit*. She explains how the Skin Horse toy tells the Rabbit what it means to be real. The script calls for her to read from a worn, beloved copy of the book: "It takes a long time. That's why it doesn't often happen to people who break easily or have sharp edges, or who have to be carefully kept. Generally by the time you are Real, most of your hair has been loved off, and your eyes drop out and you get loose in the joints and very shabby. But these things don't matter at all, because once you are Real, you can't be ugly, except to people who don't understand."[18] The passage underscores the feelings of many of Kaufman's characters. Clementine and Joel want to be loved regardless of their rough patches, and like the worn-out Rabbit, they almost give up on their search for love. Kaufman does not have a false, idealized vision of love, but accepts that along with moments of joy, is it also naturally fraught with waves of anxiety and uncertainty. His character Joel, especially, will come to understand that love does not happen all at once.

However, for some reason *The Velveteen Rabbit* speech did not translate to film, and Michel Gondry asked Kaufman to cut it down to 25 percent of the original monologue. Kaufman was excited by the challenge and what remains is still a poignant exchange about transformation and indelible love. Clementine weeps as she tells Joel not to leave her and Joel pleads with Dr. Mierzwiak (in his head) to please just let him keep this memory. Joel realizes he doesn't want to lose his memories, whether good, bad, or ugly. He screams out as if yelling at God that he wants to call the whole thing off. "Can you hear me? I don't want this anymore!"[19] One is reminded of the Biblical reference in which Christ pleads with God to take his burden away from him and change his fate.

A frustrated Joel composes himself as best he can and tells Clementine he has an idea as how to stop this heinous operation. He believes they can possibly outrun the erasure process and physically pulls Clementine away from the memory of them going to visit her Grandma. He finds himself back at Mierzwiak's office telling the doctor to wake him up, but Joel is still trapped in his own head. The doctor is professionally sympathetic but informs him that he (the doctor) is merely inside his head too and how can he possibly help him from there. Suddenly, in a corner, Joel sees the mutated, furtive, scrambled form that is Patrick. Joel realizes this is the little brat who is stealing his identity and seducing Clementine with phrases from their letters, his journal, and their private, intimate memories. Simultaneously, we see Clementine and Patrick lying on the frozen Charles River. Patrick is using Joel's previous words, verbatim, and this false, wholly contrived situation creeps up on Clementine. She knows something about this experience is wrong and quickly announces she wants to go home.

When Joel and Clementine meet up again in Joel's memory of their walk in the woods, she calmly persuades him to at least enjoy the scenery while it lasts, as he struggles to preserve their past. He manages to open his eyes for a second but his body remains helpless, still prone in his apartment while Stan and Mary dance around his lifeless body. Clementine suggests that they go to a memory that she didn't belong in, such as something from childhood. They land in a scene in which Joel is approximately 18 months old. He is crawling under a table and making pre-speech baby noises while his mother and a neighbor busily rush around preparing cocktails and party food. We, the audience, only see the adults from baby Joel's perspective and get glimpses of their legs and a 1960s-era kitchen. Clementine's idea for them to retreat to Joel's childhood seems to be working, as Clementine is substituted for his mother's friend at the time. However, Joel is reduced to a childlike nature and is consumed with getting his mother's attention. Although they seem to be safely hidden from the erasure boys in this memory, Joel echoes what Clementine said to him earlier when he implores her to not leave him. Kaufman's binary dialogue shows how their relationship is on a time loop and though it seems incurably fractured at this point in his story, maybe the circle of time will bring them back in sync. The infant version of Joel mixes up or combines his need for the safe embrace of his mother with his affection for Clementine. Transference is a powerful thing.

Meanwhile, back at Joel's apartment, Stan finally realizes that Joel is "off the map," and is essentially lost. Mary persuades him to call Howard, and although Stan wonders what Mary's motives are in doing this, he relents. When Howard arrives and takes over the computer operation, he finds Joel in a memory of being bathed in the sink as a baby. Clementine is with him in the sink as well, and through forced perspective, the characters are rendered as toddlers, small enough to fit comfortably in a kitchen sink.

When Howard inspects Joel's body, lying on the bed, he realizes that the patient's eyes are open. In a scene reminiscent of both *Le Jetee* and *Twelve Monkeys,* the doctor, Stan, and Mary surround Joel's bed and hover over him. This is a good example of how Kaufman's collaboration with Michel Gondry helped bring some of the writer's more terrifying scenes to fruition. From Joel's prone and helpless perspective, the audience sees the doctor inject Joel with a needle and we feel how isolated he is, trapped in his own mind. Immediately after the injection, Joel and Clementine are seen at a drive-in movie theater. They are having a good time when Joel snaps out of the memory and understands that the eraser boys must have found them. He tries to change the situation by once again fleeing and this time Clementine suggests that they go even deeper into his subconscious and tells him to hide her in his humiliation. Although Joel thinks back to an embarrassing scene for him as a boy in junior high school where his mother accidentally opens the door to his bedroom while he is masturbating, the erasing procedure continues and they find themselves on the deserted winter beach in Montauk. Finally, at his wit's end, Joel enters a harrowing, disturbing memory when as an eight year old, he was bullied into hitting a dead bird with a hammer, repeatedly. In the original draft of the script, the humiliating scene Joel chooses to attempt to hide Clementine in entails a memory from junior high school where a relentless bully named Joe Early hits him and he falls to the ground, covering himself. At school that day, young Joel had been trying to hide from what was sure to be a losing battle. Joel explains that after that fight, the other school kids always called him Jill. Kaufman explained that when Clementine has the idea to hide her elsewhere, it is really Joel talking to himself, but by thinking about the problem through Clementine's voice, he has more license to be adventurous. The answers coming through as though they are Clementine's ideas helps liberate him. Curiously, we, as the audience, don't know Clementine at all, as we only see her through the lens of Joel's mind. Other than the few times she is alone with the character Patrick, Joel's perception of Clementine is all we are given.

Despite their efforts to hide in deeper layers of hidden memories, Stan tracks the couple to Joel's childhood humiliations nonetheless, and just as they are playing a pretend game of mock suffocating each other—Clementine disappears. This game, where one person pretends to kill the other with a pillow, was actually a childhood game that Charlie Kaufman used to play growing up. Kaufman revealed that the object was to see who could play dead the longest, while the other person pretended to be concerned.

With the erasing procedure now under control, Stan excuses himself to go outside to get some fresh air. While this is a ruse to get Mary's attention and perhaps persuade her to join him, she stays inside Joel's apartment with Howard as she is happy to have a rare moment alone with him. Nervously, she tries to impress him with her beloved quotes from Bartlett's and goes on to quote Alexander Pope and therein, the name of the film: "How happy is the blameless vestal's lot? The world forgetting, by the world forgot. Eternal sunshine of the spotless mind. Each prayer accepted and each wish resigned."[20] Mary's reference to Pope's poem "Eloisa to Abelard" is the story of a doomed, tragic love set in the 12th century. Peter, also known as Pierre Abelard, renounced his family's military background and became a controversial philosophy teacher and theologian. Although there are several differing accounts of what really happened to the would-be lovers, it is commonly held that Eloisa was Abelard's 13-year-old student who fell hopelessly in love with him. Eloisa became pregnant and Abelard whisked her away from her uncle's home and sent her to stay with his sister, who would help raise their son. Later, the distraught Eloisa was banished to a convent while her uncle had Abelard castrated. Although some accounts refer to the lovers as having been secretly married, Abelard joined a monastery, and later in life, because of his contrarian beliefs, formed his own order.

Alexander Pope's poem, structured in the form of couplets, begins with Pope's perception of how Eloisa might have reacted to an intercepted letter from Abelard to a friend. Her undying love for him was reignited and the poem depicts a long-suffering, open wound of a tragic obsession. Her vow of silence, the company of pious nuns, and the solitude offered by her surroundings never brought her any comfort. In fact, in this repressed environment, she had no other outlet for her grief and spent her days and tortuous nights trapped in her head. Her anger at God and Abelard are palpable. Eloisa's memories relentlessly torment her, and just as Joel and Clementine believe, she trusts that she would be happier with a "spotless mind." Underscoring Kaufman's main theme in the film, Eloisa laments: "Of all affliction taught a lover yet, 'Tis sure the hardest science to forget!"[21]

In Kaufman's story, when Clementine and then Joel choose to erase their pain, they are choosing a form of metered out suicide. From Pope's view, Eloisa seems to want to choose death too, as she thinks this would be the only way to cure her tortured mind. From her convent she cries, "Yet here for ever must I stay: Sad proof of how well a lover can obey! Death only death, can break the lasting chain; And here, ev'n then, shall my cold dust remain."[22]

Many authors before and since Alexander Pope have made reference to Eloisa and Abelard's story. Scholars to this day debate the authenticity of the lovers' letters to one another. In some versions, Eloisa married Abelard against her wishes, as she did not want to preclude him from becoming a man of the church. Scott Moncrieff (Marcel Proust's translator) believed much of the letters to be forgeries. Moncrieff said of the pair, "And when, in later years, she writes him her three immortal letters, his irritation and boredom are manifest in every line of his replied." In a letter to George Moore, one of the translators of the lovers' letters, Moncrieff asserted, "The great majority of people in England think, if they think about the matter at all, that Abelard and Heloise are fictional characters invented, my dear George Moore, and very beneficially invented by yourself ... Such as it is, pray accept the offering of my part in it with every good wish, upon this your onomastico."[23] Whether or not their tragic love story was fictitious or real, the story endures, and Eloisa and Abelard finally lay side by side in the cemetery in Pere Lachaise in Paris along with Oscar Wilde, Proust, and Molière. Alexander Pope's ode to a tragically flawed yet immortal romance remains the perfect allusion for Kaufman's film tile *Eternal Sunshine of the Spotless Mind*.

In the movie, as Mary Svevo finishes quoting Pope, the editor of the film, Valdis Oskarsdottir, sews in a scene in which Joel and Clementine are watching a circus on the streets of New York. In a happy accident, as the filmmakers were making their movie, in the middle of the night, they heard that the Barnum and Bailey circus was moving its company, including an elephant, through the city streets. The scene was moved around many times, and originally, Oskarsdottir wanted Mary to be able to finish her scene as she wanted the audience to be able to stay with the emotional moment. She didn't want to take away from Mary's character, but said that ultimately, Kaufman does not see his scripts as sacred and it was decided the improvised circus scene would follow Mary's overlapping dialogue. The traveling night circus was able to serve as another poignant "memory" in the scrapbook of Joel's mind. In a funny twist, while filming the scene, people on the streets of New York had recognized Jim Carrey and were starting to yell his name and ruin the take. While the moment wasn't planned and certainly wasn't borne of Kaufman's script, he is happy that Gondry was able to capture the event and that the actors stayed in character to contribute another lovely sliver of time.

Back in Joel's apartment, just as Dr. Mierzwiak succumbs to Mary's attempt to kiss him, his wife sees their embrace through the window. When Mierzwiak abandons Mary and runs after his wife, who seems resigned to her fate says, "Don't he a monster, Howard, tell the girl."[24] This statement could easily be a reference to Dr. Frankenstein and his monster as Mierzwiak's operation can be viewed as a monstrous attempt to patch together what becomes a less than human form by his own hand. (This modern concept of a monster is also echoed in the film *La Jetee*.) A Lacuna patient becomes less than human by severing a part of themselves. Mierzwiak and his crew take on the God role just as Dr. Frankenstein did with his creation.

As Howard must now be truthful with Mary, his loving assistant is smacked in the face with the cold reality that she has been a naïve pawn. She too has undergone Lacuna's patchwork reassembling of the broken mind. However, the horrible truth is more important to Mary than the pain of her situation, as she states in the shooting script, "Patrick Henry said, 'For my part, whatever anguish of spirit it may cost, I am willing to know the whole truth; to know the worst, and to provide for it.' Patrick Henry was a great patriot, Howard ... I don't like what you do to people."[25] Kaufman drew this character as a wounded but brave soul, and her speech, though heartbreakingly funny and endearing, is never silly. Earlier in the story when Mary saw memory erasure as an abstract concept, through the lens of her love for the doctor and his easing people's pain, she thought both the process and Howard were brilliant. But now that she realizes that she has experienced the procedure first hand, she sees it as wrong and unethical. She is going to right this wrong.

When Mary decides to take matters into her own hands and distribute the Lacuna tapes to former patients, not everyone has the same reaction she does to the truth. Although she was driven to action and stood up for herself upon being confronted, Kaufman shows us that other Lacuna patients are in desperate need of ignorance. Although absent from the final film, the original draft shows that the patients who received her message and their tapes about Lacuna return to the office begging for their memories to be re-erased. They are dealing with a myriad of issues such as a little girl being lured into a car by a man with a puppy and then raped, a soldier witnessing his friends slaughtered on a battlefield, a young boy being called ignorant slurs by relentless bullies, and a heinous car accident from the driver's point of view.

Kaufman's character of Stan clearly sides with Lacuna's theory that one is better off without traumatic memories. And the "science" of memory erasing that Dr. Mierzwiak espouses in the film is not an entirely fictitious concept. In 2004, the same year in which *Eternal Sunshine of the Spotless Mind* was released, the article "The Quest to Forget" appeared in the *New York Times Magazine*. The article outlined a study by a professor at Harvard Medical School in which a trauma patient could diminish painful memories, with the use of the drug propranolol. The article tells the story of a woman named Kathleen who was admitted to the emergency room after having been run down by a bicycle messenger. After the initial shock wore off, she thought back to a trauma from eight years prior, when an armed drug addict "forced his way into her car, made her drive to an abandoned building and tried to rape her."[26] She explained that it took her almost a year's time to get past the nightmares and fear she suffered, causing her to ruminate each night and wake up still feeling like she had that gun against her head. Because she knew her tendency to get stuck in the painful past, she agreed to be part of the professor's pilot study called therapeutic forgetting.

At the Center for the Neurobiology of Learning and Memory at the University of California, Irvine, director James McGaugh conducted a similar study. He showed a test group a series of slides and then told them a story to accompany the pictures. When the stories consisted of bland, everyday life, the test group retained less recall than when they were shown the same slides but with a story about a boy being hit by a car and rushed to the hospital where surgeons frantically reattached his severed legs. Then a new group, who had been administered the drug propranolol was brought in, and went through the same process as the original group. However, this time, with the drug in their systems, the gory, exciting story versus the bland story made no difference in the group's recall. "This was the first suggestion that it might be possible in humans to interfere pharmacologically with the recollection of intense memories."[27] Kaufman's story involving Lacuna, Ltd., may not be the stuff of fiction after all. It is a revelation that propranolol may help ease the suffering of posttraumatic stress victims, especially those who have psychological damage from war. However, bioethicists question whether this renders a person robotic rather than human. One can argue that we would not be who are we without our entire past, including the ugly and humiliating parts. When Charlie Kaufman was asked if he himself would partake in such a process, if it were in fact possible, he unequivocally answered, no. He embraces the good with the bad and sees the larger picture of one's life.

Another poignant memory that Kaufman had written for *Eternal Sunshine of the Spotless Mind* but that is absent from the screen version, finds a 10-year-old Joel with his father, fishing from a rowboat. His dad, drunk and sullen, tells him, "Don't be like me, son. Don't waste your life. You'll come to a point someday where it'll be too late. You'll be sewn into your fate ... and there'll be nowhere to go except where you're headed, like a train on a track. Inevitable, unalterable."[28] Joel has placed Clementine in this memory too (to ostensibly hide her) and reveals how horrified he is that his father saw no hope for him, that his father saw failure written in his future.

When Joel summons the courage to pursue Clementine and confronts her at her job after he ran away from the beach house scene, he admits that he thought Clementine was still going to save him, even after all that had come before. In the commentary section of the high definition version of the movie, Michel Gondry mentions the fantasy of being saved by a woman. Earlier, when Joel is a toddler and crouching under the kitchen table, the adult Joel acknowledges that his drive for his mother to pick him up in her arms (in effect, saving him) is incredibly strong. In being saved, the responsibility of choice is removed. Kaufman seems to struggle with the notion of being saved and the comfort that lies therein versus taking the responsibility to save yourself. He implies that being saved is only okay if one is a child. Adults need to save themselves.

Another important dynamic in the scripts that is only hinted at on screen is Joel's relationship with his live-in girlfriend, Naomi. At various stages, Joel questions whether he should return to Naomi and their secure, yet bland existence. Once again, Kaufman (through his character Joel) makes reference to being damaged by the notion of romance in movies and the media, when in a voice-over he ruminates, "I thought about Clementine and the spark when I was with her, but then I thought what you and I had was real and adult and therefore significant even if it wasn't much fun. I saw other people having fun and I wanted it. Then I thought fun is a lie, that no one is really having fun; I'm being suckered by advertising and movie bullshit."[29] Joel then sees himself as an old man, full of regret that he didn't pick up the phone to call Naomi when he had the chance to make things right between them.

In the shooting script, when Joel debates with himself about being better off with Naomi, he wonders, "How can I continue on this path toward a living death, a life filled with obligation and guilt and responsibility, but joyless, hopeless?"[30] Just as the character Mary Svevo made reference to Nietzsche in her toast, Joel's questioning of his own life choices is another reference to the philosopher. Kaufman's work is often filled with Nietzschean modes of thought, and *Eternal Sunshine of the Spotless Mind* calls into question the self versus duty to a marriage/family dilemma as well as the phenomenon of recurrence. Just as Nietzsche asserted, Joel's metaphysical journey reflects the philosophy that one's nature, even given different circumstances, really doesn't change. Regardless of the memory erasure operation and advanced technology, Kaufman's characters will continue to make choices that will lead them down the same path. Naomi serves to exemplify the fact that Joel can never escape his true self and his given set of schemata. Although he does not want to hear the truth (Naomi's version of it), she tells him, "Whatever it is you think you have with this chick, once the thrill wears off, you're just going to be Joel with the same fucking problems."[31] Wherever you go, there you are.

Yet another dysfunctional but comical relationship woven throughout the story is that of Joel's friends Rob and Carrie. They serve as a type of tense, parental model as Carrie initially wants to protect Joel from learning about Lacuna while Rob, perhaps just to disagree with Carrie, is the one to show him the actual notice they received in the mail. Carrie is the mother figure to both men as she is the sturdy, rational one in the relationship. After the three of them return from the beach party where Joel just met Clementine, Carrie turns kindly to him, sitting in the back seat of the car as a child would, and says that she saw him talking to someone pretty. She is warm and encouraging, while at the same time able to placate her husband somewhat resignedly as she tells him to just watch the road. More examples of Carrie's maternal instincts toward Joel are illuminated in the original draft, when in the car on the way home from the beach party she asks him if he had fun, and upon dropping him off at his apartment refers to him as sweetie and says that she hopes he feels better.

Back on the big screen, the film takes the audience to Mary Svevo's final scene in which Stan finds her rushing to her car, having left Lacuna with all her cassette tapes and files. In the early drafts of the screenplay, Mary gets to confront the apathetic Howard and passionately yells at him that he made her have an abortion. Later, in response to Stan visiting her apartment after she leaves her job, she says that Howard is a thief in that he steals the truth. Although Stan calmly says that people come to Lacuna voluntarily, she responds that she won't allow it and questions what memory erasure would mean for society as a whole. "I don't want to hurt people. But these things happened. All these little sadnesses, the big ones. What if no one remembers? What does that do to the world?"[32] When she has exhausted herself, she quietly ends with the belief that indeed, *someone* has to remember.

In Kaufman's original draft, Joel and Naomi briefly reunite. They have sex and seem to quickly fall into their former dynamic. When Naomi tries to reach him on the phone on the day he has called out sick to go to Montauk on a whim, he says he just needed to take the day off to think. Naomi replies: "Long day's thinking into night" (a funny reference to Eugene O'Neill's play *Long Day's Journey into Night*). When Joel asks if she thinks her school dissertation will be published, the Kaufman wit again shines through as she replies, "I don't know. I'm not sure there's a big public demand for books on Calvinism and misogyny."[33] Although the Naomi scenes had been filmed (played by Ellen Pompeo), Michel Gondry felt it was too late in the story to introduce the audience to another character. Kaufman revealed that at this point, Joel "realizes he loves Clementine and he rejects Naomi all over again. But it's the way he does it. She keeps saying, 'Is there anyone else?' And he says, 'No.' He just won't be straight with her." Although the scenes were eventually cut, Kaufman would have preferred to included them. He added, "I fought it. I really like the complication of having her in there. I think it makes Joel more culpable."[34]

When Joel walks through one of his last memories on screen, it is actually a scene from the first time he met Clementine at the party on the beach with Rob and Carrie. Unlike the cautious Joel, Kaufman gives us another glimpse into Clementine's impulsive character as she trespasses onto a private beach home closed for the season. It serves as an opportunity for adventure and a way to be alone with Joel, while if he had his druthers, he would never put himself in this awkward situation. When he recalls this memory, he agrees that she is exciting and he is attracted to her spontaneity. However, because he ran out of the house at the time and consequently the actual experience, they cannot reconstruct a proper ending to this recollection. Clementine urges him to come back and at least make up a good-bye, but the house is literally crumbling all around her as she speaks. She tries to forge a new memory by lovingly whispering, "Meet me in Montauk."

Although absent from the final film, as a segue to the beach house scene, Clementine asks Joel if he has ever read the poet Anna Akhmatova. When he replies that he loves the writer and Clementine is jubilant that they both adore her poetry, they have to question whether they originally referenced her before or after they saw the winter beach house. Joel feels that if they did mention her beforehand, that it would seem too coincidental that way, or perhaps it was just preordained. What he doesn't yet realize is that his experience is binary. Clementine goes on to quote Akhmatova: "Seaside gusts of wind, and a house in which we don't live."[35] It may have been important to Kaufman to mention Akhmatova, because the Russian poet exemplifies a courageous soul who felt she was estranged from her memories but was forced to reconcile with her difficult past. She led a tragic life under Stalin's regime, but found the strength to stand up for herself and her work. Joel and Clementine's mutual love for the poet help them bond, and Kaufman imbues Joel with the courage to face his fears and forge onward in his relationship.

After the winter beach house memory disintegrates, the film returns to the scene in which Joel and Clementine are in Joel's car returning from a night on the frozen Charles River. Because of the mobius strip nature of the film and Kaufman's writing, the audience sees that Patrick has already tried to make inroads into Clementine's life and we hear his voice on her answering machine as she quickly grabs her toothbrush and mail on her way back to Joel's car. When she opens her mail from Lacuna and reads Mary Svevo's letter aloud, Clementine and Joel have no idea what the cryptic message means. On the audiotape, we hear Clementine's voice complaining about Joel and how she wants to erase him from her life. In the film, the tape reveals that Joel bores her and she is sick of his mopey, puppy dog face. However, in the shooting draft, Kaufman has Clementine divulge even harsher, personal stabs such as, "How could I even look at them [children] if they looked like him? How could anybody?"[36] Sitting together in the car, as far as they know, they just met each other, so hearing her bitter rant, one has to wonder if they can fully digest the pain of the Lacuna tape. Joel obviously knows he is being insulted, but does he feel the betrayal of a close, trusted friend/girlfriend of two full years of his life, or as he implies, is this a cruel trick by a deranged acquaintance? Kaufman himself questions how well a person can absorb that kind of information if they haven't yet experienced it. They both realize they have no memory of the last two years of their lives.

Clementine later seeks out Joel at his apartment to find him queasily listening to his own voice on a Lacuna tape, complaining about her. Just as he was hurt by her angrily listing his bad traits, now she hears what irked him about her. She overhears him say, "[she's an] amazing, burning meteorite...will carry you to another world where things are exciting. But what you quickly learn is that ... it's really an elaborate ruse."[37] The audiotape continues to play as Clementine apologizes and Joel expresses regret for what he said.

At the end of the final film version, Clementine is ready to walk away from Joel, because she foresees the whole drama happening again and again—that they are doomed to repeat the past, so why should she bother. Joel, feeling this new illumination (care of Mary Svevo's decision to mail the Lacuna tapes) might be the sea change they have needed, asks Clementine to wait. Although reluctant, they both seem to feel the pull of willing to try again. This could be a fresh start for them. This moment draws parallels to the ending of Munro's "The Bear Came Over the Mountain," when the husband, Grant, once again visits his wife in the nursing home. Upon this certain visit, Grant has come to terms with his wife's possible Alzheimer's disease and even goes so far as to bring her love interest back to surprise her; however, this time his wife knows him as her husband and welcomes him with open arms. She is either through punishing him or is very lucid today. She tells him, "You could have just driven away."[38] Like Grant, Joel too has the option to walk away from the relationship once he knows Clementine has had her memory erased, but both men persevere.

At the end of the movie *Eternal Sunshine of the Spotless Mind,* the final scene in which Joel and Clementine have fun cavorting on a winter beach could imply future happiness, or this may be just a scene from their past. For the hopeless romantic, it is a sign of possibility; however, at the end of Charlie Kaufman's original screenplay, the story ends 50 years in the future with Clementine once again back at the Lacuna office. On the database, we see that the older Clementine has undergone this erasure process 15 times in the last 50 years: all of them involving Joel. An elderly version of Mary is still serving as the receptionist (implying that Mary underwent the erasure process again). The last written scene depicts an elderly version of Clementine hooked up to the erasing machine, while the old man version of Joel leaves a message on her phone asking why she won't return his calls. After the phone message, one of the technicians attending to old Clementine's procedure reaches over and hits "erase."

One of the major overriding themes of the Oscar-winning screenplay is the concept of existentialism versus fate: free will versus determinism. Is Lacuna's erasure process merely faulty, or do Joel and Clementine really have a choice in the world? Are they, as Joel's father predicts, "sewn into fate"? Although their minds have been cleared of the past, they are still attracted to each other on the beach at Montauk and on the train. Despite the fact that Joel is not an impulsive person by nature, he is compelled to call in sick from work that day and take the train that will once again lead him to Clementine. Was he following his own intuition? Was he blindly playing a role in a story (his fate) that was already written? Is Joel just a puppet? One is again reminded of Kaufman's other puppets and puppeteers struggling with choice versus fate in *Being John Malkovich.*

Another of Kaufman's themes is the question of ethics. Although both Clementine and Joel both freely choose to undergo the memory erasure process, what responsibility does Lacuna have in aiding them to mutilate their brains? Is Dr. Mierzwiak acting from a core of compassion or is he a clean-up man, wiping away messy mistakes and regrets of his own? Are he and his staff exploiting their clients' pain? From the looks of their shabby office, it doesn't appear as if is he is exploiting them for monetary gain. Then again, he may have homes all over the world and simply does not reinvest his earnings into his business. His decrepit workplace may be a clever front, while he boards his yacht just off the Amalfi Coast.

Many films in modern cinema have used a form of memory erasure or memory tweaking as part of the plot. Characters in films such as *Here Comes Mr. Jordon* (1941); *Heaven Can Wait* (1978); *Down to Earth* (2001), which is the third incarnation of the same film; *Chances Are* (1989) and

Superman II (1980), all find themselves living with their minds having been altered. The only film in which the ethical question of memory erasure does not come in to play is *Superman II*, as Superman makes the decision to wipe his beloved Lois's memory of his true identity and their relationship. Although the choice is not Lois's, it is unnecessary to question Superman's motives as he has proven he only acts from truth and compassion. It is *his* sacrifice for him to erase her memory of their love for each other. He, of course, retains the memory for them both and at the end of the story, he is the only one who has to suffer the loss and return to being treated as hapless Clark Kent in her eyes. Would it have been more compassionate for Joel to allow Clementine to keep her wish to have him erased from her memory? Would that be asking too much of a mortal, and if fate is forcing Joel's hand, did he even have the choice?

Much like the works of Philip K. Dick, Chris Marker, and Gabriel García Márquez, Charlie Kaufman's scripts certainly have elements of the fantastical, but Kaufman's characters' journeys are always based in truth. In an era when a screenwriter can see the box office rewards of churning out pages on the power of talking chipmunk sequels, the hilarity of unplanned teen pregnancy, and preening pirates (with apologies to Johnny Depp), Kaufman explores eternal philosophical questions, the price of memory, and the meaning of an enduring love. The uniquely reflective modern filmmaker has said he wants the audience to have a different experience of his films upon repeated viewings. Indeed, one's experience would be quite different each time after a night of selected memory erasure from Lacuna.

The film was released in March of 2004, and although some critics found the nonlinear quality of the story to be muddled, it was mostly met with open arms. Audiences enjoyed repeat viewings of the film and the box office totaled over $70 million worldwide. Roger Ebert spoke of the film's emotional core and publications such as *Time Out New York* counted it as one of the best films of the decade. In a list that included *The Royal Tenenbaums* (2001), *No Country for Old Men* (2007), *There Will Be Blood* (2007), and *Zodiac* (2007), avclub.com ranked *Eternal Sunshine of the Spotless Mind* the number one film of the 2000s. They noted, "It's the rare film that shows us who we are now and who we're likely, for better or worse, forever to be."[39]

Whether or not it was Kaufman's fate to provide the world with *Eternal Sunshine of the Spotless Mind,* he was rewarded for his endeavor. If accolades mean that one is on the correct path in life, Charlie received the message loud and clear when in 2005 his original script won him an Academy Award. It would also garner him his third BAFTA and the prestigious PEN American Center Prize.

The long process—from pitching the idea in 1998 with a throbbing toothache, to deleting the many beloved snow scenes because the budget would not allow it, to fighting to keep the production in the United States instead of Canada, to including Paul Proch's artwork to help flesh out Joel's sensibility—culminated in something that pleased both Kaufman and audiences. The good omens started to appear in 2003 when nature or fate or some unknown force had provided the filmmakers with one of the snowiest winters in years. Kaufman got his wish and the team was able to film the dreamlike landscape of the snow-filled beach. The winter beach house was one of the first ideas Kaufman had for the eternal love of Joel and Clementine and now the weather was validating his plan. The journey from script to screen took several wrong turns along the way and could have failed many times, but Kaufman is always willing to embrace that risk.

By 2004, *Time Magazine* had listed him as one of the 100 most influential people in the world. The art of screenwriting had helped carve out a path for him, but the need to challenge himself was always close at his heels. He would spend the next four years writing and crafting a film that would serve as his feature film directorial debut.

Hope Leaves the Theater and What I Really Want to Do Is Direct

> I would bet everything I have that you will some day direct.
>
> —Charlie Rose to Charlie Kaufman

"I've had this experience where people say that I'm depressing or 'so sad' and why am I so sad. My experience in the world is that when someone has written something or articulated something that is close to me but hasn't been articulated or written and I recognize it, I feel a common humanity that's overpowering to me. It's actually a time where I feel less alienated from the human race and I feel, in a way, pleased to be part of this thing." Kaufman explained with great clarity, "And you know, when you combine it with the idea that this thing, this painting or this book might have been written two-hundred years ago and this person who created this thing is dead and has been dead for a long time … is me. And then you know that history is not this *thing,* but you know that this person was in this world and going through it with as much urgency and sadness and passion and loneliness."[1]

Before Charlie Kaufman's directorial debut, *Synecdoche, New York,* screened at the Cannes Film Festival in May of 2008, Kaufman penned two "sound shows," entitled *Hope Leaves the Theater* and *Anomalisa,* for film composer Carter Burwell. Burwell, who had previously worked on Kaufman's films *Being John Malkovich* and *Adaptation,* also tapped the Coen Brothers for his experimental staged readings for Theater of the New Ear. A sound play differs from a good old-fashioned traditional radio play in that a sound play is meant to be seen as well as heard by a live audience. As in a full-fledged play, an audience convenes to watch a performance on a stage; however, the stage is clear of any scenery and the audience is watching actors sit on stools with their scripts in hand. Carter Burwell and his seven-piece orchestra play in front of the seated actors, and a foley artist is on stage with all the props he might need at his disposal. The entire story has to be conveyed with voices, music, and sound effects.

Part of the reason Kaufman wanted to take on the project was that he was having trouble finishing writing what would be his directorial debut, *Synecdoche, New York.* He had been working on the screenplay for so long that he jumped at the chance to write something different, and the short sound plays seemed just the antidote. He was also excited about the chance to meet Joel and Ethan Coen, who were also contributing work to Burwell's project. He had always admired their work, including their films *Fargo* (1996), *Barton Fink* (1991), and *Miller's Crossing* (1990), on which Burwell served as composer.

The performance pieces from all involved ideally had to be seen and not merely heard, because (as in much of Kaufman's work) what is being said only scratches the surface of what is really transpiring. Starring the high-wattage cast of Meryl Streep, Peter Dinklage, and Hope Davis, the sound-only production plays opened in April of 2005 at St. Anne's Warehouse in Brooklyn and went on to play in London at the Royal Academy as well as Royce Hall in Los Angeles.

Kaufman's first of the two sound plays, *Hope Leaves the Theater,* is about a character named Hope (Hope Davis) talking about making an exit. The double entendre of the story is set in the exact present with the actors playing themselves, actors, and an audience. The real audience sitting out in the dark watches the fake audience react to the real actors and the characters they are playing. Somewhere, Franz Kafka is blushing.

Kaufman explained the creative collaboration:

> The play starts out in the woman in the audience's head, who's played by Hope Davis, and it's before the play starts. But they're all three [actors] sitting onstage, the house lights are up, the people are coming back in to the theater—the real people—and you start to hear this voiceover inside someone's head, and you start to hear her thinking about, oh, look, there's Meryl Streep onstage. She starts thinking about things and Meryl Streep starts thinking about Hope Davis. And then the real audience starts to hear it, and they start to listen and they start to get it. That's very palpable: the moment you feel people in the audience start to get what's going on is very exciting, and all of that is lost on radio.[2]

Kaufman had always wanted to work with Hope Davis based on her performance in Lawrence Kasdan's film *Mumford* (1999). He was taken with her portrayal of Sophie Crisp, a talented woman suffering from chronic fatigue in a small town. In a difficult role in which the character's current life was informed by depression and unexplained physical pain, Davis's innate humanity seeped through as the character she played was embarrassed to be in a place in her life where she was forced to live at her parents' home. Her empathy and authenticity was palpable as she told her doctor that everyone thinks chronic fatigue syndrome is bullshit until it happens to them.

Hope Davis, the award-winning actress, remembered when the notoriously shy Kaufman phoned her. "He called and said, 'I'm doing this thing, but you probably don't want to be a part of it.' I said, 'Of course I do—count me in.'" She also recalled learning about the experimental nature of the play: "We were all wondering and kind of worrying about what it would be like to be an audience member. There's nothing all that visual. It's actors sitting on stools. But we did it in New York for three nights and everyone I know said it was one of the most exciting evenings of theater they remembered. People were incredibly intrigued by the form."[3]

Kaufman wondered how the work would be received and Davis noted that he was nervous about the piece and wasn't sure if it was working, so he began to rewrite it. Kaufman needn't have worried and was stunned on opening night when the audience was thrilled. Part of his concern was that he wouldn't be able to sell tickets to the Los Angeles audience. Davis, however, was sure of its merit and reassured the writer/director as best she could. Of working with Kaufman at the helm, Davis added, "He's just the loveliest kind of most humble guy. We all loved the piece so much, and we had a lot of laughs. Somebody asked if we'd be willing to do it on Broadway for a couple weeks, and we all said we wanted to. It will be hard if we have to let it go."[4] Davis's costar Peter Dinklage, whose starring role in *The Station Agent* (2003) wowed critics and audiences alike, added, "It just takes you somewhere. And because it's a radio play, with the music and the sound effects, it's great when you close your eyes and listen to it. Charlie's such a brilliant man and so original. I'll do anything he wants me to do."[5]

The play was well received and the audience had a great time as luminaries Meryl Streep and Hope Davis made fun of themselves, their characters, and the audience alike. The show even got a big laugh when one of the characters said that the writer, the real Charlie Kaufman, had committed suicide.

For Kaufman's second sound play, entitled *Anomalisa,* he used the pen name Francis Fregoli. The pseudonym is a reference to a psychiatric disorder called the Fregoli syndrome, in which a person believes that different people are in fact a single person who changes appearance or is in disguise. The syndrome may be related to a brain lesion and is often of a paranoid nature. Someone suffering from Fregoli syndrome believes that a person can change their appearance and gender within seconds, leaving behind only vestiges of clues as to who they really are. An example is thinking that your ex-wife is disguising herself as your boss. Your boss looks and acts the same as he usually does, but there are ticks or telltale words he now uses that convince you that this is your ex standing in front of you. Although the playbill read that Francis Fregoli is the pen name of an established writer, who wished to remain anonymous, Charlie Kaufman's penchant for reading about psychotic syndromes bled through.

Anomalisa, starring David Thewlis, Jennifer Jason Leigh, and Tom Noonan, is a play about a man in which everybody in his life is the same person. Kaufman has always admired the work of director Mike Leigh and was thrilled to work with Thewlis, who is one of Leigh's inner circle and had starred in Leigh's harrowing film *Naked* (1993). Jennifer Jason Leigh's work had always powerfully affected Kaufman, especially her performance in the Coen brothers' *Hudsucker Proxy* (1994). They enjoyed working together so much that Kaufman went on to cast the actress again as the conniving, dusted Maria in his directorial debut *Synecdoche, New York*.

Rounding out the cast of *Anomalisa*, Kaufman was perhaps most excited to work with the enigmatic writer/director/actor Tom Noonan. The shy writer had long admired Noonan and his plays, screenplays, and films, especially his self-penned and self-directed movie *What Happened Was* (1994). Kaufman thoroughly enjoyed their collaboration on *Anomalisa*.

The program notes for *Anomalisa* open with the beginning of the epic poem *Divine Comedies* by the Pulitzer Prize–winner James Merrill: "I yearned for the kind of unseasoned telling found / In legends, fairy tales…"[6] Much like Kaufman, the autobiographical poet is known for transforming private moments of his life into plays, and the initial premise of the poem mirrors Kaufman's struggles with writing. Both writers' personal relationships inform their work, and their writing demonstrates a great understanding of life's inherent duality.

Anomalisa begins with Michael Stone, a self-help guru and book author, traveling to a conference in Ohio where he'll meet and greet fans. After holding a seminar featuring his tome about the customer service business, he holds court in a bar with his female fans. The now beyond tipsy and sleazy Stone takes fan Lisa (Jason Leigh) to his hotel room. There is something wrong with Lisa (making her an anomaly) although she doesn't want to discuss it, other than mentioning she hasn't had sex in eight years. The drunken book author falls in love and intends to leave his family for her. As he boozily murmurs her name, he slurs it into something sounding like "Anomalisa."

The sex scene generated laughs from the audience as the actors sat up on stage and moaned and breathed into the microphones. The Foley artist furiously rubbed silk sheets together as the actors escalated their moans. After a beat, the two characters' voices affected falling back onto a bed, sighing in relief as the Foley artist simulated a sound evoking a Bic lighter.

Tom Noonan, who sat between Thewlis and Jason Leigh on stage, played many different characters (in traditional radio show style), including a cab driver, and a hotel desk clerk. He also gave voice to Michael Stone's nightmare in which he believes that everyone in the world is in love with him but is actually one "group" personality who constantly needs things from him. Stone's psychotic dream and paranoid conversation with Lisa at breakfast the next morning leads us to believe that he has a form of Fregoli syndrome. During breakfast he tells Lisa that he loves her, and only her (meaning he doesn't love "all of them" from his nightmare). Stone's psychosis begins to seep through as he hears Tom Noonan's voice superimposed over Lisa's. Subsequently, Stone begins to rant ad nauseum at the conference that day and has a complete breakdown upon returning to his family.

Working with such a critically acclaimed, as well as famous cast on the sound shows, Kaufman generously admitted, "I had a very difficult time, just a few years ago even, meeting people like that. Meeting Meryl Streep before she did *Adaptation* was terrifying for me. I was terrified. And that's not an unusual thing for me. So if I imagine myself at that point in my life being able to [direct a feature], I don't think I could have done it. But I realized doing the plays, that I have ideas these people, my favorite actors, are responding to ... I overcame some personal obstacle of shyness or insecurity in that regard, which is a big deal for me."[7] Directing some of his favorite actors for Theater of the New Ear ultimately gave him the confidence to helm what would be his directorial debut, the highly anticipated *Synecdoche, New York*. After a supportive and encouraging work experience with Sony on the film *Adaptation,* Amy Pascal, Chairman of Sony's Columbia Pictures, suggested to Kaufman and Spike Jonze that she would love to see them do a horror movie together. The three got to talking and instead of planning a standard horror genre project, they considered the perhaps even scarier themes of aging, isolation, regret, illness, and mortality. Kaufman wasn't interested in genre horror, but rather a horror movie of the soul, along the lines of Todd Haynes's compelling film *Safe* (1995) or Peter Weir's atmospheric *Picnic at Hanging Rock* (1975).

In 2004, Kaufman began to put thought to paper and over two years later he emerged with a script. He had the opportunity to finish the story at Yaddo, the artists' colony in Saratoga Springs, New York. The gorgeous, upstate 400-acre estate provided a much needed peaceful, nurturing environment in which Kaufman could finish what would be his directorial debut. Other than the peace and quiet, Kaufman was naturally drawn to the hallowed halls, which since Yaddo's inception in 1900 has seen the likes of Sylvia Plath, Philip Roth, Patricia Highsmith, and Flannery O'Connor walking the grounds. In fact, Highsmith, one of his biggest literary influences, bequeathed her entire estate to Yaddo.

In titling his screenplay, he wanted the name to recall a small town where little theater was offered, such as Poughkeepsie or another upstate hamlet outside of the Big Apple. When a draft of the script was first leaked onto the Internet in 2007, the cover page read, "Schenectady, NY." Kaufman maintains that "Schenectady" was never the title for his story and that perhaps whomever scanned in the script and posted it to the net, changed his title page, possibly to avoid detection. Once a screenplay is sent to a literary agency, it is stamped with their logo, leaving an identifying mark that would have been obvious to Internet readers. As Kaufman and Sony started to do marketing for the movie, the true title, *Synecdoche, New York,* emerged. It is a play on words in that the word *synecdoche* sounds like the name of a small town in New York State, and is a figure of speech by which a part is used to describe the whole, or vice versa. When the audience sees a child's badly scuffed shoe strewn on a hot pavement amidst a vicious biker gang in *Mad Max* (1979), they don't need to see the entire pummeled child to know what has happened. We understand that the shoe is representative of the whole bloody mess.

The original plan for Sony and Kaufman was for Spike Jonze to direct *Synecdoche, New York,* but by this time, the director was already mired in the *Where the Wild Things Are* film project. As Jonze and Kaufman discussed Charlie himself as the possible new director, signing the untested Kaufman initially proved to be too risky for Sony and the film was put in turnaround. Jonze was of course still interested in directing the script, but Kaufman didn't want to wait the three years or so for his colleague's schedule to free up. Amy Pascal, always a proponent of Kaufman's work, was eager to work with him again yet was on the fence about the change in plans. Although putting a project in turnaround is usually a bad omen, Pascal's decision to free up Kaufman's script was a gracious gesture. Sony could have just as easily decided to hold on to the project for years and let it languish. By letting go of the project, Sidney Kimmel Entertainment almost immediately stepped up with the necessary financing. Kimmel was also on board to accept Kaufman as director and, in the ultimate coup for Kaufman, offered him final cut (a writer's dream come true and not something he would have been granted by Sony). Spike Jonze was available to collaborate with his friend as a producer.

Kaufman had always had aspirations to direct and was luckily at a point in his life where he no longer cared if he failed in his endeavors. Conversely, he had taught himself to embrace failure, and the concept continued to drive him. Bravely, the Oscar-winning writer asserts that the notion of failure is the true reason he does anything. To him, failure is an important component of success and he believes that one can't do anything truly interesting if one is not willing to fail. It's not a negative thing for him, as it's merely the possible result of doing something he doesn't yet know how to do. *Synecdoche, New York,* specifically, was a very personal story, and Kaufman felt he was the best choice to direct it, because he didn't think anyone would understand the script the way he did.

The movie had a dream cast including some of the most highly respected women working in film today, including Catherine Keener, Michelle Williams, Samantha Morton, Emily Watson, Jennifer Jason Leigh, Dianne Wiest, and Hope Davis. Rounding out the enviable ensemble was Oscar-winner Philip Seymour Hoffman and Kaufman's friend Tom Noonan.

For inspiration, the director suggested that Spike Jonze watch Noonan's movie *What Happened Was* for its dramatic dynamic between two people in only one room. Despite being limited to one claustrophobic setting, Kaufman was interested in the subtleties of the dialogue and characterizations. He expounded, "It's amazingly well written and acted., You can watch this very simple movie between two characters and, depending on your mood, see different things in it every time."[8]

On having the opportunity to work with Noonan again and the rest of his *Synecdoche, New York* cast, Kaufman said, "It was great to have them and they all agreed to do the film. I cast Emily Watson because I already had Samantha Morton and both of them occupy the same space in my head. So subsequently the whole casting took place like that. Samantha told me that she was cast in a movie where the director told her how much he loved her in *Breaking the Waves* (1996), and she had to tell him that it was Emily Watson. I guess it's a common mistake, but it was fun to have them together in the film."[9]

When asked if he wrote the role of Caden with Philip Seymour Hoffman in mind, Kaufman replied, "No, I sort of make it a point not to write with actors in mind. And when I was writing this, Spike Jonze was going to direct it, so I wasn't going to be doing the casting. But I don't think about actors when I write because I think what I'd do then is write what my understanding of Phil Hoffman is, as opposed to creating a character that maybe some actor can come to and enlarge with their personality." Kaufman clarified, "But that being said, he was the first person I thought of and he seems to me the perfect person to play that."[10]

In the original draft of the script, small-town theater director Caden Cotard (Philip Seymour Hoffman) mounts the play *Equus,* written by Peter Shaffer in 1973. Known for its severe emotional themes, Kaufman wanted to do a very realistic, gory, violent version of the play with animatronic horses. However, the filmmakers could not obtain the rights to this modern psychological drama. Fortuitously, once they procured the proper rights to use Arthur Miller's *Death of a Salesman,* Kaufman realized that this classical piece about the nature of identity might prove to be even better than *Equus* for his purposes. It was indeed serendipitous, but not intentional. The drama gods were in his favor, and there is something poignantly and wonderfully sad about having young people perform *Death of a Salesman.*

As the movie begins, the audience is introduced to Caden, a weary, forty-ish, greying, out of shape father. He is having trouble getting out of bed. Kaufman has always enjoyed wordplay, and Caden's last name, Cotard, refers to a medical diagnosis in which the patient believes that she or he is dead, decaying, or beyond detached from themselves and the world. The name *Cotard* is also a reference to a character in Marcel Proust's literary epic, *In Search of Lost Time.* Proust's Dr. Cottard in volume one, *Swann's Way,* displays some of Caden Cotard's characteristics: "Dr. Cottard was never quite certain of the tone in which he ought to reply to any observation, or whether the speaker was jesting or in earnest."[11]

As the film *Synecdoche, New York* opens, Caden's wife, Adele Lack (Catherine Keener), and daughter, Olive (Sadie Goldstein), are going about a typical morning as the audience hears a radio announcer comment that it is the first day of fall. Caden manages to make his way outside his house, in his pajamas, and this is the first time the audience glimpses a tall, middle-aged man, who seems to be watching Caden from across the street, or perhaps he is just taking a walk in the neighborhood. In the script, it is raining, so the stranger seems out of place and looming.

When Kaufman was reworking the scene in which Caden, Adele, and Olive are in the kitchen together in the morning, he decided he would include the real newspaper headlines from that day, as a way of grounding the beginning of the movie in reality. The Schenectady, New York, newspaper he's holding is dated October, giving the audience a clue that time is already passing quickly, much quicker than the time it takes to simply rise and retrieve a newspaper. Kaufman himself misread the headline that morning and thought for a second that Harold Pinter had died, when in reality, he had just won the Nobel Prize. Kaufman also made it a point to have Caden mention other news that day, such as the Avian flu being found in Turkey and a female track athlete who had died, because he liked the idea of moving from the real, documented world of the newspaper, which one could verify, to a more surreal examination of what is fictional, such as the *year* on the paper, 2040. What appealed to him is that it *had* to be made up.

Other than the very tangible date on the newspaper versus the time referenced by the radio announcer, Kaufman also depicts the subjective nature of time by including various shots of clocks. The clocks are set to disparate times as the date on Caden's newspaper changes while he reads it. Kaufman explores the idea of time passing, and passing faster as one ages. Caden is also living in a state of depression, and experiences time differently because he is stuck in a painful period. On the passing of time in the film, Kaufman said, "There is definitely a difference between emotional time [and chronological time]—or maybe there is only emotional time. One of the things that I do in the movie is have time move more quickly as the character gets older. I've had that experience in my life. Summer vacations lasted for thirty years when I was nine. My years go by in days now, which is kind of terrifying once you realize what is at the end of that. There are two reasons for this. One is the aspect of [life] running away, and the other is how interchangeable our days are, the habitual existence that we live in."[12]

While some critics try to squeeze existential meaning out of every line of *Synecdoche, New York*, Kaufman said he made certain choices simply because they were funny to him. Examples of his wordplay are evident when characters mistake words like urologist and neurologist as well as psychosis and sycosis. Kaufman once walked by a clock graffitied on a wall in a city and believed he was late for an appointment. He found that funny and decided to use it in the movie.

He also sees the realistically comedic nature in a scene in which Caden's wife, in a half awake state, thinks Caden is talking about a stool in his office rather than blood in his fecal matter. Unafraid to include real human behavior in his films, where he once depicted the thorny subject of masturbation in the movies *Human Nature* and *Adaptation,* in *Synecdoche,* he unflinchingly presents other messy but nonetheless true and necessary bodily functions.

> I think there are things that aren't represented in movies that are a big part of everyone's life. This is a movie about health and about the body, so I wanted to have the body represented, and that was the way to do it. It was in keeping with the character to have this sick relationship with his bowel movement ... you're dealing with the body, and you're dealing with bodily functions. We romanticize everything about people in movies, and I decided that one of the things I don't like in movies is that people feel alone with their bodily functions in the real world, as if people in the movies don't do these things. We had a lot of fun making the different artificial feces in the prop department.[13]

When Caden bends down near the faucet to perform the everyday ritual of washing his face, a piece of the sink slams into his head, causing blood to rush all over his face. This scary episode begins a physical and psychological slide into poor health and chronic depression. Caden's excessive focus on his perceived failing health or hypochondria extends to everyone around him. When his four-year-old daughter's bowel movement is green, he projects his own obsessive worries onto her, but doesn't want to upset her. However, he can't hide the alarm on his face. Similarly, when Adele coughs for the first time, the audience knows that Caden will think the worst. To him, a simple cough is the equivalent of a cough in a Western—a symbol of imminent death.

Kaufman had mined this rich territory before when writing for the television show *Ned and Stacey* back in 1997. In the episode entitled "Where My Third Nepal Is Sheriff," one of the main characters cannot commit to traveling to Nepal with his good friend because he is wracked with fear that something might happen to him while he's away from his family and that he will never see them again.

In *Synecdoche, New York,* Caden attempts to control his surroundings and possibly get a grip on his health issues by cleaning and scouring his home. After Adele has left him and taken their daughter Olive with her, Caden begins his day by brushing his teeth and then seamlessly starts to scrub a rusted, paint-splattered table. This action can be seen as an attempt to clear away Adele's left-over debris and perhaps to clear his mind of the painful abandonment. Kaufman further explained, "As I'm writing, I start to see connections, and themes I didn't see, and that sparks other things. So then I go back and rewrite things or alter them. It's a combination of intuition and a lot of finessing. It becomes a combination of the rational and the irrational. I always go in circles. I have OCD to a certain extent, so I tend to do a lot of circular thinking. I think I do have OCD a bit."[14]

Kaufman's penchant for writing about psychotic syndromes crops up again when Caden finds himself at Adele's apartment door in New York: the name on the door reads Capgrass. Similar to the aforementioned Fregoli syndrome, Capgras delusion or syndrome is the belief that a loved one or close friend has been replaced by an exact duplicate or an identical-looking impostor. The Capgras delusion is classified as a syndrome that involves the misidentification of people, places, or objects, and it mostly occurs with schizophrenia but is also connected with brain injuries and dementia. An example in film can be found in *Invasion of the Body Snatchers* in which loved ones are being replaced by exact duplicates.

When Caden obsessively cleans Adele's apartment at the end of the story, this behavior could be symbolic of the only connection he has left to her. It could also be a manifestation of his guilt that he let time slip by and didn't do enough to find his wife and especially child when they first left the country. He can only communicate with her through the inane notes that she writes to her cleaning lady.

In the movie, Kaufman shows Caden's beloved Hazel (Samantha Morton), who runs the box office for his play, reading Proust and Kafka (she mentions *The Trial*, specifically), as a way to express an aspect of her character. In the original script, she is reading *Ulysses* but says she can't seem to get past the first line. She initially takes on these challenging tomes because she wants to impress Caden as well as improve herself. Kaufman liked the idea that the audience can see all the volumes of Proust near Hazel. When she asks Caden to recommend a book to her, it is implied that he mentioned Kafka, but we don't know for sure. Kaufman finds it an endearing quality of her personality that although she can't get through all of her books, she's damn well going to try. She wants to be someone more than her present identity allows for.

At one point in the film, Hazel is seen at her desk with a dog sleeping behind her in a little bed. In a subsequent scene, the dog is gone. Although most of Kaufman's original script is realized on screen, an unused scripted scene that would have helped the continuity shows Hazel driving home from a cast party after the play, and finding a severely wounded dog in the road. She brings him home to die a comfortable death (as comfortable as a dog *can* be with a tire track embedded in his body). On screen, although the movie audience never learns about the dying dog, the scene in which she is crying in her car is telling of her character nonetheless. Although Caden rejects Hazel's love at this point in his life, he later realizes that she is the one who offered to nurse him through his depression, just as she took on the responsibility of comforting a mangled dog at the end of its life. In a bit of Kaufman irony, the dog (aptly named Squishy) and Caden are the only ones alive at the end of the original script.

When Caden has an appointment with his therapist, Madeleine Gravis (Hope Davis), they talk about a man who committed suicide. Caden asks her why he killed himself, to which the therapist replies, "Why did *you?*"

Her reply begs the question Is Caden dead? Is this merely a misunderstanding or part of his therapist's cold, unsettling style of analysis. More intent on relentlessly marketing her new self-help book than listening to her client, she seems untrustworthy. Importantly, her last name, Gravis, is another of Kaufman's symbolic wordplay examples as the word *gravis* means "actively poisonous or intensely noxious." Often used in medical terminology, the word is usually connected to a vicious insect bite or a malignant disease. Dr. Gravis is seen with an increasingly bad skin condition on her leg but makes no notice of it. Is her decaying skin a reality or something Caden only sees as an illusion? Perhaps he sees the truth about her. In a very funny scene, she offers him a new copy of her book, and after he thanks her, she promptly tells him the price.

After the tepid success of Caden's staging of *Death of a Salesman,* he wins a generous genius grant from the MacArthur Foundation and rents a massive hangar in New York City to mount an ambitious theater piece depicting his real life as it happens to him. Charlie Kaufman has always valued writing about human issues as they occur in whatever phase of life he may be in at the time. He feels that writing about personal events while you are experiencing them lends real merit to illuminating the truth of the matter. To write about an emotional event that happened to you 15 years ago, with all the perspective and hindsight that time affords, is a bit of a cheat according to him.

In mounting his ambitious, giant construction of his version of New York City within the parameters of the abandoned warehouse, Caden hires Claire Keen (Michelle Williams), who played Mrs. Loman in his *Death of a Salesman,* to play his wife Adele. The name Keen, which is in direct opposition to his wife's name Lack, suggests exactly what Caden needs in his life: someone who is warm, alert, impassioned, and devoted. The new woman in his life, as her last name implies, brings him enthusiasm. The director and lead actress fall in love, marry, and have a daughter named Ariel. However, Caden soon realizes that he should now cast actors in the roles of his new wife and himself. This performance piece, now spiraling into a play within a play within a play, takes on the definition of the literary term synecdoche.

As part of Caden's loss after his marriage dissolved, he can no longer effectively communicate with Adele or their daughter Olive. When he attempts to call Adele in Europe, she pretends she can't hear him on the phone and in a great comic moment hangs up on him after she says: "I have to go, I'm famous!" In a heartbreaking scene in which Caden tries to find his now adult daughter, he finds her working in a seedy strip club and literally can't communicate with her as she is dancing behind a plastic barrier. He ends up screaming and pounding on the plastic case in an effort to get her attention, but she does not even recognize him. Communication issues arise in several of Kaufman's films. For example, the character Clementine angrily yells at the mumbling Joel in *Eternal Sunshine of the Spotless Mind* that she can never hear him. Similarly, in *Being John Malkovich,* Dr. Lester's receptionist, Floris, claims she can't understand a word that Craig Schwartz is saying. She does, however, seem to be able to apprehend quite effectively once she has a lustful interest in him. Ironically, when he gently rebukes her, she returns to her nonsensical wordplay as if her confused hearing and incomprehension is a protective shield. Kaufman implies that people only listen to you when they have something to gain. In *Synecdoche, New York,* Caden and his daughter have fallen so far from any semblance of connection that they literally no longer speak the same language. On Olive's deathbed in the hospital, she can only speak German as he struggles to communicate his regrets through a translator. As his daughter dies, never having forgiven her father, he stares at her tattooed flower and watches a petal fall from her body onto the bed and wither. This moment of surreal and metaphorical imagery perhaps most aptly showcases Kaufman's directorial imprint on the film.

Unlike his adult daughter, young Hazel manages to bring great comfort to Caden throughout his life. After his father dies, it is Hazel whom he seeks out for consolation. Although she has her own life now and has moved on despite his ambiguity toward her, she takes the time to talk him through his grief. He asks her what he should do, as if she knows the lines that will steer his life, and consequently his play, down the correct path. Early on in the story, when they share a drink on her couch, he finds some relief in passively taking direction as she tells him to get on his knees in front of her.

At the end of the story, the audience hears the character Millicent (Dianne Weist) give Caden directions in his earpiece, and he doesn't question this new character's motives. When she introduces herself as Ellen, the audience knows that this is also the name of Adele's housekeeper. Although ostensibly Caden only recently met her when she auditioned to play the part of the maid for his play, it is easier for him to be complacent and follow for awhile rather than forge ahead by his own design. Kaufman has said he is unsure who Millicent is and why she behaves the way she does. He goes so far as to say she seems somewhat sinister, and yet Caden accepts her without a fight. As in dreams, we don't stop to question a motive, but accept our immediate surroundings, however incongruous. This is similar to the way he accepts that Sammy (Tom Noonan) has been stalking him for decades and that Sammy knows Caden better than he knows himself. Instead of being horrified by this discovery, it is a relief to the exhausted theater director that someone else has in a sense been taking notes, and that he is not truly alone in the world and with his thoughts. The character's name, Sammy Barnathan, may be a clever play on the name of a Rabbi in the Talmud. Rabbi Samuel bar Nathan had a prayer leader removed from guiding a religious service because of his excessive bowing. This overly submissive posture greatly angered the Rabbi, and in turn he fired the cantor from his position. Tom Noonan's character Sammy essentially fires Caden from his life as his passivity is unacceptable. The physically stronger, charismatic Sammy replaces Caden in his work and personal relationship with Hazel. He becomes a type of twin as he capably steps into Caden's shoes. This reflects Charlie Kaufman's interest in twins and duality, also evident in his film *Adaptation.*

Kaufman asserts that we are all on a continuum. In relation to the end of *Synecdoche, New York,* he says, "There is this correlation between Caden's life and Ellen's life, between his loss of his daughter and her not ever having her daughter, between all those elements to the point where [Caden and Ellen] became the same person at the end of the movie. He apologizes to the actress who plays her mother for disappointing her and is in the process getting comfort and being told by this person who isn't his mother that she's proud of him, and this gives him inspiration to move forward, and he gets a new idea for how he's going to do his play. It's actually his first new idea since Hazel dies, and it never gets realized."[15]

Although Kaufman was able to see most of his original screenplay come to fruition, he did need to cut some scenes for the sake of time. One especially poignant scene absent from the final film is scripted directly after Caden is left standing alone in an alley in Berlin. After seeing piles of discarded, unopened birthday and Christmas gifts he has sent his daughter over the years, he meets a young French film student who brightens his day and gives him perspective. Kaufman explained that he had written the character as a woman who would serve to offer Caden an objective viewpoint and help crystalize what he had been experiencing. However, because of time constraints, this was one of the first things he chose to cut from the story.

Just as the character Lawrence of Arabia in David Lean's 1962 epic famously sighed, "I've come to the end of myself," Kaufman's Caden Cotard utters at the end of *Synecdoche* that he thinks he is here on the end of his life. A kindly woman in the original draft of the script understands his predicament and tells him that she sees the world moving in fast forward and that there are so many moments unobserved and therefore heartbreakingly lost. However, if they do go unnoticed, they do not create change. The two share a meal together and although the woman is quite young and Caden is an older man at this point in the story, they connect like we haven't seen previously. As they exit the cafe, a speeding car hops the curb and hits the woman. She dies as Caden attempts to comfort her. Although this scene had to be struck from the final film for time reasons, its content is incredibly telling. Although Caden only knew this woman for a short period, their platonic encounter gave him the connectedness and understanding he had been searching for.

To those critics who deemed the work too much of a dreamscape, Kaufman explained, "I find that I wake from dreams profoundly affected in ways that I don't usually experience in my waking life. Sometimes I'm so despairing after a dream, or sometimes I'm so joyful in the morning, and I don't necessarily remember all the details of the dream. I just wake up with a feeling of a hole in my heart for example, which is a really common thing for me and it follows me throughout the day."[16] Kaufman followed up this remark on *The Charlie*

Rose Show in the autumn of 2008, when he noted that the movie is based in dream logic and dream imagery. He cites the scene is which Hazel sweetly seduces Caden on the couch and she asks that he beg for a kiss. This is unlike previous behavior we would expect from her, and hence the scene becomes scary. Kaufman likens it to a dreamscape in which, for example, we can fly, and we just accept it instead of stopping the action to ask if we could always fly. He also mentioned that he is an excellent writer in his dreams, because he can finish a story in 15 seconds whereas in real life it takes him two years to write a script.

Although Kaufman doesn't like to explain definitively what the story means for him (because he wants the audience to have their own personal experience), he does offer, "Not only is Caden's play a synecdoche, but so is every work of art. There is no way to convey the totality of something, so every artistic creation is at most a representation of an aspect of the thing being explored. As for the part about this project mirroring Caden's, I can certainly see the obvious parallels, but I am not Caden. Perhaps he represents part of me and in that sense, he is a synecdoche of me."[17]

The reason Caden cannot finish the play is because, as in reality, new information is constantly introduced into his life. His experience mirrors the personal issues that Kaufman himself is dealing with in his life and wants to explore and analyze. As Kaufman changes, grows older, and experiences different things, his truth changes. By offering his audience such personal fair, the writer/director tries to get closer to a complete representation of the world as he sees it. However, he realizes he can never fully achieve his goal because, just as Caden, he continues to evolve.

Some of Kaufman's advisors didn't understand the dream logic of the film, especially the ending. Although Kaufman had final cut, he felt pressured to change the end and bring Adele back into the fold for proper closure or tweak the final scenes so that they appeared less bleak. Kaufman did not want to reconfigure the story to merely lure a larger audience to his film, yet he wrote a new ending that industry people loved, and he found money in the budget for reshoots. However, it was Philip Seymour Hoffman who gave Kaufman the courage to stick to his original plan. Of shooting the new ending, Hoffman said that he would shoot whatever Kaufman wanted, but he was of the strong opinion that the director should listen to his instinct to not change the ending. Due to the fact that Hoffman carried the film in that he appeared in every scene, Kaufman has great respect for him as an actor and a person. In a sense, Hoffman became his closest collaborator as the director and lead actor spent weeks talking about the characters, aging, mortality and illness. Hoffman helped give his director the confidence to say no to filming a more commercially viable ending to the saga. The studio, however, was unhappy with Kaufman's decision and even urged him to film the new ending and then decide later if he wanted to use it or not. Ultimately, the director held his ground and realized that if he shot an alternate ending that he might be forced to use it. Regardless of what some of his producers might say, he feels he made the proper choice.

Synecdoche, New York received passionately positive reviews after it screened at the Cannes Film Festival in May of 2008. Highly touted as one of the most anticipated features on the schedule, Richard Corliss at *Time* entitled his review: "Finally! An Instant Cannes Classic." The respected film reviewer happily reported, "For nine days the 61st Cannes Film Festival had been doddering along into a premature senility ... The Riviera fortnight has been so stodgy that we almost welcomed a wild, four-and-a-half hour misfire like Steven Soderbergh's *Che*. But now our (my) patience has been rewarded, our (my) biliousness calmed. One good movie can do that ... This year the savior is Charlie Kaufman's demanding, rewarding *Synecdoche, New York*."[18] A. O. Scott of the *New York Times* championed the film as well, noting of Kaufman, "He has created a seamless and complicated alternate reality, unsettling nearly every expectation a moviegoer might have about time, psychology and narrative structure. But though the ideas that drive *Synecdoche* are difficult and sometimes abstruse, the feelings it explores are clear and accessible. These include the anxiety of artistic creation, the fear of love and the dread of its loss, and the desperate sense that your life is rushing by faster and faster than you can make sense of it. A sad story, yes, but fittingly for a movie bristling with paradoxes and conundrums, also extremely funny."[19]

Although the film was chosen for a Friday night viewing at the festival (considered a lucky slot, previously held by *Pulp Fiction*), Sidney Kimmel Entertainment and UTA decided to screen the movie early for buyers. This move proved to be risky as Kaufman and his producers left France without a distributor. However, to put that experience in perspective, no American film garnered distribution that year on the croisette, including Steven Soderbergh's noteworthy and embattled biopic about Che Guevara. When the news came out of Cannes that *Synecdoche, New York* failed to find distribution, a wave of misinformation hit the wire as it was taken out of the context that 8 of the 10 specialty film companies were going out of business and the 2 remaining were looking for an indie comedy. Some of the news coming out of Cannes included Hollywood Elsewhere's Jeff Wells's review criticizing even the title of Kaufman's directorial debut. Wells claimed that a possibly unfamiliar word in a film's name would equal commercial suicide. He wrote, "Titles should always convey something that your average dumbass can understand—this one doesn't ... and later with the shots of pink urine and bloody stools sitting in the toilet ... I'll put up with no more than one human waste shot in a film. Here there were three." Wells added, "I was watching it, realizing after a time that there was no escape from the hangar, and wishing more and more that something else would happen. A visitor who isn't in the play upsetting the apple cart, say. Or a 747 crashing into the hangar and blowing it all to hell."[20]

Synecdoche, New York's producer and longtime Kaufman colleague, Anthony Bregman, shot back in a post on www.hollywood-elsewhere.com, "What piercing criticism you have for your readers! The title is too complicated for 'your average dumbass'? You'll put up with one but not three shots of bodily waste per film? There's no 747 crash in the story to make the film more entertaining? Now there's some meaningful suggestions for how to make better films. Such a shame Charlie Kaufman didn't consult with you before putting his finishing touches on the script. Or maybe it's just a matter of taste—after all, you did pretty much pan *Eternal Sunshine of the Spotless Mind* back in 2004."[21] When I spoke with Mr. Bregman on the phone in November of 2008, he admitted that he was exhausted and angry when he wrote the response, but he confirmed that he did indeed write it and that he stands by his thoughts on the matter. The producer of *Synecdoche, New York; Eternal Sunshine;* and *Human Nature* (and teacher at Columbia University's Graduate Film School) upholds his faith in moviegoers and shows a fierce loyalty to his friend and colleague Charlie Kaufman. Kaufman's response to Jeff Wells was that he simply doesn't think of people that way (as dumbasses, that is), and learning a new word, such as synecdoche, is never a bad thing.

Overall, the experience at Cannes hurt Kaufman personally because he wanted the distributors and audience to know how hard his cast and crew had worked on this project. He wanted recognition not for himself but for them, their talent, and commitment. He explained, "It was hard because the producers decided to screen the film for distributors a week before the official screening for the critics and the public. So when the film didn't sell, it became a stigma of the film that didn't sell and that really hurt us. Even though none of the U.S. films got sold, but it got stuck on us. There was a lot of speculation as far as why it didn't sell. So by the time it got to the screening, we had this negative press about us which is upsetting."[22] Soon after Cannes, however, the distribution house, Sony Pictures Classics recognized the obvious merits of the film, and scheduled a U.S. release date in time for Oscar season.

If the title *Synecdoche, New York* was problematic for some, Caden Cotard's ideas for a title for his play were some of the more comedic highlights of the film. Throughout the story, and as Caden ages, he mentions several new possible names. First, he tells Claire he is thinking about calling the project *Simulacrum*. When she admits she doesn't know what that means, he offers another title, *The Flawed Light of Love and Grief,* which is from Louise Bogan's poem "The Alchemist." Bogan, who survived an impoverished East Coast childhood to become a poetess in the 1930s and 1940s, manages to embody much of *Synecdoche's* sensibility: "I burned my life, that I may find / A passion wholly of the mind."[23]

Just before Caden auditions women to play the role of Millicent, he asks Hazel what she thinks of the possible title *Unknown, Unkissed, and Lost.* This reference is from Geoffrey Chaucer's book, one of the epic love poems, *Troilus and Criseyde.* In true Kaufman form, the story of Troilus and Criseyde focuses on the end of a doomed love affair. Just as Hazel abandons Caden for another man in *Synecdoche, New York,* so too does Criseyde leave her love. Known for its deep humanity and metaphysical posits, this epic poem seems apropos for Caden's purposes of a title: "You may weep here alone and cry and kneel: but love a woman so she knows it not, and she'll repay you with what you cannot feel: unknown, unkissed, and lost, is what's unsought."[24]

Just before Hazel's death, when she and Caden are sitting in bed enjoying a tender, quiet moment, he tells her he recently thought of another name for his play: *The Obscure Moon Lighting an Obscure World.* This title is a reference to a Wallace Stevens's poem called, "The Motive for Metaphor." Hazel replies that she thinks it might be too much. The modernist poet from Reading, Pennsylvania, always appealed to Kaufman, and perhaps he thought the poem helped sum up his character Caden's regrets: "The obscure moon lighting an obscure world / Of things that would never be quite expressed."[25]

After much pondering about the title of his own project, Kaufman told Salon.com, "I came up with a new understanding of what the title means, and it wasn't intentional. It occurred to me that every work of art is a synecdoche, there's no way around it. Every creative work that someone does can only represent an aspect of the whole of something. I can't think of an exception to that. So that means that this movie is a synecdoche, as an exploration of this man's life."[26]

After premiering at Cannes, publicity for the film was largely foisted onto the director, who was occasionally accompanied by Philip Seymour Hoffman and Catherine Keener. Embracing his role as director and in essence the film's champion, Kaufman embarked on an international tour schedule to introduce sold-out screenings and field queries during question-and-answer sessions. At the North American premiere of the film at the Toronto International Film Festival, Kaufman was met with favorable reviews and left feeling reinvigorated. "It's weird," he observed. "I've seen the movie now with a lot of audiences, and they're all different. In Toronto, audiences were laughing the whole way through. What I'd heard before, at all the screenings, was that the beginning of the movie is funny and then it gets really serious for the next hour and a half. At Toronto everyone was laughing through the whole movie, and I'm thinking, 'Oh yeah, that was a joke!' So it does vary, and can be taken in different ways."[27]

Often he was asked how he viewed the difference between the writing and directing experience. "I like writing but it's very lonely sometimes, and it requires a lot of discipline. It's the opposite of pragmatic, and directing is enormously pragmatic. It's also very structured. And it's managerial, so I have to figure out how to talk to people on an individual basis. It's not like there's one way to talk to actors; they're all different. I also have to let go of my natural personality traits, which are sulking and moodiness, and kind of become an adult, because that's required."[28]

The director also likened the experience to being a parent: "I'm the father of ... Well, she's eight now, but parenting is a relatively new experience for me, and I feel like there is that same kind of thing. It's kind of like, 'Okay, this is my job here. I can't be so insane around this person. She needs me not to be.' That comes across in all sorts of ways, like my trying really hard not to transmit my concern, because I have a lot of anxiety about medical things for example. It can be somewhat gratifying too, because I don't have that relationship with other adults where I need to comfort them or they come to me for that."[29]

What resulted from Kaufman's directorial debut was a highly personal, idiosyncratic, challenging view of the meaning of life and the nature of art. Initial viewings polarized critics, leaving the writer-turned-director feeling understandably exposed and spent. The *New York Times'* Manohla Dargis was moved by its ambition and existential scope, declaring, "It's extravagantly conceptual but also tethered to the here and now ... to be here now, alive in the world as it is rather than as we imagine it to be, seems a terribly simple idea, yet it's the only idea worth the fuss, the anxiety of influence and all the messy rest."[30] Two months later, the film still weighed heavily on the critic's mind and on the last day of the year 2008, Dargis wrote another piece on *Synecdoche, New York,* in which she said, "The film doesn't answer its riddles in one sitting, which makes sense given it's about one of the greatest mysteries: a human life. Its dense texture, thicket of literary references, medical terms, mordant jokes, eccentric images and myriad preoccupations are not there simply to drive you crazy (though they might) or show you how smart Mr. Kaufman is, or make you feel clever for watching its allusions. Rather, the film is a representation of Caden's inner world, or I'm guessing, Mr. Kaufman's, which of course would make it a synecdoche."[31]

In what Roger Ebert himself called an unconventional review, the veteran movie critic wrote, "This is a film with the richness of great fiction. Like *Suttree,* the Cormac McCarthy novel I'm always mentioning, it's not that you have to return to understand it. It's that you have to return to realize how fine it really is. The surface may daunt you. The depths enfold you. The whole reveals itself, and then you may return to it like a talisman."[32] Rex Reed, currently a columnist at the *New York Observer,* on the other hand, left the screening of *Synecdoche, New York* well before it was even over, and yet commented, "It's interesting, in a sadistic sort of way, to watch good actors crawling through quicksand, and this dreck is full of them." In his description of one of the characters, he wrote, "he uses a quirky look-a-like (Emily Watson) named Tammy, who in real life is a weirdo box office attendant named Hazel (Samantha Morton), whose house is literally and figuratively on fire and going down in flames."[33] While I myself haven't heard the word *weirdo* used since the third grade, it is refreshing to find someone wise enough to question reading Kafka and Proust. Many longtime readers of the *Observer* as well as fervent bloggers called for Reed's immediate expulsion from the newspaper and questioned why such irresponsible rants still merited a salary.

Beyond general misunderstanding, some critics and audiences may have been harshly divided because they were waiting for a safety valve or a hand up out of the deep recesses of Caden Cotard's mind. Kaufman explained that he intentionally didn't provide the audience with a 'hook' this time. In the way that he felt *Eternal Sunshine of the Spotless Mind* might be reduced to the explanation of someone's memory being erased, he didn't want *Synecdoche* to be summed up so easily. Moviegoers may have been waiting for a twist at the end of Caden Cotard's life, which would clarify his choices, but Kaufman felt that would be cheating. A tacked-on ending would be too glib and dishonest for the writer who esteems truth above all things.

As audiences have been force-fed a movie studio's three-act structure template and a guaranteed story resolution over the years, Kaufman understands that modern audiences may find *Synecdoche, New York* challenging. "I remember when I was a little kid in school, you'd be given an open-ended assignment, and there was this panic, like 'What do they want? I don't know what to do. What do they want me to do? I don't know what the assignment is.' We have to get over that. I've always said, 'There's no wrong way to look at this movie.' It's yours as a viewer. Immerse yourself in it. This is what I have to offer at this point in my life, and as much as possible, I'm going to separate my ego from it."[34]

In an inevitable comparison to his arguably more famous, previous directors, Eric Hynes, from IndieWire noted, "As director, Kaufman doesn't have the whimsical or ironic touch of Gondry or Jonze, making *Synecdoche, New York* a much heavier affair. Wherever they stand in the funhouse, regardless of absurd dress or situation, Kaufman's actors sell the truth of each particular moment. As a result, and seemingly against all reason, *Synecdoche* has a crashing emotional power. Masked in age-enhancing latex, awkwardly enjoying themselves beneath the sheets and coughing away smoke as the surrounding house burns down, Hoffman and Morton exchange vows of love and regret, and somehow it's the saddest, loveliest thing I've seen all year."[35]

Another frustration the director encountered was the consistent question at Q&As at screenings regarding the meaning of Hazel's constantly burning house. Unsatisfied with the notion that dream logic is ambiguous by design, audiences demanded a clear-cut answer. Above all else, Kaufman wants a moviegoer to impart his or her *own* experience, not his. A member of his crew told him that he understood the burning house in a very profound way, in that it represented his life. Hazel herself tells Caden that the end is built into the beginning. Kaufman explained, "She made a choice about her death by moving into that house; she died because of that house. It took a long time but she planted the seeds. The realtor even says to her, 'You

know it's an important decision how one wants to die.' At the very beginning of the movie Hazel decides this thing that is going to effect her forty
years later in her death. That's sort of like when the preacher says, 'You
make these choices and you may not know what's going to happen because
of these choices for twenty years. You may never know. You may never be
able to trace it back to their source.'" He continued, "But that's not what
this guy reacted to about that burning house. He reacted to the idea that
you make choices in your life and in some cases you know that they are the
wrong choices but you just don't know how to get yourself out of them, so
you make them your home. You live this thing that's obviously a hindrance,
whether it's a relationship or whatever, and you work around it and find
yourself there." Of the comedic side, Kaufman explained that yes, he sees
the silliness of putting yourself in that situation because the sellers are motivated regardless of faulty wiring, corroded pipes, or an eternal blaze in the
living room. A hurtful life experience that many women and men can relate
to is the that fact that Hazel wants a home of her own, but realizes she will
probably have to make this monumental decision without her loved one.
Kaufman recognized, "It's about Hazel making a decision because she feels
that in her life she is not going to have someone to buy a house with. She
has to settle for something that's not great because she's decided that this
thing isn't going to happen with [Caden]."[36]

Having traveled the world to promote *Synecdoche, New York* since its debut
at Cannes in May, at one point toward the end of the publicity tour, during
the last week of October 2008, Kaufman had finally had enough. He started
to tell the American and Canadian press that he was through with show business. Borne out of frustration and exhaustion, he told the *Los Angeles Times,*
"I feel embarrassed for even doing this in the world. I put this thing, that is
like me, my soul, in the world and I just feel like it's trampled. It makes me
feel like I don't want to do this anymore. I certainly don't want to try to sell
them, but I don't want to make them anymore either."

More than once, Kaufman has asked, "Why am I trying to seduce how
many millions of people for this thing to be worthwhile to the people who
invested? ... this business crap. Hollywood Oscar watch ... this thing that
people want to rip down because it's gotten too successful. It seems heart-
less to me. It's not based on anything to do with anyone's heart. It has to do
with anger. Everybody is really angry all the time. It makes me angry. I don't
want to be angry."[37]

Perhaps the single, universally embraced and agreed-upon moment of
brilliance uniting critic and audience alike, was the Pastor's sermon in the
funeral scene toward the end of the film. The scene does not appear in any
of the drafts because as producer Anthony Bregman will attest, Charlie
Kaufman wrote it the night before it was shot. Producer Spike Jonze was
surprised to see it in dailies and was moved by its poignancy. The actor
who delivered the page-long monologue (Christopher Evan Welch) had

auditioned for a different role in the film he didn't win, but was quickly faxed the new scene and asked to be ready to perform the next day.

In an appropriate blurring of the real and unreal, when *Synecdoche, New York* opened in Los Angeles in the fall of 2008, the Montalban Art Gallery announced an exclusive exhibition of Adele Lack's micro paintings and a private opening reception. The show was entitled, "Small Miracles" and consisted of 27 paintings. Visitors were, of course, supplied with magnifying glasses. Measuring approximately one-inch square in size, each painting was listed with a corresponding year of the work—ranging from 2005 through 2024. The Montalban also hosted a screening of the film the same evening they debuted Adele Lack's first West Coast exhibit. Her bio read that she was born in New York and hadn't had a major show until the age of 41 when she first brought her work to Berlin. Her major show *Adele Lack: Anstriche* was then displayed at Kunst Galerie. In Hollywood, the Montalban Gallery, which in reality is a Nike Sportswear store on Vine Street with an extra room upstairs, showcased badly copied printouts of the work of the real artist, Alex Kanevsky.

To achieve the look of Adele's tiny paintings for the actual film, Kaufman hired Kanevsky, who had studied mathematics at Vilnius University in Lithuania and painting at the Pennsylvania Academy of Fine Arts.

Since Adele Lack's art exhibition had been advertised in several places including a Variety.com blog as well as *Juxtapoz Art & Culture Magazine* online, attendees may have been expecting the real artwork from the feature film. A review of the "opening night show" posted on the Web site criticaldarling.wordpress.com was entitled "Small Disappointments." However, lending credence to the accompanying screening, Spike Jonze and Tom Noonan were in attendance.

By November of that year, a mere few weeks after he was ready to quit the business altogether, Kaufman was able to put his pain aside, and as he is wont to do, see the bigger picture. He also revealed that given a choice going forward, he wasn't eager to give one of his scripts to another director unless he needed to in order to pay the mortgage. In an article for *Interview* magazine, he expressed his wish to continue directing his own scripts as he told director David Cronenberg, "One of the things that I found really helpful, at least in my mind—and I've never discussed this with the actors or with the people I work with is that being a neophyte in directing, I feel like I have a kind of authority simply because I'm the writer as well. If I were doing somebody else's script or I adapted a book by Philip Roth, on set there would be a million different interpretations of the material and people could argue with me. Certainly on *Synecdoche, New York* we had discussions and arguments, but I felt like I had authority."[38]

Soon after Kaufman changed his mind about staying in the "Business we call Show," another change of heart occurred. Film critic Jeffrey Wells, who had initially said that *Synecdoche, New York* left him in an epic, saturnine funk, made a complete and utter about-face when he wrote, "The best film I saw at this year's Austin Film Festival turns out to be one of the best movies I've seen all year. *Synecdoche, New York* is a cinematic experience that I expect to stick with me for some time to come."[39] What a difference a few months, not to mention multiple viewings, make. Producer Anthony Bregman, who had followed Wells's evolving view of the film with interest, was pleased that with some time to digest the movie, people saw the merit in expanding their initial reaction. Indeed, it is one of Kaufman's long-held goals that if a person can glean something new or different from repeat viewings of his work, then he is doing his job correctly.

During the fall of 2008, Kaufman escorted his film to the 52nd London Film Festival, where he taught a master's class on filmmaking. The class had been sold out for weeks, and yet hundreds of people lined up outside the National Film Theatre attempting to get a seat. Periodically showing clips from his films and taking questions from the students, he spoke of his time working in television and his frustration with the media. He described an incident years ago, when he had trusted a writer from *Time* magazine and confided in her that he was picked on in school when he was young. Subsequently, the writer named the piece something similar to "Revenge of the Nerd," and he was offended that it had nothing to do with his actual work in film. He also revealed that he has thought about working in television again because he's interested in telling a story in long form over a long period of time, which doesn't often happen in movies. He would be interested in following a character over several decades.

On December 2, two months after the London Film Festival, actors Jason Bateman and Sandra Oh announced the nominations for the 2009 Film Independent Spirit Awards (formerly known as the Independent Spirit Awards) at the Sofitel Los Angeles Hotel. *Synecdoche, New York* was nominated for Best Screenplay and Best First Feature. Perhaps even more exciting was the news that *Synecdoche, New York* won the coveted Robert Altman Award. Established in 2007 shortly after Mr. Altman's death, the award symbolizes unique cinematic vision. *Synecdoche, New York* is only the second film to win this prestigious title, as in its first year the award went to Todd Haynes's film *I'm Not There.*

At the end of the year, in a *Time Magazine* article entitled "The Top 10 Everything of 2008," *Synecdoche, New York* found a proud spot as the second best film of the year, second only to Pixar's *WALL-E.* Richard Corliss wrote, "Ambition. That's what most independent films lack, and what the directorial debut of screenwriter Charlie Kaufman has, ad infinitum, ad gloriam ... The movie keeps getting bigger and weirder and denser and sadder and funnier, till all the pressure on Caden leads to a final implosion. A movie so human you'll want to argue with it, spank it, take it home or give it some Xanax, *Synecdoche* is the richest, most devious—I'll cut to the chase and say best live action film of the year."[40] Other than the beautiful review, Corliss also pointed out that Caden Cotard's name, other than referencing Proust's character Dr. Cottard from *Swann's Way* and the psychotic syndrome Cotard, is also an anagram for Acted Candor.

With candor to spare, to round out the year 2008, Kaufman broke one of his own rules and granted a television interview to someone other than the beloved Charlie Rose. On December 9, Kaufman was a guest on Stephen Colbert's eponymous TV show, *The Colbert Report*. Colbert, with whom he once worked on *The Dana Carvey Show,* asked Kaufman what the new movie *Synecdoche, New York* was about, and more importantly checked his notes and told him to make sure to use the phrases *feel good* and *sassy Chihuahua* in his explanation. Colbert cheekily asked what it would mean for him if he didn't "get the film": would that make him dumb? Kaufman's reply was that Colbert (and the audience) could not be wrong about what their experience of the film was. You could only be right.

One of the things Caden's subconscious was right about, if nothing else in his life, was that Harold Pinter *did* die—just not before he became the Nobel Laureate. On Christmas Eve 2008, the distinguished playwright died from cancer at the age of 78. Just as Kaufman dislikes offering an explanation of his work, being disinclined to impose his perspective on an audience, or simply not wanting to dilute it, so too did Pinter. Hesitant to explain the motivations in their work, both writers talk about how the writing process is just as mysterious to them as it is to an audience. In his speech upon accepting the Nobel Prize for Literature in 2005, Pinter attempted to explain his reluctance to divulge the meaning of his stories and how he realized his characters:

> It's a strange moment, the moment of creating characters who, up to that moment have no existence. What follows is fitful, uncertain, even hallucinatory, although sometimes it can be an unstoppable avalanche. The author's position is an odd one. In a sense, he is not welcome by the characters. The characters resist him, they are not easy to live with, they are impossible to define. You certainly can't dictate to them. To a certain extent you play a never-ending game with them, cat and mouse, blind man's bluff, hide-and-seek. But finally you find that you have people of flesh and blood on your hands, people with will and an individual sensibility of their own, made out of component parts you are unable to change, manipulate or distort.[41]

Whether audiences and critics loved or hated the characters and the story of *Synecdoche, New York,* it inspired passionate debate about identity and the meaning of existence. Kaufman concluded, "I think as you get older you start to—I've always been preoccupied with issues of dying and illness. All that stuff is not new for me, but it does become more a part of my life as I get older and watch people I know die and get sick. It's a real thing and it's a universal thing. No matter where you are in life, it dictates your decisions." The writer/director revealed, "I know that as a very young child, I was afraid of death. Many children become aware of the notion of death early and it can be a very troubling thing. We're all in this continuum: I'm this age now, and if I live long enough I'll be that age. I was twenty once, I was ten, I was four. People who are twenty now will be fifty one day. They don't know that! They know it in the abstract, but they don't *know* it. I'd like them to know, because I think it gives you compassion."[42]

From *Being John Malkovich* to *Synecdoche, New York,* Kaufman's compassion for his characters is unshakable. Like we all do, his characters make the same mistakes over and over again, yet the writer shows them nothing but tenderness and respect. Despite the comically absurd turns his stories may take, his protagonists nearly drown with the highly personal and yet universal questions of identity, mortality and free will versus fate. Throughout their complicated and exasperating journeys, their creator allows them to remain as deeply flawed as real people and yet he never judges them.

Though Kaufman doesn't offer an explanation, his interest in subjects such as doubles and duality in such projects as *Adaptation* and *Synecdoche, New York,* is perhaps borne of his childhood love of acting and inhabiting a different self for a while. Just as it was a great comfort for Kaufman to act in plays as a child and shed the painfully shy part of himself, his character Caden Cotard finally finds relief in life when strangely enough, a stalker offers to take over his identity. Similarly, the writer's invention of a twin brother, Donald Kaufman, was *the* construct that allowed him to push through the seemingly impossible assignment of adapting *The Orchid Thief.* The conceit of a twin saved the real Charlie Kaufman from losing the writing career he had worked so hard to achieve. Of his many achingly human characters, it is Donald who sums up the hard-won, underlying message of compassion throughout Kaufman's oeuvre: You are what you love, not what loves you.

I don't pretend to understand all of Kaufman's motivations and would be suspicious of anyone who claims they do, but it is clear that his drive for understanding his own truth and his willingness to embrace the possibility of failure make him a force to be reckoned with. At barely 50 years old, his profound influence on working screenwriters is palpable. From *I Heart Huckabees* (2004) to *I'm Not There* (2007) to *Cold Souls* (2009), stories dealing with the metaphysical are touted as "Kaufmaneque." Although these movies pale in comparison to Kaufman's relentless stare into the abyss, his name in cinema has come to mean existential fare and a highly advanced sense of comedy. His name also stands for a certain integrity so rare in the film industry. His willingness to write amidst the immediacy of his true life experiences rather than offer them through the filter of the safer distance of hindsight, sets him apart from the poseurs. He cuts deep, but his unsettling, unflinching emotional bravery allows us to get closer to our core selves and in turn connect to each other.

It is our immense gain that he is brave enough to make himself so vulnerable in his writing. His work will always remain relevant because he is unafraid to voice our greatest fears: that we made the wrong choices; that we were loyal to the wrong people; that we wasted our lives.

Although Charlie Kaufman is wary of labels because they are so reductive, the shy little boy from Long Island has become the philosopher laureate of the film world. While the press may claim that he is not forthcoming about his personal life, one only needs to read one of his richly crafted screenplays or watch any of his films to realize that there is no one more generous.

Notes

CHAPTER 1

1. Jim Windolf. "Interviewing Charlie Kaufman (As Brian Lamb)." *Vanity Fair.* October 20, 2008.
2. Ibid.
3. Ibid.
4. Stephen Applebaum. "Charlie Kaufman Interview: Life's Little Dramas." *The Scotsman.* May 9, 2009. http://thescotsman.scotsman.com/entertainment/ Charlie-Kaufman-interview-Life39s-little.5246560.jp.
5. "Lenny Bruce." *Absolute Astronomy.* http://www.absoluteastronomy.com/ topics/Lenny_Bruce.
6. "In Loving Memory of Humphrey Bogart." *BeingCharlieKaufman.com.* http:// www.beingcharliekaufman.com/index.php?option=com_docman&task=cat_ view&gid=50&Itemid=136.
7. Ty Burr. "Being Charlie Kaufman: The Writer Talks About Directing His First Film." *The Boston Globe.* November 2, 2008.
8. Peter Keough. "Outside the Frame: Charlie Kaufman Interview." *The Boston Phoenix.* November 7, 2008. http://thephoenix.com/Blogs/outsidetheframe/ archive/2008/11/07/charlie-kaufman-interview-part-i.aspx.
9. Kevin Maher. "Is Charlie Kaufman Out of His Head?" *Times Online.* October 4, 2008. http://entertainment.timesonline.co.uk/tol/arts_and_entertainment/ film/london_film_festival/article4867578.ece.
10. John Del Signore. "Charlie Kaufman, Director: Synecdoche, New York." *gothamist.* October 23, 2008. http://gothamist.com/2008/10/23/charlie_kaufman_ director_1.php.
11. Secher, Benjamin. "Charlie Kaufman's Mutant Horror Film." *The Telegraph UK.* May 15, 2009.
12. Maher. "Is Charlie Kaufman Out of His Head?"
13. Burr. "Being Charlie Kaufman."
14. Shari Roman. "It's Just An Interview, Charlie Kaufman." *Fade In* 7. no. 4. (2004).
15. Ibid.
16. Paul Proch and Charles Kaufman. "Eggboiler." *National Lampoon,* April 1984.

17. Paul Proch and Charles Kaufman. "God Bless You Mr. Vonnegut." *National Lampoon,* October 1983.
18. Ibid.
19. Jonathan Marlow. "You Say Synecdoche: Charlie Kaufman's *Synecdoche, New York.*" *Green Cine.* October 22, 2008. https://www.greencine.com/central/charliekaufman.
20. Evan Henerson. "A Date With Charlie Kaufman. Screenwriter Sweats the Details of a Star-Studded Staged Reading at UCLA." *Daily News* (Los Angeles, CA). September 14, 2005.
21. "Biography." *BeingCharlieKaufman.com.* http://www.beingcharliekaufman.com/index.php?option=com_content&task=view&id=31&Itemid=34.
22. Jeff Grimshaw. "Journey into Madness." http://grimshaw.jeff.tripod.com/journeyintomadness.html.
23. "Biography." *BeingCharlieKaufman.com.*
24. Ibid.
25. Burr. "Being Charlie Kaufman."
26. Mike Russell. "Kaufman Sweats." *In Focus.* April 2002. http://www.natoonline.org/infocus/02April/kaufman.htm.
27. Dean Adams. "Program Guide." *Get a Life.* July 1995. http://www.nyx.net/~dnadams/guides/get-a-life.
28. Dean Adams. "Prisoner of Love." *Get a Life.* December 14, 1991. http://www.nyx.net/~dnadams/gal/gal-script28.
29. Windolf. "Interviewing Charlie Kaufman."
30. Jason Tanz. "The Kaufman Paradox." *Wired.* November 2008.
31. Windolf. "Interviewing Charlie Kaufman."
32. Russell. "Kaufman Sweats."
33. Tanz. "The Kaufman Paradox."
34. Russell. "Kaufman Sweats."
35. James Ponsoldt. "The Play's the Thing." *Filmmaker Magazine.* Fall 2008. http://www.filmmakermagazine.com/fall2008/synecdoche.php.

CHAPTER 2

1. Mike Sager. "The Screenwriter." *Esquire.* December 1, 2002.
2. Jason Tanz. "Charlie Kaufman: Hollywood's Brainiest Screenwriter Pleases Crowds by Refusing to Please." *Wired Magazine.* October 2008.
3. Peter Kobel. "Film; The Fun and Games of Living a Virtual Life." *The New York Times.* October 24, 1999.
4. Annie Nocenti. "Writing *Being John Malkovich.*" *Scenario Magazine.* November 1, 1999.
5. Charlie Kaufman. Interviewed by Jason Tanz. "Storyboard: A Profile of a Profile of Charlie Kaufman [audio]." *Wired Magazine.* September 10, 2008. http://www.wired.com/storyboard/2008/09/the-complete-in/.
6. Yama Rahimi. "Interview: Charlie Kaufman (*Synecdoche, New York*)." *Ion Cinema.* October 22, 2008. http://www.ioncinema.com/news/id/3381.
7. Jared White. "Interview: The Stars of *Being John Malkovich.*" *University Wire.* October 27, 1999.

8. Michael Sragow. "Being Charlie Kaufman." *Salon*. November 11, 1999. http://www.salon.com/ent/col/srag/1999/11/11/kaufman/.

9. Barbara Vancheri. "Quirky Twists Surprised Even *Malkovich* Screenwriter." *Pittsburgh Post-Gazette*. May 1, 2000.

10. Mal Vincent. "Being Me! Actor John Malkovich Plays Along with The Idea That Other Characters in Film Can Get Inside His Head." *The Virginian-Pilot* (Norfolk, VA). November 12, 1999.

11. Dennis Lim. "Have You Been This Man? Spike Jonze, Charlie Kaufman and John Malkovich Have Made the Most Extraordinary Movie." *The Independent* (London, England). February 27, 2000.

12. Sarah Gristwood. "So What's It Like Being John Malkovich." *The Scotsman*. March 10, 2000.

13. Vincent. "Being Me! Actor John Malkovich Plays Along."

14. Charlie Kaufman. *Being John Malkovich* [screenplay]. (London: Faber and Faber, 1999).

15. Charlie Kaufman. "Being John Malkovich [early draft]." *Daily Script*. n.d. http://www.dailyscript.com/scripts/beingjohnmalkovich.html

16. Kaufman. *Being John Malkovich* [screenplay].

17. Ibid.

18. *Being John Malkovich*. Directed by Spike Jonze. Written by Charlie Kaufman. USA Films. 1999.

19. White. "Interview: The Stars of *Being John Malkovich*."

20. Kaufman. "Being John Malkovich [early draft]." *Daily Script*.

21. Ibid.

22. Barrett W. Sheridan. "Being Charlie Kaufman. Picking the Minds of Kaufman and Director Michel Gondry." *Stanford Daily*. April 2, 2004. http://www.stanforddaily.com/cgi-bin/?p=1014298.

23. Kaufman. *Being John Malkovich* [screenplay].

24. Ibid.

25. Jeff Otto. "IGN Interviews Charlie Kaufman." *IGN Movies*. March 16, 2004. http://movies.ign.com/articles/499/499468p1.html

26. Kaufman. *Being John Malkovich* [screenplay].

27. Ibid.

28. Ibid.

29. Ibid.

30. Cynthia Rose. "Interview: John Malkovich." *Arena Magazine*. 1990. http://www.muchacreative.com/Journalism/Malkovich.html.

31. Kaufman. *Being John Malkovich* [screenplay].

32. Kaufman. "Being John Malkovich [early draft]." *Daily Script*.

33. Kaufman. *Being John Malkovich* [screenplay].

34. Clifford Odets. *Waiting for Lefty and Other Plays*. (New York: Grove Press, 1933).

35. Sragow. "Being Charlie Kaufman."

36. Kaufman. *Being John Malkovich* [screenplay].

37. Kaufman. "Being John Malkovich [early draft]." *Daily Script*.

38. Ibid.

39. Kaufman. "Being John Malkovich [early draft]." *Daily Script*.

40. Kaufman. *Being John Malkovich* [screenplay].
41. Sragow. "Being Charlie Kaufman."
42. Kaufman. *Being John Malkovich* [screenplay].
43. Ibid.
44. Philip K. Dick. *The Philip K. Dick Reader.* (New York: Citadel Press, 1987).
45. Kaufman. "Being John Malkovich [early draft]." *Daily Script.*
46. Ibid.
47. Stephen Schaefer. "It's Tough Being John Malkovich; Cast Gets Inside Actor's Head in Quirky New Film." *The Boston Herald.* October 27, 1999.
48. Kaufman. "Being John Malkovich [early draft]." *Daily Script.*
49. Kaufman. *Being John Malkovich* [screenplay].
50. Nocenti. "Writing Being John Malkovich."
51. Kaufman. "Being John Malkovich [early draft]." *Daily Script.*
52. Ibid.
53. Ibid.
54. Ibid.
55. Ibid.
56. Vincent. "Being Me! Actor John Malkovich Plays Along"
57. Kobel. "The Fun and Games of Living a Virtual Life."
58. Sragow. "Being Charlie Kaufman."
59. Tom Carson. "The Last Great Movie of the Century." *Esquire.* October 1999.
60. Rahimi. "Interview: Charlie Kaufman."
61. Laura Burton. "It's Just a Big Mess Inside My Head." *guardian.co.uk.* April 18, 2009. http://www.guardian.co.uk/film/2009/apr/18/charlie-kaufman-interview.

CHAPTER 3

1. Kaufman. *Being John Malkovich* [screenplay]. Introduction.
2. Sean Nelson. "Nothing Against the Masses." *The Stranger.* April 11–17, 2002.
3. Warren Curry. "Hairy Situation: An Interview with *Human Nature* Writer Charlie Kaufman." *Cinema Speak.* April 9, 2002. (Web) Last accessed November 11, 2008.
4. Moira Macdonald. "Malkovich/Human Nature Writer's Head Has No Simple Portal." *The Seattle Times.* April 8, 2002.
5. Michel Gondry. "Michel in Dreamland." *Creative Review.* October 1, 2001.
6. Scott Tobias. "Interviews: Michel Gondry and Charlie Kaufman." *AV Club.* March 17, 2004. http://www.avclub.com/articles/michel-gondry-charlie-kaufman, 13859/.
7. Roman. "It's Just an Interview, Charlie Kaufman."
8. Ibid.
9. Ibid.
10. Russell. "Kaufman Sweats."
11. Elizabeth Weitzman. "Rhys Ifans: The Actor With a Mad Poet Lurking Inside." *Interview Magazine.* May 1, 2002.
12. Russell. "Kaufman Sweats."
13. Brett Buckalew. "Interview: The Inner Depths of Human Nature." *University Wire,* April 11, 2002.

14. Russell. "Kaufman Sweats."
15. Charlie Kaufman. *Human Nature: The Shooting Script*. (New York: Newmarket Press. 2002).
16. Ibid.
17. Charlie Kaufman. *Human Nature*. First draft. May 20, 1995. Available from http://www.beingcharliekaufman.com.
18. Kaufman. *Human Nature: The Shooting Script*.
19. Ibid.
20. Ibid.
21. Ibid.
22. Kaufman. *Human Nature*. First draft.
23. Kaufman. *Human Nature: The Shooting Script*.
24. Ibid.
25. Franz Kafka. "A Report to an Academy." *Franz Kafka: Collected Stories*. (New York: Everyman Libraries, 1993).
26. Ibid.
27. Ibid.
28. Kaufman. *Human Nature: The Shooting Script*.
29. Ibid.
30. Ibid.
31. Ibid.
32. Gondry. "Michel in Dreamland."
33. Ibid.
34. Mary Corliss. "Beggar's Banquet. Cannes Review 2001." *Film Comment*. July/August 2001.
35. Rob Feld. *The Shooting Script Adaptation*. (New York: Newmarket Press, 2002).
36. Tobias. "Interviews: Michel Gondry and Charlie Kaufman."
37. Ibid.
38. Ibid.
39. Ibid.

CHAPTER 4

1. Kimberly Jones. "Are You There World? Watching Charlie Kaufman Try To Work It All Out." *The Austin Chronicle*. November 14, 2008. http://www.austinchronicle.com/gyrobase/Issue/story?oid=oid%3A702338.
2. Fred Topel. "An Unorthodox Adaptation: Deciphering Charlie Kaufman." *Screenwriter's Monthly*. February 2003.
3. Mike Sager. "The Oddest, Most Innovative Mind in Hollywood Belongs to a Hirsute Recluse Named Charlie Kaufman." *Esquire*. December 1, 2002.
4. Susan Orlean. *The Orchid Thief. A True Story of Beauty and Obsession*. (New York: Random House, 1998).
5. Kaufman and Kaufman. *Adaptation: The Shooting Script*.
6. Ibid.
7. Ibid.
8. Ibid.

9. Ibid.
10. Sarah Boxer. "*New Yorker* Writer Turns Gun-Toting Floozy? That's Showbiz." *The New York Times*. December 9, 2002.
11. Charlie Kaufman and Donald Kaufman. Revised *Adaptation* draft. November 21, 2000. Available from http://www.beingcharliekaufman.com.
12. Kaufman and Kaufman. *Adaptation: The Shooting Script*.
13. Lynn Smith. "Being Robert McKee, Both On Screen and Off." *Los Angeles Times,* November 3, 2002.
14. Kaufman and Kaufman. *Adaptation: The Shooting Script*.
15. Ibid.
16. Orlean. *The Orchid Thief*.
17. Charlie Kaufman and Donald Kaufman. "Swamp Ape Draft: Second Draft: Revised *Adaptation* draft. September 24, 1999." *BeingCharlieKaufman.com*.
18. Ibid.
19. Ibid.
20. Ibid.
21. Kaufman and Kaufman. "Swamp Ape Draft."
22. Mark Peranson, Anya Kamenetz, Dennis Lim, and Ed Park. "The Heart of The Meta." *The Village Voice,* December 4, 2002.
23. Rebecca Murray and Fred Topel. "Writer Susan Orlean and Producer Edward Saxon Talk about *Adaptation* and *The Orchid Thief*." *About.com*. n.d. http://movies.about.com/library/weekly/aaadaptationintc.htm
24. Boxer. "*New Yorker* Writer Turns Gun-Toting Floozy?"
25. Murray and Topel. "Writer Susan Orlean and Producer Edward Saxon."
26. Murray and Topel. "Director Spike Jonze and Screenwriter Charlie Kaufman."
27. Ann Hornaday. "Script Witch Doctors; with *Adaptation,* Charlie Kaufman and Spike Jonze Turn Writing and Filmmaking Inside Out. Or Upside Down. Or…" *The Washington Post,* December 15, 2002.
28. Rebecca Murray and Fred Topel. "Meryl Streep Talks About Adaptation." *About.com*. n.d. http://movies.about.com/library/weekly/aaadaptationinta.htm
29. Smith. "Being Robert McKee."
30. Claude Brodesser, Jill Feiwell, and Geoffrey Berkshire. "Backstage Notes." *Variety.com*. March 23, 2003. http://www.variety.com/article/VR1117883243.html?categoryid=1043&cs=1.
31. Kaufman and Kaufman. *Adaptation: The Shooting Script*.
32. Peter Travers. "Review of *Adaptation*." *Rolling Stone*. November 28, 2002.
33. A. O. Scott. "Film Review: Forever Obsessing About Obsession." *The New York Times,* December 6, 2002.
34. Stephanie Zacharek. "*Adaptation* and The Perils of Adaptation." *Salon*. December 16, 2002. http://www.salon.com/ent/movies/feature/2002/12/16/adaptation/index1.html.
35. Topel. "An Unorthodox Adaptation."
36. Kaufman and Kaufman. *Adaptation: The Shooting Script*.
37. Murray and Topel. "Meryl Streep Talks About Adaptation."
38. Carter Burwell's official Web site. *Adaptation* soundtrack liner notes. http://www.carterburwell.com/projects/Adaptation.shtml#Carters_Notes

CHAPTER 5

1. "Kaufman Cusses Clooney: There's No Love Lost There." *Empire*. April 1, 2004. http://www.empireonline.com/News/story.asp?nid=15727.
2. Howard Feinstein. "IndieWIRE Interview: *Synecdoche, New York* Director Charlie Kaufman." indieWIRE. October 24, 2008. http://celebrifi.com/gossip/indieWIRE-INTERVIEW-Synecdoche-New-York-Director-Charlie-Kaufman-indieWIRE-220949.html
3. Jones. "Are You There World?"
4. Chuck Barris. *Confessions of a Dangerous Mind*. (New York: Hyperion Books, 2002).
5. Nev Pierce. "Interview with George Clooney." *BBC News online*. www.bbc.co.uk/george_clooney_confessions_of_a_dangerous_mind_interview.shtml.
6. Anne Thompson. "Man With a Mission: Get the Film Made." *The New York Times*. December 22, 2002.
7. Barris. *Confessions of a Dangerous Mind*.
8. Ibid.
9. Ibid.
10. Peter Andrews. "The Hating Game." *The Saturday Review*. March 29, 1980.
11. Charlie Kaufman. "*Confessions of a Dangerous Mind*. Third draft (revised) May 5, 1998." Available from www.beingcharliekaufman.com.
12. Barris. *Confessions of a Dangerous Mind*.
13. Kaufman. "*Confessions of a Dangerous Mind*. Third draft (revised) May 5, 1998."
14. Ibid.
15. Ibid.
16. King Kaufman. "Topic Reality TV: Chuck Barris." *Salon*. March 6, 2001. http://archive.salon.com/people/bc/2001/03/06/chuck_barris/.
17. Kaufman. "*Confessions of a Dangerous Mind*. Third draft (revised) May 5, 1998."
18. Barris. *Confessions of a Dangerous Mind*.
19. Kaufman. "*Confessions of a Dangerous Mind*. Third draft (revised) May 5, 1998."
20. Ibid.
21. Ibid.
22. Ibid.
23. Ibid.
24. Ibid.
25. Eccles. 9:10 (King James).
26. Kaufman. "*Confessions of a Dangerous Mind*. Third draft (revised) May 5, 1998."
27. George Clooney, Chuck Barris, and Sam Rockwell. "Behind the Scenes." *Confessions of a Dangerous Mind*, DVD. Directed by George Clooney. Burbank, CA: Miramax Home Entertainment, 2003.
28. Jeff Jensen. "The Associates." *Entertainment Weekly*. November 15, 2002.
29. Spence D. "Being Chuck Barris." *IGN Movies*. January 23, 2003. http://movies.ign.com/articles/383/383542p1.html.
30. Barris. *Confessions of a Dangerous Mind*.

31. Kaufman. "*Confessions of a Dangerous Mind*. Third draft (revised) May 5, 1998."
32. Joel Stein. "Chuck Barris: Lying to Tell The Truth." *Time*. January 7, 2003.
33. Ibid.
34. "Kaufman Cusses Clooney."
35. Joshua Balling. "It's a Wrap: A Smooth Run for Nantucket Film Festival 9." *The Inquirer and Mirror*. 2004. http://www.ack.net/600iminthisissuestory.html.
36. John Powers. "Dangerous? Not Really: Clooney/Kaufman/Barris's Confessions Doesn't Quite Live up to Its Hype." *LA Weekly*. December 26, 2002.
37. "Movie Marketed As Six Different Genres." *The Onion*. March 5, 2003. http://www.theonion.com/content/node/31332.
38. Neil Smith. "Inside Screenwriter Kaufman's Mind." *BBC News* online. April 28, 2004. http://news.bbc.co.uk/2/hi/entertainment/3664683.stm
39. 1 Cor. 13 (King James).
40. Philip K. Dick. *A Scanner Darkly*. (New York: Random House, 1977).
41. Ibid.
42. Ibid.
43. Charlie Kaufman. "A Scanner Darkly. First draft December 20, 1997." Available from http://www.beingcharliekaufman.com.
44. Dick. *A Scanner Darkly*.
45. Ibid.
46. Ibid.
47. Emanuel Levy official Web site. "Interview: Kaufman on *Synecdoche, New York*." October 1, 2008. http://www.emanuellevy.com/search/details.cfm?id=10012.
48. Marlow. "You Say *Synecdoche*."

CHAPTER 6

1. Charlie Kaufman. "Commentary." *Eternal Sunshine of the Spotless Mind*, DVD. Directed by Michel Gondry. Universal City, CA: Universal Studios, 2007.
2. Charlie Kaufman. *Eternal Sunshine of the Spotless Mind: The Shooting Script*. (New York: Newmarket Press, 2004).
3. Charlie Kaufman. "*Eternal Sunshine of the Spotless Mind*. First draft, undated." *Beingcharliekaufman.com*.
4. "A Conversation with Screenwriter Charlie Kaufman." *The Charlie Rose Show*. PBS-TV, Los Angeles. March 26, 2004.
5. Chris Marker. *La Jetee*. (New York: Zone Books, 1992). Original script 1962.
6. Kaufman. *Eternal Sunshine: The Shooting Script*.
7. Ibid.
8. Ibid.
9. Tom Waits. "9th & Hennepin." *Rain Dogs*. Compact disc, Island Records, 1990. Original release date 1985.
10. Walter Chaw. "Riding a Mental Rollercoaster with One of Our Heroes." *Film Freak Central*. October 26, 2008. http://www.filmfreakcentral.net/notes/ckaufmaninterview.htm
11. Kaufman. *Eternal Sunshine: The Shooting Script*.
12. Alice Munro. "The Bear Came Over the Mountain." *The New Yorker*. December 27, 1999.

13. "Heartbreak Theory, II: Even Great Filmmakers Get the Blues." *The Stranger.* March 24, 2004.
14. Italo Svevo. *As a Man Grows Older.* (New York: Putnam, 1932).
15. Kaufman. *Eternal Sunshine: The Shooting Script.*
16. Ibid.
17. Ibid.
18. Margery Williams. *The Velveteen Rabbit or How Toys Become Real.* (Cohasset, MA: Vermilion, 1995).
19. Kaufman. *Eternal Sunshine: The Shooting Script.*
20. Alexander Pope. "Eloisa to Abelard." *Poetical Works.* (New York: Oxford University Press, 1966).
21. Ibid.
22. Ibid.
23. *The Letters of Abelard and Heloise.* Introduction by Betty Radice. (New York: Penguin, 1974).
24. Kaufman. *Eternal Sunshine: The Shooting Script.*
25. Ibid.
26. Robin Marantz Henig. "The Quest to Forget." *The New York Times Magazine.* April 4, 2004.
27. Ibid.
28. Kaufman. *Eternal Sunshine: The Shooting Script.*
29. Ibid.
30. Ibid.
31. Ibid.
32. Ibid.
33. Charlie Kaufman. "*Eternal Sunshine of the Spotless Mind.* First draft, undated."
34. Charlotte O'Sullivan. "Charlie Kaufman: An Extra-normal, Extraordinary Scriptwriter." *The Independent.* May 7, 2004. http://www.independent.co.uk/arts-entertainment/films/features/charlie-kaufman-an-extranormal-extraordinary-scriptwriter-562483.html
35. Anna Akhmatova. *The Complete Poems of Anna Akhmatova.* Edited by Roberta Reeder. (Somerville, MA: Zephyr Press, 1989).
36. Kaufman. *Eternal Sunshine: The Shooting Script.*
37. Ibid.
38. Munro. "The Bear Came Over the Mountain."
39. Noel Murray, Keith Phipps, Nathan Rabin, Tasha Robinson, and Scott Tobias. "The Best Films of the '00s." *A.V. Club.* December 3, 2009. http://www.avclub.com/articles/the-best-films-of-the-00s,35931/.

CHAPTER 7

1. Chaw. "Riding a Mental Rollercoaster with One of Our Heroes."
2. Burr. "Being Charlie Kaufman."
3. Henerson. "Charlie Kaufman Sweats."
4. Ibid.
5. Ibid.
6. James Merrill. *Divine Comedies.* (New York: Atheneum, 1976).

7. Del Signore. "Charlie Kaufman, Director: Synecdoche, New York."
8. Kaufman. *Adaptation: The Shooting Script.*
9. Rahimi. "Interview: Charlie Kaufman (*Synecdoche, New York*)."
10. Del Signore. "Charlie Kaufman, Director: *Synecdoche, New York.*"
11. Marcel Proust. *In Search of Lost Time. Volume 1 Swann's Way.* (New York: Random House, 1992).
12. Ponsoldt. "The Play's the Thing."
13. Feinstein. "Interview/*Synecdoche, New York* Director Charlie Kaufman."
14. Ibid.
15. Ponsoldt. "The Play's the Thing."
16. Michael Guillen. "*Synecdoche, New York*—Interview with Charlie Kaufman." *Twitch.* October 23, 2008. http://twitchfilm.net/interviews/2008/10/synecdoche-newyorkinterview-with-charlie-kaufman.php.
17. David Carr. "The Universe According to Kaufman." October 17, 2008. http://www.nytimes.com/2008/10/19/movies/19carr.html.
18. Richard Corliss. "Finally! An Instant Cannes Classic." *Time.* May 24, 2008.
19. A. O. Scott. "Soderbergh and Che, Provacateurs." *The New York Times.* May 23, 2008.
20. Jeff Wells. "Way Back When." *Hollywood Elsewhere.* http://www.hollywood-elsewhere.com/2008/05/synecdoche_baby.php.
21. Anthony Bregman. "Anthony Bregman Says." *Hollywood Elsewhere.* http://hollywood-elsewhere.com/2008/05/synecdoche_baby.php
22. Rahimi. "Interview: Charlie Kaufman (*Synecdoche, New York*)."
23. Louise Bogan. *The Blue Estuaries: Poems 1923–1968.* (New York: Farrar, Straus & Giroux. 1968).
24. Geoffrey Chaucer. *Troilus and Criseyde.* (New York: Penguin Books, 1984)
25. Wallace Stevens. Selected Poems. (New York: Random House, 2009).
26. Andrew O'Hehir. "Who Names a Film *Synecdoche*?" *Salon.* October 24, 2008. http://www.salon.com/print.html?URL=/ent/movies/btm/feature/2008/10/24/kaufman
27. Ibid.
28. Burr. "Being Charlie Kaufman.
29. David Cronenberg. "Charlie Kaufman." *Interview Magazine.* November 25, 2008. http://www.interviewmagazine.com/film/charlie-kaufman.
30. Manohla Dargis. "Dreamer, Live in the Here and Now." *The New York Times.* October 24, 2008.
31. Manohla Dargis. "Mirror Reflections on Time's Dualities." *The New York Times.* December 31, 2008.
32. Roger Ebert. *"Synecdoche, New York." Chicago Sun-Times.* November 5, 2008.
33. Rex Reed. "Could Synecdoche, New York Be the Worst Movie Ever? Yes!" *The New York Observer.* October 21, 2008.
34. Scott Tobias. October 22, 2008. http://www.avclub.com/articles/charlie-kaufman,14322/
35. Eric Hynes. "A Self-Made Man: Charlie Kaufman's *Synecdoche, New York* [review]." *Indie Wire.* October 22, 2008. http://www.indiewire.com/article/review_a_self-made_man_charlie_kaufmans_synecdoche_new_york/.
36. Ponsoldt. "The Play's the Thing."

37. Rachel Abramowitz. "The Critical Words? Every One Stings. *The Los Angeles Times.* October 26, 2008. http://articles.latimes.com/2008/oct/26/entertainment/ca-kaufman26.
38. Cronenberg. "Charlie Kaufman."
39. Jeffrey Wells. "AFF08: *Synecdoche, New York.*" *Hollywood Elsewhere.* November 21, 2008. http://www.hollywood-elsewhere.com/arthouse/2008/10/aff08-synecdoche-new-york.php.
40. Ibid.
41. Harold Pinter. "Harold Pinter." *Nobelprize.org.* http://nobelprize.org/nobel_prizes/literature/laureates/2005/pinter-lecture-e.html.
42. O'Hehir. "Who Names a Film *Synecdoche?*"

Index

About the Author

DOREEN ALEXANDER CHILD was raised in Philadelphia and holds a BA in English from West Chester University. Her work has been published in newspapers and literary magazines, and she has produced independent films and a television pilot. Currently she lives in Los Angeles and serves as managing editor of *CinemaEditor* magazine.